Praise for *Transforming Your Leadership Culture*

"Leaders expecting to guide their organizations through a cultural transformation by creating an environment for team success while satisfying the customer would greatly enhance their likelihood of success by reading *Transforming Your Leadership Culture*."
—**Gary E. Black,** president and CEO, Lenoir Memorial Hospital

"At last, a book that addresses a whole new leadership competence: creating a leadership community that through its collective intelligence transforms the organization. A compelling integration of leadership and organizational development."
—**Tex Gunning,** former CEO, Unilever, and managing director, Decorative Paints, Akzo Nobel N.V.

"'Inside-out' change is one of the most profound and powerful concepts for guiding cultural transformation that I've ever come across. Fundamental and sustainable transformation requires transformation within people—in their values, beliefs, and professional identities—not just in their conforming to a new set of organizational structures, systems, or policies. This ground-breaking book makes it clear why that's so, and shows how to use that knowledge to create twenty-first-century capabilities for your organization."
—**Rich Hughes,** senior author, *Leadership: Enhancing the Lessons of Experience*, and coauthor, *Becoming a Strategic Leader*

"Building on years of hands-on experience with real organizational leaders, the authors have written a breakthrough book that blends individual leadership transformation, organization development, and the power of community into a potent formula that truly has the power to transform organizations and empower employees."
—**David Noer,** Frank S. Holt Jr. Professor of Business Leadership, Elon University

"In today's world of unprecedented market dislocation and volatility, with multidimensional change in competition driven by quantum changes in technology, computing power, and product innovation, the need for human talent, alignment, and leadership has never been more important. McGuire and Rhodes provide the knowledge, insight, and roadmap for creating sustainable success in today's uncertain world."
—**Kelly Martin,** chief executive officer, Elan Corporation, plc

"Finally someone gets it! Leadership and culture—you can't transform one without the other, and just as with any worthwhile endeavor, the first rule is to 'show up!'"
—**Scott A. Snook,** Harvard Business School

"Twenty-first-century leadership requires a clear understanding of leadership culture in all organizations. *Transforming Your Leadership Culture* is an excellent resource for redefining and reframing the essence of leadership, and it provides a fresh approach to developing a more effective organization."
—**Michael A. Cafasso,** Colorado president, director,
    American Bank of Commerce

"John McGuire and Gary Rhodes make crystal clear the reason organizational change efforts rarely work—the lack of leadership culture change. Practical and inspirational, their Culture Development Cycle is a first-rate contribution to fostering transformation through collective learning and expanded ways of thinking and being."
—**Pamela Shockley-Zalabak,** chancellor,
    University of Colorado at Colorado Springs

"This book from McGuire and Rhodes is required reading for all executive leaders within your organization. Crisp, concise, and practical, it provides a framework that will enhance organizational change and transformation beyond best intentions."
—**Jon C. Abeles,** senior vice president, talent management and
    diversity, Catholic Healthcare Partners

"Times of stress exaggerate the tensions between managing and leading that exist within an organization. This book offers great insight into how to enhance an organization's ability to balance these tensions, resulting in more effective leadership."
—**Elmer L. Doty,** president and CEO, Vought Aircraft Industries

"This book fills a critical void regarding change leadership and why most large-scale change processes are unsuccessful. It showcases substantive research that illuminates the blind spot in transforming cultures and demonstrates how to practically apply developmental theory in support of major organizational shifts."
—**John D. Schmidt,** CEO, Avastone Consulting

"My expectation was one of great anticipation on what I could learn to help build a leadership culture. However, my revelation was that the learning goes far beyond an individual or an organization, to how people can connect, build community, evolve, and achieve. But it starts with me!"
—**Chuck Moore,** senior vice president, human resources, KONE Inc.

"I highly recommend this book for its innovative approach and distillation of years of research and experience. *Transforming Your Leadership Culture* is the kind of read that appeals not only to the expert but also to anyone interested in what makes for an adaptive and inspired change environment. Though they aim at whole culture change, McGuire and Rhodes model the collaborative inquiry mode their book advocates throughout by engaging the reader personally in exploring the issues and challenges presented. Overall, a highly accessible and well-written book that invites readers to consider novel distinctions in creating a new social discourse that applies to collective change efforts."
—**Susanne R. Cook-Greuter,** principal of Cook-Greuter and
    Associates

"At last a leadership book that recognizes that organizational culture reflects executive leadership. For teachers, coaches, and executives, this discussion of theory and practice demonstrates practical methods for transforming institutional culture that fully engage leadership at all levels."
—**Martha Romero,** leadership consultant, Collaborative Ventures

"Through the work my management team and I have done with Gary Rhodes, I have personally experienced the power of the strategies presented in *Transforming Your Leadership Culture*. This book is an indispensable tool for any manager wanting to run a highly functioning company."
—**Jason DeSalvo,** CEO, Strategic Outpatient Services, Inc.

"A must-read for executive teams and consultants facing organizational change or transformation."
—**Brent Manssen,** T.A.B. Associates, Inc.

"In the context of today's crises and uncertainties, *Transforming Your Leadership Culture* is a must-read for all leaders in all types of organizations wishing to successfully lead efforts of meaningful and lasting change."
—**Melanie-Anne Taylor,** Center for Executive Development, Inc.

"*Transforming Your Leadership Culture* provides unique insights into organizational change from a cultural frame."
—**David C. Bangert,** Shidler College of Business,
    University of Hawaii

"The financial system's near-collapse is but one example of the complex and uncertain world we face. *Transforming Your Leadership Culture* demonstrates that a new breed of leaders—able to sincerely transform themselves together with their organizations—will be the ones best suited to thrive in these times."
—**Cynthia A. McEwen,** Avastone Consulting

"A watershed book for 'serious people' looking for 'serious change' in their organizations."
—**Daniel C. Buchner,** vice president, organizational innovation,
    Continuum

Transforming Your Leadership Culture

John B. McGuire
Gary B. Rhodes

JOSSEY-BASS
A Wiley Imprint
www.josseybass.com

Center for
Creative
Leadership
www.ccl.org

Published by Jossey-Bass
A Wiley Imprint
989 Market Street, San Francisco, CA 94103-1741—www.josseybass.com

Readers should be aware that Internet Web sites offered as citations and/or sources for further
information may have changed or disappeared between the time this was written and when it is
read.

Limit of Liability/Disclaimer of Warranty: While the publisher and author have used their best
efforts in preparing this book, they make no representations or warranties with respect to the
accuracy or completeness of the contents of this book and specifically disclaim any implied
warranties of merchantability or fitness for a particular purpose. No warranty may be created
or extended by sales representatives or written sales materials. The advice and strategies
contained herein may not be suitable for your situation. You should consult with a professional
where appropriate. Neither the publisher nor author shall be liable for any loss of profit or any
other commercial damages, including but not limited to special, incidental, consequential,
or other damages.

Jossey-Bass books and products are available through most bookstores. To contact Jossey-Bass
directly call our Customer Care Department within the U.S. at 800-956-7739, outside the U.S.
at 317-572-3986, or fax 317-572-4002.

Jossey-Bass also publishes its books in a variety of electronic formats. Some content that appears
in print may not be available in electronic books.

Library of Congress Cataloging-in-Publication Data
McGuire, John B.
  Transforming your leadership culture / John B. McGuire, Gary B. Rhodes.— 1st ed.
      p.   cm.
  Includes bibliographical references and index.
  ISBN 978-0-470-25957-3 (cloth)
      1. Leadership.   2. Organizational change.   3. Corporate culture.   I. Rhodes, Gary B.
  II. Title.
  HD57.7.M3956   2009
  658.4'092—dc22
                                                                    2008053155

Printed in the United States of America
FIRST EDITION
HB Printing   10 9 8 7 6 5 4 3 2 1

A Joint Publication of
The Jossey-Bass Business & Management Series
and
The Center for Creative Leadership

For Boyd E. and Ross,
whose graceful wisdom,
advice, and support guided us in our own
development toward bigger minds

Contents

Acknowledgments

This book represents the contributions of many people over many years, and we acknowledge our appreciation to them here. Writing this book has been for us an Inside-Out experience— growing bigger minds and engaging colleagues and clients alike at a deep level—the same experience we anticipate you will have in reading this book. We have grown to appreciate that writing is indeed a joint, collaborative effort based on the knowledge generation of the entire community. Foremost in our gratitude is our close colleague, our inspirational and most generous friend, Charles J. (Chuck) Palus. As project manager in the CCL Connected Leadership project for many years, Chuck has provided the intellectual continuity and integrative backbone for all of our collective work. He has been an exemplary change guide and has ceaselessly encouraged us with his creative spirit and brilliance. Using integrative approaches spanning multiple frameworks to arrive at practical, usable products and services has made this journey deeply meaningful and great fun. Chuck's worldview is deep and funny, serious and humble. He has an enormous mind. We think Chuck's work is available as a happening fractal of what we all could be and ought to become: a modern-day river rider, an alchemist with an edge, a transformer extraordinaire. Thank you, Chuck, for a great ride. What a long, invigorating trip it's been!

The core team of this project is composed of extraordinarily gifted and dedicated harbingers of the new direction of organizational-level collective leadership. Cindy McCauley initiated the CCL Connected Leadership project, and she also took the lead in our case study research in interdependent leadership cultures and practices. She and Bill Drath doggedly led our work in developing the ideas and publication of our groundbreaking ontology of leadership as direction, alignment, and commitment, opening the door to leadership as a collective activity and well beyond the tired belief of the individual as the center of gravity in leadership. We're indebted to Patricia O'Connor for lighting the way in group action-learning development work and for her tireless application of extending this creative methodology with clients. We also acknowledge our group director during the tough times, Richard Hughes, currently U.S. Air Force Academy transformation chair, for his profound commitment to both doing the work and providing unflagging leadership support during the challenging times in our work. We owe special thanks to Ellen Van Velsor for her steadying hand and reliable intellect in keeping this work on a track of common sense and relevance.

Kate Beatty has been, and will remain, the heart and soul of dedication in the effort to extend CCL into this field of organizational leadership. Her tireless strategic efforts on behalf of CCL's Developing the Strategic Leader program and her seminal book with Rich Hughes, *Becoming a Strategic Leader*, are foundational to our core advancement into this emergent field. Kate, Rich, Bruce Byington, and Laura Quinn have pioneered the concept of strategy as a learning process, and the emerging reality of leadership strategy as the linchpin of change in the twenty-first century.

As we advanced our robust prototyping of services and tools development in this practice, we thank Dave Altman and Jennifer Martineau for their enthusiastic support and their deep belief in the value of this project. They have provided the gift of time and resources to bring it forward, and we acknowledge deep appreciation.

We are grateful to our learning partners. William (Bill) Torbert has been an adviser to the project for several years. He has become a close partner, and we owe special thanks for all his encouragement, sage advice, and friendship. Suzanne Cook-Greuter has been enormously helpful in administering assessments to our clients' senior teams and assisting us with the team development based on the profiles and the coaching she has provided. Ken Wilber added tremendous value through his generous time with us in conversation, providing inspiration to pioneer new territory and brilliant insight to advance the integral theory into the collective potential of leadership for the benefit of humanity. Bernice McCarthy's 4MAT learning cycle was invaluable in our applications to collective learning in leadership and informed our explication of the Culture Development Cycle.

We can never express the depth of our appreciation for our client collaborators and long-term learning partners at Abrasive Technology Inc. (ATI): Butch Peterman and Tanya Patrella; and at Lenoir Memorial Hospital: Gary Black and Jim Dobbins. All the members of the change leadership teams at both organizations are too numerous to mention here, but we know your names, hearts, and minds, and we are grateful for our partnerships with you and your engagement to re-create your organizations. In this writing journey, we could not have wished for greater invitation, guidance, and support than what we received from our CCL editor, Peter Scisco. Pete, you talked us out onto the ledge—and then you talked us down from it—and our gratitude is immense. We're grateful for the encouragement and support of Martin Wilcox, the director of CCL's publications group, and all the staff members who got us through. We are also indebted to the assistance of the professionals at Jossey-Bass, notably Kathe Sweeney and Byron Schneider, and to our developmental editor, Alan Venable—we thank you.

Finally, for those who supported us through this effort that took us away too much, the deepest gratitude for our dearest loves and best friends, Christy Furman and Lynn Rhodes. We acknowledge what you know—we could never have done it without you. We love you forever.

The Authors

John B. McGuire is a senior faculty member at the Center for Creative Leadership (CCL). His diverse work history includes senior business management positions in corporate settings— Digital Equipment Corporation and Fidelity Investments, among others. He has also operated his own leadership and organizational development consulting business, garnering extensive experience across industries and in private, public, and nonprofit sectors. He formerly kept a psychology practice in family systems.

John's current work focuses on organization-wide change through leadership. He is research and development practice leader for the Change Leadership team, practicing organization culture transformation through balancing change management with change leadership. This practice focuses on developing corporate cultures, leadership strategies, and core organizational capabilities. A key tenet of this practice is assisting clients in overriding the high failure rates in change management by connecting leadership across the organization in its key outcomes of setting direction and achieving alignment and commitment.

His results-oriented work with teams and organizations combines thirty years of practical corporate line and staff experience with research-based approaches to help solve clients' business problems. John is interested in providing clients' teams and organizations with sustainable solutions while simultaneously providing practical results at each step in the process.

John holds master's degrees from Harvard and Brandeis universities and has received recognition for his service in corporate, public, and nonprofit institutions.

Gary B. Rhodes is a CCL adjunct and retired senior fellow. He is a principal with Leading Edge Solutions, a consulting firm specializing in the design and delivery of high-impact executive leadership programs for individuals, teams, and organizations, from a systems perspective. In his continuing work with CCL, he is focused on action research in support of intervention designs that are systemic and systematic, and that focus on organization and leadership development as a learning process. His current research, writing, and presentations emphasize linking strategy as a learning process to individual, team, and organizational change in building responsive, sustainable, innovative leadership cultures. He is skilled in individual, team, and organizational assessments.

Gary has worked with hundreds of organizations worldwide, including Boeing, the Japanese Management Association, Bank Negara Malaysia, International Centre for Leadership in Finance, Novartis, Genentech, Elan Pharmaceuticals, Amgen, General Motors, Daimler Benz, BCG, Vought Aircraft Industries, FMC, United Defense, and the World Bank. His nonprofit clients include the Council on Foundations, Council of Jewish Federations, American Red Cross, CARE, and the Prudential Spirit of Community Leadership Initiative.

Gary has done extensive consulting, training, and publishing on leadership and supervision in nonprofit organizations, including coauthoring the textbook *Competent Supervision: Making Imaginative Judgments*. He holds a master's degree in social work from the University of California at Los Angeles and an interdisciplinary master of philosophy in social science and social policy from the University of Michigan.

INTRODUCTION

For us in the beginning it was being, and only
later it was thinking. *First, we are*, and then we
think, and we think only inasmuch as we are, since
thinking is indeed caused by the structures and
operations of being.

—Antonio Damasio

One of the largest financial institutions in North America
recently took on a large-scale, organization-wide change program. At the outset, each of its independently operating business
units had its own human resource (HR) functions. The aim of
the program was to shift HR from this decentralized, distributed
system to a centralized operation offering fee-for-service to the
units.

The enterprise had retained a prominent consultant (one
who had truly earned the honorific of *guru*) who was pioneer-
ing new approaches in the field of change management. As part
of the firm's heavy investment in preparing for the change, the
consultant worked closely with executives and the firm's entire
HR community. A series of small- and large-group interventions
had been held in order to "train up" the departments and their
constituents in the theory and practice of the change they were
about to make. Planning and preparation were thorough and
exhaustive. Senior management prepared operational systems
and had secured the buy-in of subsidiary business units. A centralized, shared-services operation was ready to swing into action.

On a Monday morning at 8:00 A.M., the company threw the
switch, and the new shared-services system went operational.
On Friday at 5:00 P.M. the change program was cancelled, the

senior vice president who had sponsored the program resigned, and the organization development staff representing the changes in the business units were about to be sacked.

Shortly after, the HR consultant held an evening speaking session at a local hotel. He was featuring his models and, in that context, was considering the failed attempt at change in this organization. During the Q&A following his remarks, we asked him, "When you plan a major change program, do you ever consider how that change fits with the culture current in the enterprise?" He stopped, looked up at the ceiling for what seemed an interminably long time, and finally looked us straight in the eye. "No," he answered.

We appreciated his stark honesty. We suspected strongly that a problem of the culture of leadership lay behind the failure. But we were equally sure this well-respected consultant was and is not alone in ignoring the role of culture in organizational change. Change management practices have been carefully designed and analyzed for decades by company leaders and their advisers, but few of them, even today, consider the power of culture, especially the organization's leadership culture, to affect and even derail enterprisewide change efforts.

The field of organizational development, spawned over forty years ago, has developed practices in change management that regularly fail to achieve any significant results. Since the 1990s, as many as three-quarters of organizational change efforts have failed. Studies suggest that organization-wide failure rates range from 66 to 75 percent, and one study revealed that only one-third of organization-wide change initiatives achieve any success at all (Beer, 2001). It is no wonder that executives are jaded about making big investments in organization change programs. These change management programs are primarily focused on external systems, structures, and processes.

In their recent review of the organizational development field, Bradford and Burke (2005) indicate that some say we are witnessing the final demise of this ailing discipline. We see it differently—not as a setting sun but as a new dawn, an advent of a new approach to organizational change through developing leadership culture. Understanding and tapping the power of leadership culture triggers a nearly unstoppable vigor in the spirit of human systems. Agility, speed, execution, unification, readiness—all the things that CEOs dream about—are available to leaders willing to transform their organization's leadership culture toward interdependence.

Granted, it is rare to find approaches to organizational change that focus on and work through leadership. And, more precisely, it is exceptional to find change initiatives focused through the development of senior leaders themselves. We believe this is the new trajectory of successful organizational change.

Consider what you have heard or read about traditional change management pathways, and ask yourself this question: "Even if I aligned all the management systems and structures in this organization toward a specific strategy and bolstered it with vision, is this organization's leadership capable of facing the next uncertain future with all of its endlessly unfolding requirements for new systems and structures and process changes?" If you answer no or are unsure, then we pose this challenge: perhaps the change you need is in your organization's leadership mind-set, not just in its systems and structures.

We suggest that the field of leadership development is emerging as a new agent through which to achieve sustainable organizational development. Granted, challenging executives' mind-sets and inviting their developmental requirements as a core means to organizational change doesn't have the history of forty years of organizational development. Neither does it have the history of 75 percent failure rates. And if our experience and work with several organizations that have attempted deep, sustainable change is any measure (and we believe it is), then organizational change through leadership culture change is not doomed to repeat that history.

In this book, and in our work in general at the Center for Creative Leadership, we are redefining the field of leader development beyond individuals to embrace the leadership development of collectives that together set direction, get alignment, and commit to imperative change results. Imagine the power of leadership as a unified force for adaptable, sustainable, organizational change, and you can see why we say, "Change the leadership culture, and you change the organizational culture."

What If

This orientation answers the endless operational challenges of organizational viability and unleashes the leadership imagination:

- What if we acknowledged that all operational systems find their source in human systems?
- What if organizations are human systems first, and then they manifest human ideas in operational systems?
- What if those human systems are carried forward through leadership culture?
- What if senior leaders were willing to rise above the complacency of success and the insecurity of uncertain futures to find the maturity to lead together?

Edgar Schein (1992) writes that leading the culture is what leadership does, and that makes the human system pretty much the sole territory of leadership. Developing the values and advancing the beliefs of the way people make decisions and operate in an organization is ultimately the most powerful operating system the organization possesses. And yet it appears that even Schein does not believe in the possibility of transforming a culture. We do, and we have hard evidence to justify our belief.

Losing Control

Since the twentieth century, there have been only two basic kinds of organization and leadership cultures in the West. The first is command and control, with its roots in early management principles and the military-born experience of World War II. Our postindustrial era in the West lives with this hangover of hierarchy. It seems that collectively, we still need heroes and we depend on them when the heat is on. We defer our power, and we expect the individual leader to command and lead followers as the primary way to achieve goals. The imperative is to get control and to conform.

The second, emergent, breakout organizational alternative that in the 1970s began to poke through the encrusted command-and-control cocoon is the achievement-based organization. W. Edwards Deming's early influence continues in the lean manufacturing of Toyota, and the innovation cultures exemplified in Apple and Google are illustrative. These continuous-improvement organizations hold independent thought and action as core beliefs and principles. Advancing beyond the hero-led mind-set of command and control, a cluster of heroes can cooperate and coordinate activities and win—together—when direction is aligned. The imperative is to get competitive and achieve.

We are now perched on the threshold of a new world order that continues to unfold. At this writing, for example, the price of oil and its effect on the global supply chain may challenge some of the most basic assumptions about flat worlds, fluid labor, and free capital. The meltdown in financial markets exposes our interconnectedness as never before. Businesses' challenges today barely resemble those of thirty years ago. The technical education many of us received is already failing us. We must either face up to a serious shift in our identities or continue to perish professionally and organizationally at alarming rates.

In response to these unfolding consequences, a new kind of organization can be imagined. And to judge from the results of our work, it is already emerging: the interdependent-collaborative organization. Every CEO wants fast, capable response to the challenge of change. Faster, better, cheaper is impossible without collective leadership capability to reframe dilemmas, reinterpret options, and reform operations—continuously. Cross-boundary, horizontal, customer-centric value chains are not just the currently demanded reality that executives face; they are the harbingers of transformation. Institutions, organizations, and governments are going to need this adaptive, quick-footed, see-around-the-corner capacity. The imperative is to collaborate and transform.

Not everyone is ready to collaborate. A key purpose of this book is to assist leaders in understanding the pathway to get to the collaborative, transformative organization. For many of them, moving from the command-and-control mind-set into the achievement mind-set is the necessary next step. We want to help you imagine and implement a readiness pathway that makes change feasible for you and your organization. Leadership culture can be cement walls with steel ceilings that are always in your way, or leadership culture can generate and expand into a unified force for a promising, innovative, and sustaining future.

Three Things in This Book You Won't Find Elsewhere

What is really new and different in our method of change? For one, the way we approach clients with a balance of discovery, challenge, and support has freshness. Our combinations of intervention content and the integration of developmental theory within our research-based tools that measure collective mind-sets are assuredly new, if not unique. But what is really new and different and reflected in this book are three things.

First, *executives do the change work first*. Executives can't delegate culture transformation work to others. Not anymore.

Without first wading into the cultural morass of internal beliefs themselves, and then making common sense of it in dialogue with others, executives and senior leaders have a poor chance (the odds are one in three or four) of achieving durable organizational transformation. We insist that executives involve more than themselves in the change process. We are adamant that they lead by engagement and example. We follow two simple principles: (1) Do not ask others to do what you are not willing to do yourself. (2) If you want something different, then become something different.

Second, *a critical mass of the leadership culture becomes the change and takes change to the middle*. Serious people connected together in change leadership commit to the mutual risk of collectively initiating new leadership beliefs and practices that generate change. Developing leadership to the next level of maturity while implementing strategic imperatives is the glue of change. It bonds a critical mass of senior leaders to demonstrate alignment toward the change they expect of others by discovering and navigating a joint future together. Then a solid coalition of connected leadership shows up and stands up to advance this increasingly clearer organizational direction into the organizational middle, where core operations are carried out day to day. Together, senior leaders engage both nominal and potential leaders in generating new leadership beliefs and practices that create new aligning mechanisms that advance strategic intent and goals. The viral momentum of seeing is believing spurs movements.

Third, *everyone gets bigger minds*. If not unique, our practice is unusual in its dedication to the advancement of higher orders of human potential in organizations. We stand on a platform of advancement toward more interdependent, collaborative leadership cultures, their beliefs and practices, and the organizations they are intended to serve. This platform orients organizations toward a connected, collective leadership capability in which everyone in the organization can share.

From this support, leaders individually and leadership collectively can shake loose from the complacency of individual success and elevated organizational position to deal with the reality of telling the truth, finding deeper wisdom in the way things really are, and accepting accountability for the sustainability of the whole organization. Understanding and facing that new situation requires increasingly more complex and bigger minds that are willing and capable of dealing with the increasing complexity of an ever-changing world. The willingness to learn is the only requirement to getting a bigger mind.

Whom This Book Is For

Connected human potential is endless. As human beings we want and need to drive and thrive to the next level, the next potential, the next fulfillment. It is our nature. Even so, this book addresses first and foremost executives and organizational leaders of all kinds, who see that change is necessary but have become skeptical that lasting, sustainable change—transformation—lies within their reach.

We think that when you believe that leadership culture is in you and that leadership can be a boundless, emergent, imagining creative force for change, you can construct endless new orders of human and operational potential that transcend boundaries and are limited only by your willingness and then your ability to realize them. We have seen and heard and felt and experienced this potential in leaders and organizations willing to believe in the possibilities of their spirit, vision, and determination.

Are you ready?

Part One

YOU, YOUR TEAM, AND TRANSFORMATION

1

TRANSFORMATION

Can It Be Done?

> We can easily forgive a child who is afraid of the
> dark. The real tragedy of life is when men are afraid
> of the light.
>
> —*Plato*

In 2002, Technology Inc., a high-tech manufacturer of precision tools, pushed its chips into the center of the table and went all in. Already number one or two in niche markets, the company wanted to keep that position and develop new product lines. At stake was the company's hope for the future: to become more innovative and create a better working environment for all employees. The company gambled that it could shift its structure from a traditional hierarchy—a command-and-control, vertical structure—to a flat, customer-focused, process-centered organization. It committed to transforming its leadership culture as a means of transforming the organization itself. The game's last card—the river of dreams—was revealed only after much dedicated work, but the wager paid off. Among Technology Inc.'s organizational winnings, which are still being tallied, are these:

- Turnover rates that dropped from double-digit numbers to near zero
- Previously poorly performing plants suddenly making and sustaining group-variable compensation

- A shift in metrics themselves to only three core measures
- Fifty percent reduction in product returns year after year for five years running
- A state-of-the-art talent management system that includes peer reviews; individual, group, and organizational-level compensation; coaching; and assessment and learning systems
- Zero recruitment costs due to 100 percent internal referrals of new hires
- Hierarchical, conformance-based culture transformed into a process-centered organization with a collaborative culture

Leaders today, especially senior leaders, are living in an increasingly complex and shifting new world order. The compelling challenge for leaders individually and as collectives is to develop bigger minds—new mind-sets that can anticipate and prepare organizations that secure new capabilities to address successive future challenges. This means that as a senior leader, your role is shifting too. We imagine that you experience an unsettled feeling. Gone are the days when you could simply lead and delegate from the top. You too now are a primary object of change, and you must personally take on this challenge in order to guide your organization into a demanding future. This new world has thrown its gauntlet at the feet of all leaders: it challenges everyone to face it, develop, and emerge to advance their professional cause. There is a new call to action for and new identity of leadership.

Yet a key element is missing from this discussion of how leadership faces a shifting world order. Organizations have grown skilled at developing individual leader competencies but have mostly ignored the challenge of transforming their leaders' mind-sets from one level to the next. Today's horizontal development within a mind-set must give way to the vertical development of bigger minds. Parochial mind-sets concerned only with the immediate environment cannot deal with the complexity the new world order has foisted on us all. Getting better at what you already do is not good enough—not because it is wrong, but because it is inadequate.

The upward development of individual leaders is necessary but not sufficient. The continuing failures of organization change efforts testify to a willful ignorance of this harsh reality. The new world order requires new consciousness to deal with it. This book is about getting those bigger individual and collective minds. Serious change is for serious people, and we are introducing a view and a process that challenge all of us to show up, stand up, and grow up.

We hold to this self-evident truth: human beings seek advancement, adaptation, and development toward increasingly complex knowledge, mastery, and harmony in their environment.

When we talk about change in this book, we mean change beyond basic adaptive improvements in response to ongoing pressures and opportunities. We mean transformation. We mean creative new leadership beliefs and mind-sets and the new orders of leadership practice they generate that are capable of permanently advancing and altering the way leadership is experienced and accomplished. Limited change can take place without altering an organization's basic culture. Big change means a major intended shift upward in the organization's culture. Change may be incremental and may occur daily, but transformation is quantum change. Just as the butterfly transcends but includes the caterpillar in its transformation, individual leaders, teams, and entire leadership cultures can transform their current mind-set into a new one.

Consistently in our experience, transformation begins with a major step up in the beliefs and practices within the organization's leadership culture. *Change leadership's beliefs, and you change the culture.* We know that sounds simplistic, and we don't say it's easy. If it were, we would not be wondering (as you may be too) why so many modern organizations are so bereft of adaptation and learning. Why *does* change come so hard?

Voice of Change

Imagine if the people in your leadership culture were unanimous in their response to this survey item: "Our work is united by a common goal." At Memorial Hospital, one of the cases in this book, 90 percent of the respondents strongly agreed with this statement about a commonly held organizational direction. They also agreed that "the work of each individual is well coordinated with the work of others," and "we are putting our shared success above our individual success." What would you give to have this kind of shared alignment and commitment in your leadership culture and in your organization?

This chapter lays out the framework of the main ideas for seeing your organization's leadership overall. It begins by describing how leaderships and their cultures reflect differing consistent logics and how change in those logics can be impeded by certain mind-sets. From there, it explains why changes in leadership culture must begin with the senior leaders. The chapter then lays out three basic types of leadership culture, one of which almost certainly describes your own organization. After that, it tells where your focus needs to be throughout a process of cultural change and what to make of tensions between roles of managers and leaders. Finally, it presents an overview of a general process or path to successful transformation.

But first, understand this now: change, especially large-scale organizational transformation, starts with you. You can no more delegate, defer, or demand culture change of others any more than you can delegate someone else to eat your food or drink your water.

If that sounds intimidating, then consider this piece of good news from our own experience: organizational leadership that takes on and follows through on the process of cultural transformation in support of other large changes consistently succeeds in terms of larger performance goals, while other organizations generally fail to change and struggle to survive. Think of this book as your survival guide to leading change.

Leaders, Logics, and Transformation

There is a logic to any persisting culture. A culture's collection of beliefs and norms fits together in a meaningful way. For this reason, in the Introduction, we proposed the concept of leadership logics: distinctive, consistent mind-sets that tend to pervade the culture of leadership in every organization. For example, one system of leadership logic, which we call Dependent-Conformer, centers on the idea that a leader gives an order for someone else to carry out. This type of culture excludes nonofficial leaders from participating in the leadership collective. It leaves them and their potential waiting indefinitely to emerge.

> What potential could you add by tapping the talent of unofficial leadership, allowing it to join and add value to the leadership culture?

It's often useful to think of leaders as including people whose titles may not suggest "leader." This idea of nontitled leaders and their potential for joining in and advancing leadership

---

"Lead, Follow, or Get out of the Way"

That motivational statement for decades has betrayed a belief that leadership is about few leaders and many followers. We profess that that very old idea severely limits any organization's future. Followership maintains that the most effective human system for the maintenance and distribution of power and influence is the command-and-control hierarchy. Management control through the chain of command used to work in a stable world and still holds on in many organizations. But followership is rarely effective or efficient in a fast-and-tumble new world. We need as many leaders as we can get. The successful organizations we work with want everyone to have a shot at leading, and they regard followers as unsuccessful employees.

logics raises the question of how to think of and define what all kinds of leaders have in common. We believe that the best way to do this is to talk about outcomes.

The Outcomes of Leadership: Direction, Alignment, and Commitment

We define leadership in terms of outcomes: what leadership brings about. As a collective human process, leadership can best be described as what is done to set direction, achieve alignment, and get commitment (Drath and others, 2008). *Direction, alignment, commitment:* we shorten the three to the acronym DAC:

• *Direction.* Setting direction usually implies some measure of change, from incremental to major. For a senior leader, setting direction means charting a course of vision for the organization. Strategy addresses where you are going and how you are going to get there, so setting direction is part of strategy. All significant enterprisewide change emanates from vision and strategy. In organization transformation efforts, your leadership strategy is as important as your business (or organizational) strategy. Your *leadership strategy* is your organization's implicit and explicit choices about the leadership culture, its beliefs and practices, and the people (talent) systems needed to ensure success.

• *Alignment.* Alignment produces the right configuration of beliefs and talent in the systems, structure, and processes that enable your organization to head in the direction you have set. When leadership practices are jointly shared by the collective leadership, such alignment becomes a powerful force for change. One vital alignment is that between business strategy and leadership strategy. It provides an integrated strategic intent for the whole organization.

• *Commitment.* Commitment is getting the leadership culture and then the whole organization on board, believing and devoted to the direction set by your vision and strategy.

DAC as Qualities of Human Systems

It's important to note that direction, alignment, and commitment originate as qualities of human systems. If you don't believe us, try getting commitment from a computer operating system. Traditional management functions focus on just operational tasks. It's important to notice that a manager's tasks of planning, staffing, and budgeting are very different from the leader's work in achieving the outcomes of directing, aligning, and commitment, even though all may cohabit the same human body and mind—yours.

It is often difficult to stay aware of the difference in the day-to-day press of action, but leaders of change must discern it. More often than we can count, we (and perhaps you too) see company officers spend the vast majority of their organizational time in encounters about managing changes in organizational structure or systems and almost no time focused on human system changes in the organization's leadership culture.

Edgar Schein (1992) writes that what leadership really does is lead the organization's culture, which makes the human system pretty much the sole territory of leadership. But he and many other experts have been reluctant to suggest or verify an actual pathway for transforming culture. We advocate developing and advancing the values and beliefs of your informal organizational culture because these are the guides by which people operate and make decisions and are, ultimately, the most powerful operating system your organization possesses.

Attitudes and Assumptions That Get in the Way

"Change the culture?" you ask. "You have got to be kidding me. How can I do that?"

You can start by examining your attitude, assumptions, and beliefs about change.

During successful organizational transformation, the leadership culture serves as a unified force for new direction, alignment, and commitment. In our experience, four general attitudes can get in the way of embarking on change. As you look at where your leaders are now, think about the extent to which any of these might be a problem.

"*Just Let George Do It*": The Myth of the Great Person (CEO). You or others may believe that meaningful, sustainable organization change, including culture transformation, is possible—but only if someone like Jack Welch or Lou Gerstner is there to make it happen.

It is easy to come by this myth. The popular press and many business books extol the actions of larger-than-life Great Person executives. The media document their achievements and hold them in high regard. It's a powerful image. In some organizations,

Voice of Change

Many clients come to us seeking some kind of creative, unconventional assistance with developing leadership and changing their organization, and yet the majority of them think about change in conventional training and development terms. "What programs do we need?" they ask. "Do we have the right competencies?"

Conventional thinking is not your friend when it comes to transformation. Classroom training alone won't get you there, and neither will a focus on developing individual leader competencies. Sustainable change means developing new organizational-level capabilities. That's what DAC offers: a different way toward developing the leadership culture you need. A few powerful organizational capabilities are much more than a cluster of individual leader competencies. Without continuity for sustained collective learning in the leadership culture, the chances for change in your organizational success are slim. Sharing direction, alignment, and commitment is not easy; if it were, everybody would be doing it. It is possible, however, and it defines a pathway to transformation.

employees are so conditioned to it that they look to the CEO as a parental figure—someone to show the way, make all the risky decisions, and provide a safety net for others.

We call this the "just let George do it" attitude because it defers change to somebody else. In our work, we see senior vice presidents defer to executive vice presidents, who defer to the chief operations officer, who defers to the chief executive. It's amazing to watch people give away their hard-earned power rather than stand up and lead. But leaders do give it away when they buy into the Great Person myth.

"Yes, But": Requiring No Loss in Control. Imagine a wave of people ready to make the changes you say you want. Imagine them eager to join with you as soon as you raise the ceiling so that you and they can stand up for change. Are you willing to give them real space? Executives often tell us they feel reluctant to make this kind of invitation. They worry that they don't know which way the wave will break. We call this the "yes, but" attitude: when there's no assured control over how things are going to turn out, leaders often get deeply disturbed. Right now, is your own anxiety about possible loss of control making you want to postpone a big effort to change?

"Either-Or": A Feeling of Not Enough Time. You may be too busy keeping up with operational changes and making the numbers this quarter to make time for messy culture work. Besides, even if you could get time and could get a grasp of all that's needed, making any lasting change to your organization's culture would take forever—if it happens at all. We call this the "either-or" mind-set. Time pressures force people into a false choice: either change the operations, or change the culture—there isn't time to do both (Beer, 2001).

Leaders sometimes fall into the either-or attitude even though they value the idea of cultural transformation. Most modern human organizations do poorly even at adaptive, incremental change and learning. Few are true "learning organizations" that continually adapt, learn, and readily grow in response to external change. But yours can get there.

"Are We There Yet?": Basic Impatience. Leaders come to us asking at the outset how long their organizational change will take and meaning we should be practically there—hence the name of the "are we there yet?" attitude. But lasting change will most likely take time and serious intention. If it took thirty years for an organization to develop to its current stage, it's pretty clear that it's going to take more than thirty days of work to take it to the next level.

You might summarize these four, often robotic mind-sets in a larger, debilitating belief about cultural change that might be called simply "not me, not now."

> If you're feeling not-me-not-now right now, is one or more of these mind-sets at play in you?

Change Begins with You

If you expect change in others and in the culture of your organization, then buckle your seatbelt and get ready to change yourself—first. Your change is the pivot around which culture change swings. If you keep the work of culture change at arm's length, then real, lasting change won't occur. The reason is simple: everyone else in your organization is sitting around with their arms folded, doing nothing too—just like you.

Culture change is a show-up, stand-up, participative, put-yourself-on-the-line personal process. Culture isn't an object or system out there. It's internal. You are in the culture, and the culture is in you. It's a meaning-making interpretation process that you and others perform for survival. We want you to take that personally. Sustainable and durable change begins and ends with you and your commitment.

Of his experience leading change at Honeywell, Bill George, executive vice president of control systems and later CEO of Medtronic, says, "When I faced my self in the mirror I realized that Honeywell was changing me more than I was changing Honeywell" (2003, p. 50). This is bound to be true. In the process of changing the culture of your organization, you will change. You must; you are that much part of the culture.

Culture work is intimate and will reveal your vulnerabilities. You can't manage and control real change the way that you can manage a benefits system. Your team can't fix culture or manipulate it like a software system, a business plan, or a budget. You can try to "fix" or manipulate it, and a lot of managers do. But those efforts mainly account for the dismal failure of so many change efforts. People don't like being manipulated. They prefer to be engaged. Isn't that your preference? Wouldn't you rather be engaged in a participative human process than be manipulated like a part in a machine?

Three Leadership Logics and Cultures

Vertical development of connected, or unified, leadership from one level or mind-set to the next is a practical matter. This is not just something that is nice to have. Venturing into transformation from one pattern or logic to the next is serious business. The endeavor is worth it only if you have to have a new, bigger mind-set, or logic, in order to face the future and execute your strategy. As we have suggested, a leadership logic is a set of beliefs and interpretations that underlies the choices made by and through the leadership culture. It is a supra-sense making, or collective rationale of culture through which the leadership society understands its situations and surroundings, and the principles by which it processes information and discerns outcomes.

In this book we look at three cultures, or logics, that range from earlier to later stages of development and complexity: Dependent-Conformer, Independent-Achiever, and

Interdependent-Collaborator. Most likely you will see fairly quickly which one applies most closely to your organization:

- *Dependent-Conformer.* In a Dependent-Conformer leadership culture and logic, authority and control are held at the top. Honoring the organization's code takes precedence over applied learning that may threaten the status quo. Success depends on obedience to authority and loyalty. Mastery and recognition of work operate primarily at the level of technical expertise. Mistakes are treated as weaknesses, and feedback tends to be negative and from above and is not sought or valued.

- *Independent-Achiever.* Independent-Achiever culture and logic distributes authority and control through the ranks. It focuses on success in a changing world and adapting faster and better than the competition. Success means mastery of systems that produce results in an individual's own domain and eventually contribute to the success of the organization. Recognition of good work honors systems thinking. Mistakes may be treated as opportunities to learn. Feedback may be multilateral and is valued when it develops the individual's ability for advancement and success.

- *Interdependent-Collaborator.* In the Interdependent-Collaborator leadership culture and logic, authority and control are shared based on strategic competence for the whole organization. The mind-set tends toward collaborating across boundaries in a changing world so that new orders and structures can emerge through collective work. Success means collaborative mastery of integrating systems that produce results now and into the future. Mastery and recognition of work tend to be at the integrated systems level. The system as a whole is intended to work effectively for the benefit of all across the whole value chain. Mistakes are embraced as opportunities for individual, team, and organizational learning, and both positive and negative feedback are valued as essential tools for collective success.

None of these three is better than the other two in an absolute sense. Each leadership logic has been and can be successful when the context is right. But there is an order of progression among the three. Reaching a new logic starts with recognizing where you are right now. And most senior leaders tell us that what they need today is Interdependent-Collaborative leadership because the new world order in which they lead is so complex. They tell us that they require a collective leadership working as a unified force for change. Everything about the increasing complexity of their competitive situation and environment calls for it. But few say that an Interdependent-Collaborative culture is what they have right now.

Three Frameworks for Transformation

In practical terms, three frameworks of focus guide effective work at cultural change. Each receives a chapter of its own, but we want you to have the three in mind from the start. We call them *Inside-Out*, *Readiness*, and *Headroom*.

Inside-Out

The source of transformation is your internal, intuitive, emotional, creative spirit realm of your deepest experience of being; it is subjective territory. Beliefs and meaning come from within (Inside-Out). In contrast, Outside-In is what operations are made of—the objective, empirical stuff. Inside-Out is the source of deep, sustainable change.

Readiness

By *Readiness* we mean your preparedness as a leader to face the challenge of change. Your degree of readiness depends on assumptions and beliefs that either enable or cripple your personal chance at transformation. In Chapter Five, we elaborate on what we call the three forces of Readiness: your assumptions about the nature and use of time; the degrees of your felt need for control over self, things, and others; and your deepest intentions—how serious you really are. Your personal readiness for change will determine your ability to guide others through change.

Headroom

Headroom is our term for the space and time created to allow systemic development of the leadership culture. Expanding Headroom assists everyone to acquire the bigger minds that meeting challenges requires. Headroom is about having genuine and creative multilateral, multilevel connections with others in the course of transformation. It depends on internal and group dialogue, authentic public engagement, and collective learning. Headroom means a new social reality in the leadership culture. You know it is there when you actually believe (and believe in) each other and the new organizational reality and capability you are creating.

> ### Voice of Change
>
> Advancing your organization's leadership culture is about executing your strategy while developing your leadership talent. By choosing the right level of leadership culture for the future, your leadership collective will advance to new levels of organizational capability that secure the organization through successive future challenges. Inside-Out development of leadership beliefs must come into balance with Outside-In leadership practices. Creating room for that talent to grow changes your organization's systems and processes.

Transformation and Management

What are you: Leader or manager? Your answer is probably "both," and you know before we say it that your head has a problem with wearing two hats. You're right. It does, and we need to consider why.

Change *management* gets a lot of play in business books and articles and academic theories. Much of the literature about organizational core capability focuses on global competitive ability and the associated management infrastructure required to achieve it. A short list of organizational core capabilities would answer the question, "What few underlying, inherent charac-teristics does this organization exhibit that make it effective?" Change management focuses mostly on external systems, struc-tures, and processes.

Change *leadership* gets much less attention. We urge our cli-ents continually toward a balance between change leadership ability and change management skills—between leadership's creative change outcomes and management's control-oriented technical operations. That balance is basic to successful trans-formation because both are required. Figure 1.1 may help you to visualize it.

Figure 1.1 Leadership Culture and Organization Transformation

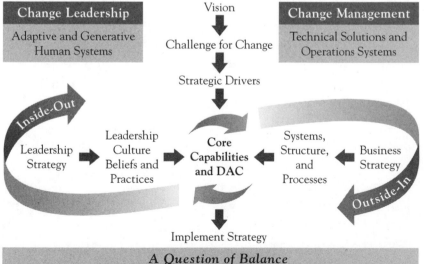

Change Leadership
Adaptive and Generative Human Systems

Vision
Challenge for Change
Strategic Drivers

Change Management
Technical Solutions and Operations Systems

Inside-Out

Leadership Strategy → Leadership Culture Beliefs and Practices → Core Capabilities and DAC ← Systems, Structure, and Processes ← Business Strategy

Outside-In

Implement Strategy

A Question of Balance

As the figure suggests, everything in organizational change is driven by a change in vision, strategic direction, and the need for alignment and commitment to achieve it. When change leadership and change management are in balance and working in sync, an organization's leadership can ensure the direction, alignment, and commitment that enable the development of new core capabilities.

On the left side of Figure 1.1, leadership comes together as a unified collective, implements a new leadership strategy, and alters or reforms leadership culture. Leadership strategy is the organization's approach to advancing the leadership culture, practices, and people systems needed to ensure future success. That approach reflects leadership's conscious, Inside-Out intent about what the new leadership collective will look like and how it will be developed through conscious choices. In its absence, the same old recurrent unconscious choices will continue to be made.

On the right side of the figure, change management looks after changes in systems, structure, and processes that the business strategy requires. Operations are changed and reengineered. New product markets may be opened. The figure calls these changes "Outside-In" because management is concerned with the many external factors of operational systems.

Both change leadership and change management are needed to make progress in a new organizational direction. When you are asking when and how much of each is required, you are on the right track toward a chance at lasting change.

At the center of the figure are the leadership outcomes of DAC and the core capabilities that your organization requires. Core capability means what few key qualities and things your organization needs to have and be able to do in order to implement the business strategy and be successful in navigating the new organizational direction.

Change *management* is not for the faint of heart. It requires mental toughness along with technical and analytical skills, and it demands your making calculated decisions and moving forward based on the best information possible. Change *leadership* requires similar qualities but also demands something different. It requires showing up and engaging personally in public ways and taking on risk and vulnerability in social settings in ways you probably did not learn about in business school or anywhere else. The vulnerability of public learning makes most of us far more uncomfortable than does managing the numbers, making business decisions, or performing most other management tasks.

The Need for Clarity About Management Versus Leadership

Almost everywhere we go, we ask senior leaders to do a quick audit of their calendars. We ask them to list the percentage of their "change" time this month they spent on operational systems versus the percentage on human systems. What we usually get is knowing laughter and shaking heads as they reveal they have scheduled and spent the vast majority of their time in operations and precious little, if any, time on people, culture, and the real source of change. In our experience as well, most U.S. managers in the baby boomer generation spend most of their time managing, with leadership as a secondary priority.

The work of management is about predictable, results-oriented work. Managers are paid to target goals, measure progress, and make it happen. Managing is technical work using objective tools and measures that lower uncertainty and minimize risk. Managers make the numbers.

Leader work is categorically different. It deals with uncertainty, taking risks, herding changes through the organization's culture, and making those changes operational as new leadership practices in order to achieve the aspirations that management alone will never accomplish (Kotter, 1996).

Consciously and actively recognizing the difference between management and leadership in your daily work life is the most essential quality you can foster in yourself and among your leaders. It's what we will call in Chapter Two the "zone of intentional transformation," in which intended change can happen.

Increasing Your Odds of Success

We mentioned in the Introduction that the chances of success in directed organizational change currently run about one in three or four. Our experience with clients and other research we have conducted or reviewed suggest that behind these poor odds is the reality that people in charge of change spend most of their time managing the technical systems and process changes required in the business operations, and precious little time on the changes required in the culture and the human systems.

Why does this happen again and again? It's tempting to view this as a problem of "the" manager duping "the" leader and undercutting what the leader tries to do. But if you are a manager *and* a leader, then you must be duping yourself! Could that be true?

> Are you undermining yourself by allowing your management side to take over and deny your leadership side its full potential?

So, you may ask, "Balancing leadership with management is key to successful transformation, but most change leader-managers aren't doing it?" Yes. That's why, throughout this book, as with our clients, we insist on working toward a balance between the Inside-Out of every leader's role and the Outside-In of every manager's external reality.

The Path We Follow

In our work with clients, based on successes and failures, we've developed and improved a path that begins with analyzing the feasibility of changing the organization. It starts with your organization's conscious decision to pursue a new business strategy (or, if you are public or nonprofit, an organizational strategy). At that point you can begin to ask what general type of leadership is needed to carry it off and how far your current leadership culture is from one that can carry it off.

The questioning begins with individual self-examination, personal dialogues, and exercises such as ones we suggest in Chapter Three. From there, it moves to similar processes with your senior team, testing out where the team stands in terms of a shared sense of worldview, intention, genuine truth telling and listening, and sense of the time required for change. In this process, the team works toward creating or redefining itself as a leadership team for change.

As the senior team goes through this process of learning, members need to continually ask to what extent they are willing to fully participate in and demonstrate in public learning and other ways that may make them feel exposed, just as they will be opening vulnerabilities in the people they are guiding in the change. Not every senior leader may want to come along. Not everyone can or will make the journey.

We believe that almost all organizational cultures can change to some degree, but feasibility and the readiness to change cannot be taken for granted. At many points along the path, you will need to weigh and monitor them. Weighing the feasibility and measuring readiness to change are fundamental steps in creating a leadership strategy that you can implement.

There is a practical reason to weigh feasibility early and often. We witness many organizations investing huge amounts of money, time, and people resources in changes that are destined to fail. Business process reengineering is a good example: from the 1990s into this decade, failure rates in implementation of reengineering have ranged around 90 percent. Companies lunged after efficiencies that consultants said they would reap from Outside-In process changes, without regard to or knowledge of the often huge Inside-Out stretch required by the human system process and the logic of the current culture. If you do good feasibility work on the culture at the outset, you can save a lot of money and heartburn in the long run.

Recall that your leadership strategy is your organization's implicit and explicit choices about the leadership culture, practices, and people systems needed to ensure enduring organizational success. Conventional leadership training and development curriculum supports this definition, but this view of strategy goes beyond those conventions as well. Defining leadership strategy this way makes it about collective leadership aspirations and worldviews and about the connected role of organization champions who enable change with a shared understanding and develop the values and beliefs that support them. Here again is the recurrent theme of your challenge to develop new beliefs.

Whatever leadership team leads your change needs to design and sponsor the leadership strategy for the organization's collective of leaders. With that, the leadership team moves out to the wider project of transforming your organization's broad leadership culture. As that work succeeds, it extends the unity of approach to the organizational middle and eventually can involve everyone in the organization. These levels of work can make use of seminal, large-group events at which the top team hosts and takes active part with the entire leadership community; action development teams in which, for example, nonexperts from across functions are asked to tackle vexing strategic issues that may reside primarily within a function; and learning time-outs in which leaders step back from the heat of action to reflect on operations development.

The path is not circuitous, but neither is it serial or direct. Because it is born of strategy and informed by learning along the way, you may have to alter the route or even reinvent it. It is an unfolding process of discovery and navigation through territory never before encountered. Plans give way to their next iteration, based on what you learn. It is a process of creating the future but does not rule out taking advantage of change that you see already occurring at lower levels in the organization.

Chapter Two will say much more about the nature and power of cultures. In later chapters we present feasible approaches to changing your organization by first changing leadership culture. You'll get direct talk and no-nonsense challenges that can help you be realistic about what is possible. You'll also examine supportive frameworks and tools to help you build your understanding about change, and read about how other organizations have approached leading organizational cultural transformation efforts—some successfully and some not.

Exercises

Learning Journal

Purchase a journal that you will use to record your reflections, insights, questions for further exploration, and experiences in applying the lessons from this book in your leadership to guide transformation in yourself, your senior leadership team, and the leadership culture of your organization.

This personal learning journal is a technique to probe your experiences for lessons you're likely to miss if you're not writing them down. While you're busily engaged in the "doing" of an experience, you may miss some powerful lessons. Reflecting on the experience and writing about it can lead to useful insights about important aspects of your life. These insights give you better information for future choices and help you develop an internal feedback system.

Journaling has several best practices:

- *Establish a routine.* If you don't make time for the journal activity, it will not happen. Realize it may feel awkward at first, but try to dedicate ten to fifteen minutes at some point in your day to reflect.

- *Periodically reflect on your reflections.* Try to set aside a larger block of time, perhaps twenty to thirty minutes every ten days, to look over your cumulative record. This allows you to add other learnings and gives you the opportunity to look for patterns and themes.

- *Break out of the mold.* Remember that the purpose of the journal is your own learning. If the structure you have adopted is not facilitating that learning, try something new.

Questions

- How do you feel about culture change starting with you?
- What is your organization or business strategy? How much and what kind of change in the organization does it demand?
- Does your organization have a leadership strategy? What do you think it is? Is it in alignment with the business strategy?
- Does your organization have the leadership talent needed to implement these strategies?
- Are you capable of implementing these strategies?

Calendar Audit of Time in Leadership Versus Management

Open your day planner or PDA for the past month. Look at your daily schedule, and determine what percentages of your time you spent on leadership and management. Record both percentages:

Percentage of time spent in leadership activities _____

Percentage of time spent in management
activities _____

Total   100%

- Based on the distribution, what would you change in order to involve yourself on a weekly basis with your organization's business strategy, its leadership strategy, and influencing leadership culture development in your organization?
- What specifically will change in your weekly calendar?

2

ORGANIZATIONAL CULTURE

Beliefs That Drive Behavior

> You're so busy grasping technology in one hand
> and science in the other, you have no hand left to
> grasp what's really important. It's the human spirit,
> that's the challenge, that's the voice, that's the
> expedition.
>
> —*John Travolta as George Malley in the*
> *film* Phenomenon

The purpose of this book is to shed light on the dark subject of culture, which people know in their gut is important but don't know how to deal with. We bet you have that feeling too. Academic and technical studies of organizational culture abound, but few practical readings are available to executives on leading change in organizational culture. Why so few?

One reason is the common and popular myth that change in organizational culture is beyond the reach of mere mortals. Executives have come to believe that significant change in their organization's culture is simply unattainable—or that if it is "possible," it would take unfeasibly long to accomplish. But would executives apply this sort of thinking and reach this conclusion if they were considering a technical change such as a new enterprisewide system? Probably not. So why is the transformation of organizational culture regularly dismissed as impossible? A second reason for the unavailability of practical information about organizational culture change is that the academic research community also buys the myth, which adds to its natural tendency to endlessly seek further proof of ideas from which we can already draw much practical advice.

Thus, we have a cycle of "We don't believe it" from executives and "We can't prove it" from researchers. This book aims to break that cycle. There is, in fact, a stream of research, knowledge, and anecdotal stories that can guide and inform executive options. This book is a step toward making that learning available for practical use now. The point is to understand the cultural, human, and especially the internal side of "how."

To that end, this chapter expands on the idea of culture as an agent of stasis, change, or transformation. The goal is to more deeply understand the power of this often hidden dimension and

Voice of Change

From Glen, CEO of Memorial Hospital, one of the cases in this book:

At a recent health care conference, I tried to talk to my CEO counterparts about organization-level leadership, but they just glazed over—they're still sending a few senior people to training classes and expect things to change. How do you talk to CEOs to get their attention about real change through the leadership culture? I told them we use organization leadership to execute strategy, change everything in operations, and provide a healthy environment to grow talent—but they don't know what I'm talking about!

I tried to discuss the investment of time with them—that time is a resource to develop collaborative leadership culture. All we have is time, and we don't ever run out of that. It's about what you do with the time that counts. We have just kept using time to try new things.

The one thing this organization leadership work does is make the organization fast! Man, every CEO wants that. You want an organization that can move quickly—you want fast, fast, fast. If you need a task force or committee to get things done, and they can move fast, then that's it, because there are so many things that need to get done simultaneously. Organization leadership has made us fast!

how changing it needs to begin Inside-Out. But first, let's listen in on a client's story of chairs and culture.

Belief Drives Behavior

Mike, a vice president at National Bank, a prestigious financial organization, tells the story of what came out of an all-day meeting of a group of vice presidents at headquarters: "We brought in VPs and directors from all our locations. We needed to use the largest conference room in the building and had to get special permission to do so."

At National Bank, "permission" wasn't simply an issue of scheduling. The large conference room was located on the top floor of the building and used exclusively by senior executives, not by vice presidents. The vice president and director offices were on the floors below; lower-ranked employees were lower still, filling in the middle floors; the ground level housed administrative and support operations. The furnishings in the building changed by floor too. The top floor featured leather chairs, high-quality wood desks and tables, artwork, and attractive kitchen and washroom facilities. Below that level, floors housed progressively less expensive furnishings.

The night before the meeting, Mike was working late in his office finishing up his presentation: "A couple guys from our maintenance staff kept walking past my office with chairs from the meeting room down the hall. I didn't think much of it until the next morning when I arrived on the top floor for our big meeting. The maintenance staff had replaced all the leather chairs in the executive conference room with the fabric chairs from our floor."

Here the power of culture reveals itself: no one had told the maintenance staff to trade out the chairs. There was no policy or precedent for doing so. The maintenance crew made its own decision, based on its understanding that certain chairs went with certain levels of status. Without question, they simply followed that cultural norm. The cultural value of authority and the trappings of status were so embedded in the organization that it didn't even occur to them that vice presidents might sit in executive chairs while meeting on the executive floor.

Whether explicit and conscious or not, belief systems drive behavior. Organizational culture holds your organization's aspirations and the spirit of the place. Its beliefs and values define the organization's core. We use the chairs anecdote here not because it is a spectacular example but because it is a small one, illustrating how endemic the force of belief is within a culture. And when executives embark an organization on change initiatives bigger than lending out a conference room—as big, say, as changing major systems, products, markets, and processes—they are asking people to alter their company's cultural beliefs in some significant way. To implement a strategy that requires people to change the way they do things, leaders need to work beyond the operational plan and plan to change culture as well. Change won't take hold in operations without change in culture to back it up.

Cultures channel choices and guarantee repeated results, whether awareness is present or not. The leadership challenge is creating a culture that supports the new operational direction rather than one that undermines or stalls it. You're more likely to succeed at that if you keep in mind why a culture tends to persist even though it may no longer seem highly productive.

Voice of Change

Have you found yourself among the many who say that for the organization to survive and thrive, we must transform the culture—but that seems impossible? Our experience with leaders in a variety of organizations suggests that you may be capable of much more than you think—but the journey starts with you. To do this, you will be embracing new beliefs as well as letting go of some well-established assumptions from your education and experience that are no longer helpful.

Swimming in the Soup

Culture is basically Inside-Out, subjective in how it influences thought and behavior. Once we are part of a culture, it's not just something "out there." This distinction between Inside-Out and Outside-In is important. We regularly find senior leaders who cannot distinguish an Inside-Out, subjective leadership experience from an Outside-In, objective, analytical management practice. The Inside-Out is basically about perceptions interpreted through social relationships; the Outside-In is basically about tasks. We think that distinguishing the difference between relationships and tasks is the most important thing that leaders do. If you approach relationships as just another task, you are likely one of those people who can't tell the difference between the overt sensory dimension and the hidden dimension of change.

Everyone in your organization swims in its cultural soup. Not only are you and everyone else *in* the culture: you *are* the culture.

Try to think of the difference between being in a culture and being an enterprise software system. Sounds like a silly request? Still, it reminds you that you can't be a software system. You wouldn't want to be. But you are always going to be in and part of the human system in which you operate, strategize, relate, lead, and make sense. So you need to know what culture surrounds you just as you need to know what software you are counting on.

In sum, culture is personal. You'll never be able to entirely objectify it because you're one of its subjects. This is a very different relationship from managing things from the Outside-In, and it's a relationship you need to understand and master because it will make or break the change your organization wants to make.

Culture, Survival, and Bureaucratic Hierarchy

Our introductory definition of culture encompasses two ideas: that beliefs can require certain behaviors and that they can exclude others. It is important to keep the second, limiting function in mind because in that sense, every culture is inherently averse to change.

In its most basic form, culture is a mechanism for sustainability and survival. "Because it works, we all get paid" reflects our belief in that basic position. Belief is a part of the culture's immune system, so to speak, which rejects alien ways of doing things and protects behaviors that are already accepted. When individuals persistently do things too differently, they risk their own survival within a society or organization.

Conformity and Survival

American courts provide a good example of how Dependent-Conformer logics and conformity to cultural norms set boundaries that may favor survival of a society. If you have ever been called to court in the United States, you've probably heard the call, "All rise!" For what? For the entrance of the judge, of course, the one who makes or governs all decisions in the room and whose level of learning is ritually held above that of all others. If your behavior deviates from his or her standard, you may be held in contempt of court solely based on the judge's assessment, and punished.

In the United States we often complain about the ordeal of visiting government bureaucracies. We describe such trips as visits to the land of the living dead, Kafkaesque daytime nightmares filled with Zombie-like automatons performing their routine tasks in slow motion, devoid of any human connection to the public they're supposed to serve. A primary reason that courts, too many public schools, and other government institutions work in this fashion is that they are driven by law or formal rules. And most U.S. citizens buy into this culture without much question because they see how conformity and rule of law promote general public order—and thereby everyone's survival.

This is not to say that conformist culture is always best even for governmental functions. Many states have adopted less obviously regimented practices, such as easing waiting lines by allowing drivers to make license renewals from their computer.

But the survival factor remains. By and large we accept "how things are done around here," and we fear that change can threaten survival. This is true for the individual who wants to keep her job and get paid, and it's also true for the collective of people who all want the same thing.

Culture Eats Strategy

When a big part of a strategy changes the infrastructure in ways that don't support survival, the culture will kill that change. Culture is the elephant in the room. As one of our clients cheerfully noted, and as Illustration 2.1 suggests, "Culture eats strategy for breakfast."

An organization's culture has the hidden power to devour strategic change initiatives. But it also has the power to cultivate change when it is understood and worked with from the inside. As a matter of enlightened self-interest, the culture can help or hang executives in big change initiatives. The help can be harnessed for your benefit if you are willing.

Your leadership culture may dictate respect for hierarchy so that most decisions are

Voice of Change

When we began working with Memorial Hospital, its leaders mostly experienced leadership as a command-and-control hierarchy; at best, leadership meant joining the ranks for personal success. Today at Memorial, leadership means an alliance designed to help the whole organization win. Can you imagine the leadership collective in your organization becoming a coherent, united force for change? Belief precedes action.

Illustration 2.1 Culture Eats Strategy for Breakfast

Source: Bruce Flye. Used with permission.

made at the higher levels. Or you may have an open-door policy that demands noncritical, positive communications across levels. Your culture may be somewhat clannish and require a high level of involvement, or it may be primarily business and results driven with a no-nonsense market focus. Your culture might even engender and create a bona-fide learning organization.

Whatever kind of culture you work in, it's important to understand its beliefs and practices before you try to change them.

General Electric and IBM: Bureaucracies Transformed

Consider the stories of GE and IBM. If you have followed their histories, you would probably not deny that those two organizations were, prior to being led by Jack Welch and Louis Gerstner, respectively, averse to change. They were overgrown, lumbering corporations whose loyalty to a bureaucratic code was pushing them rapidly to their demise. In both of these Fortune 50 companies, collective behaviors determined by social beliefs limited their learning and channeled their choices toward irrelevance and extinction in the marketplace. Both companies needed to learn new ways to be and do, and both leaders helped them become more limber, independent-minded companies.

New leadership at GE and IBM appears to have transformed them into organizations whose social beliefs expand behaviors and learning, broadening choices and new meaning. At GE, a demand for emergent executive learning changed a set of beliefs about "the way things are around here" toward a performance-based culture. At IBM, emergent social beliefs and behaviors moved from producing a slew of product-centered programs without much accountability toward a service-led strategy and a major reengineering effort that demanded increasingly sophisticated levels of capability. Louis Gerstner (2002) regarded changes in beliefs as key to changing IBM: "I came to see . . . that culture isn't just one aspect of the game—it *is* the game" (p. 182).

If you look at the Fortune 500 today in terms of how their cultures limit or expand their potentials, you can quickly and easily begin to see how different these kinds of organizations and their cultures are. Compare, for example, the U.S. automotive industry and airline industry companies with many of the newer entrepreneurial high-tech companies. Compare them in view of your own experience. From your customer's perspective on responsiveness and quality, what is it like to drive or to fly with the biggest U.S.-based organizations in the automotive and airline industries? Does that quality of experience compare to the level of innovative product and service support you receive from the top three suppliers of your computer equipment and service?

These two examples come from the private sector, but we assure you that there are most definitely differences in organizational cultures within every sector—public, private, profit, nonprofit—and with those differences come possibilities for transformations in every sector. It's a myth that only the private sector can exercise meaningful and influential change. Transformation depends as much on the type of culture an organization starts out with as it does on the sector in which the organization performs.

The Hidden Is Powerful

Too many leaders, and so too many organizations, have a bias for action. From that point of view, taking action is often the starting point, end point, and every place in between when it comes to organizational change. Action-oriented senior leaders who are faced with a need to create change often adopt furious, extended sprees of change management. They roll up their sleeves and brace themselves for the tough battle ahead, and they focus on the technical systems and process changes required in the business operations. A bias for action becomes an obsession filled with activity and the appearance of progress.

But much of culture is largely unconscious. The way to implement change successfully is to give this hidden dimension of it the same attention as the stuff of operations. To do something different (an external outcome), you must be something different (an internal outcome).

That core of beliefs is so strong that it drives decisions in ways that the decision maker may not even be conscious of because similar decisions and the process that guides them are practiced throughout the organization day by day and year by year. People become unconsciously competent at valuing the system of beliefs. Because these beliefs are so embedded and because they drive behaviors that determine decisions linked to survival, leaders really have to get people's attention to get them to make different decisions and engage in culture change.

Two primary faculties in decisions are reason and emotions, and emotion appears to trump reason according to multiple streams of recent research in neuroscience. Also, pattern recognition, or the arrangement of data from our environment (how we read our world), repeats patterns of how we see things and eventually, with a lot of repetition, becomes our truth (Hawkins, 1995).

Unexamined beliefs can control an organization and prevent any meaningful change. Years of valuing hierarchy, status, authority, and control—even if unstated—can lead to assumptions and behaviors that are unnecessary, unhelpful, and at odds with stated goals. Interestingly, in Mike's story, the bank's executive team (the "owners" of that top-floor turf) expressed surprise and some amusement at the chairs story, but all of them saw how company culture had driven the decision. If unspoken culture determines who gets to sit in what, just imagine how powerfully it may influence higher-risk, more complex situations.

Your unconscious mind is one step ahead of your conscious mind (Peck, 1992). When decisions are made without conscious reflection, they are in great part determined by beliefs that are unconsciously shared in your culture and the decision patterns already formed and reinforced by shared practices. By increasing your awareness of your experience and your relationships with both people and things, you can expand your conscious realm and get greater access to the power of your unconscious realm. Only through your relationships and the knowledge of cause and effect can you be fully effective in leading change.

Through our grounded theory research in client work, we've found that individuals and organizations that intentionally unearth and examine beliefs, values, and assumptions are able to address the culture factor as a strategic imperative alongside operations strategy. They draw out hidden or unconscious drivers for what is happening—or not happening—in the organization. So let's look at one way to increase conscious awareness in organizational culture.

Take Time for Learning

Raising awareness requires shifting your sense of time and slowing down enough to reflect on what is actually going on in yourself and with others. Doing so can allow you access to the internal experience of culture. But most people in organizations, including its leaders, don't do that. Instead, culture just happens to them, and they aren't very much aware of it. Or, stated more accurately, they don't take the time to be aware of it.

Figure 2.1 demonstrates the situation. Regardless of how hidden (how conscious or unconscious) our own values and beliefs are, they direct what we do. "Operating space" refers to where and how we do our work every day. In that dynamic space, we make each of our daily decisions, whether or not we are actually conscious of each particular decision. Our mental and emotional boundaries are managed, largely unconsciously, in this space as well. Here also we perceive and react in response to both invitations and inhibitions to change. When you are more aware, the operating space can be a playground for forming new beliefs in action development and change.

We would all like to attribute our decisions to our conscious analytical prowess, backed up by our conscientious study of market demand and supply-side reading of performance numbers in our databases and spreadsheets. But many other things are going on. To the extent that beliefs and values remain

Figure 2.1 Inside-Out: The Driver of Results

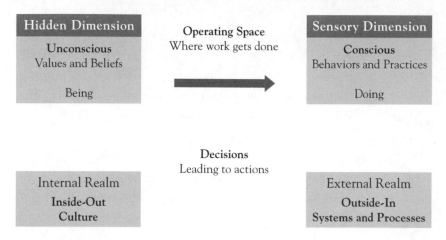

hidden, influence passes unconsciously from left to right, and unconscious organizational culture transmits beliefs into observable actions. Beliefs and repeated patterns are the root cause; our actions are the effect. As a rule in daily organizational life, we make dozens of decisions without much conscious observation of them or any conscious truth-telling process within ourselves or with others. What we believe to be true goes mostly unchecked by our reason.

So in the figure, the arrow points to the right. Should an arrow point from right to left also? In other words, don't practices, systems, and structures also affect our values and beliefs? Don't operations affect the culture? They do, but as long as the left, internal side is hidden, our way of detecting or judging its effect is very limited, so we and the organization are simply at their mercy.

We contend that making the hidden dimension less hidden and more conscious does not dilute its power. Rather, it places that power more nearly within a leader's grasp to influence outcomes. As another of our clients observed, "The culture always wins."

In the Long Run

Organizational challenges are human challenges first, and then they are operational challenges for the humans to deal with. Many companies have that backward. The current crisis in most organizations is the outcome of many years of repeated failures of outdated solutions applied toward newly emerging complex challenges. When the heat is on, organizations revert to what they know: managing numbers and structures. We've seen companies on the long, slippery slope of incessant reorganizing. One company executive said to us, "Yes, we've done it so much I think restructuring is the strategy—the only one."

But Tex Gunning (2006), CEO of Unilever, suggests that the ultimate bottom line of a business is whether it survives in the long term, not whether it meets its short-term targets. History shows that most businesses don't survive and therefore don't meet their ultimate bottom-line goal.

If organizational long-term sustainability is not your ultimate bottom-line goal, then what is? Is not a senior leader's primary responsibility the strategic guardianship of the organization?

Zone of Intentional Change

In Figure 2.2 we add what we call the zone of intentional change to our depiction of how beliefs direct what we do. What we mean to suggest by the zone is that one can increase one's power of conscious awareness within the operating space and so make more of it subject to conscious intentions. By doing so, one also makes the outcomes of decisions more effective in reaching conscious goals. One of the ways we talk about this is "creating headroom," which we discuss in Chapter Six.

By giving more conscious attention and weight to internal dimensions, leaders introduce the possibility of new ways of perceiving, thinking, and feeling about them that can give way to new

Figure 2.2 Expanding Inside-Out Conscious Awareness and Decisions with Outside-In Performance Results

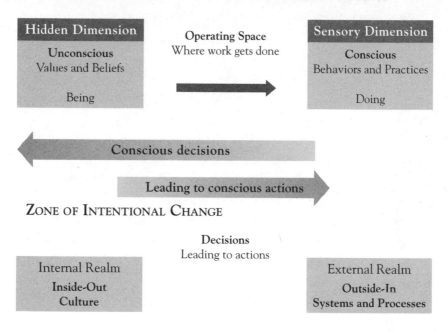

beliefs—and therefore new decisions and new behaviors. Leaders create a larger mental and emotional space for change, allowing unexpected decisions to be made. The bigger the operational change is, the more the culture space needs to expand. You have to grow up into this space as you create it for yourself and for others.

The zone of intentional change represents what we also call intentionality. In Chapter Five, we'll describe intentionality as one of the three key elements of readiness for transformation.

We make our best decisions within the zone of intentional change. You have probably already made several decisions today. Pick one or two of them and pause to examine them. Of each, ask:

How did the norms of my culture determine what I decided to do?

How did the beliefs and norms determine what I did not do but that might have been more effective?

Your answer to the second question may be more revealing than your answer to the first.

Decisions translate cultural beliefs into action. Core beliefs often drive decisions in subtle and automatic ways such that the decision maker is not, or is barely, conscious of them. In other words, the decision may be largely nonrational. It still has its own logic, but not a logic that we command. Actually the logic may be mostly emotional and reactive.

As we noted earlier in the chapter, data are mounting that emotions play a much bigger part in decision making than previously understood, and new studies suggest that emotions rule decisions more than reason does. The research is telling us that parts of the brain associated with early evolution and development of humans honor feelings over reason as a matter of survival. The obvious conclusion of this evidence is that immediate instincts that honor survival are more important than strategic long-term consideration in the immediate reaction to situations that demand decisions (DeMartino, 2006).

Getting a Bigger Mind

Figure 2.2 emphasizes how increasing your conscious awareness both increases your operating space and provides a more conscious bridge of decision making between your being and your doing, or between beliefs and practices. By increasingly opening up your awareness of beliefs, you can be more conscious of and about the decisions you are making and the impact of those decisions on your behaviors and practices. We call this process "getting a bigger mind." It expands your awareness of what's really going on and enables you to perceive more complex interconnections and respond with both long-term strategic acuity and elevated knowledge of how your next decision brings the environment you want to create more fully into existence.

Culture as Your Bottom Line

As a senior leader, the culture of your organization can help you or hang you. Organization cultures have jettisoned as many CEOs, executives, and senior leaders as boards of directors have. Through its survival response to change, the organization's culture will determine the destiny of any executive, no matter how powerful he or she appears to be.

Many leaders who find themselves on the outside have used language that tiptoes around culture: "Innovation is our future," "In challenging times, we need to pull together," "People are our most important assets," and so forth. But after that perfunctory nod toward the human element of change, these leaders quickly move to the operations element of Outside-In structural change depending solely on the usual tools of operations. It is as if they believe that when the job is done right, the culture will follow. Likely, it will not follow, as research on failure rates of structural change bears out.

The Inside-Out approach to culture change fits side by side with conventional Outside-In operational strategies. When leaders examine beliefs and thinking, they increase awareness of why and how they make decisions. They gain new insight into what is working operationally and what is not. You, your team, and the leadership culture can begin to consciously build a bridge between the hidden, internal drivers and the visible, external actions. By using reflective learning processes to factor in the power of culture, people are able to view a situation in a new way. Honoring both sides—integrating leadership and management— provides the magic to face unfolding challenges effectively. This approach creates the space and time and the conscious intention where genuine change and transformation occur.

In the next chapter, we'll start down the road toward an Inside-Out perspective and give you the tools so that you can begin to develop that perspective in yourself. The result will be that bigger mind that makes more of your unconscious conscious and available for transforming organizational culture.

Exercises

Questions

- How would you characterize the current leadership culture in your organization?
- How does your leadership culture enhance or inhibit operational implementation of the business strategy?
- How intentional is your leadership culture in developing itself toward its performance goals?

Culture and Systems Readiness Audit

Fill out the answers to the questions that follow from your point of view. Then do the same process with your senior leadership team or your team at a staff meeting, or both. Discuss from the perspective of why, what, and how to make changes that would increase the success factors for changing your organization and its leadership culture.

Has your senior leadership team agreed on what your leadership collective needs to be capable of? To what extent have you reached agreement?

1	2	3	4	5	6	7	8	9
Little			Somewhat			Substantially		

To what extent do these agreements incorporate and support leading change?

1	2	3	4	5	6	7	8	9
Little			Somewhat			Substantially		

To what extent is your vision statement supported by this shared understanding of leadership capabilities?

1	2	3	4	5	6	7	8	9
Little			Somewhat			Substantially		

To what extent does your organization have an explicit leadership strategy that is connected with and supports the business strategy?

1	2	3	4	5	6	7	8	9
Little			Somewhat			Substantially		

To what extent does your talent management system directly leverage the collective leadership capability you need to execute strategy?

1	2	3	4	5	6	7	8	9
Little			Somewhat			Substantially		

To what extent does your organization manifest intentional collective learning that supports strategy, leadership development, and change?

1	2	3	4	5	6	7	8	9
Little			Somewhat			Substantially		

Journal

Write an assessment of why to change, what to change, and your initial thinking about how to change to move any ratings below 7 in the readiness audit toward the other end of the scale. What role will you commit to play in acting on your analysis and ideas for implementation to bring about change?

3

BIGGER MINDS

Developing from the Inside Out

We are embedded in new learnings that have emotional impact, and then we separate from them so we can understand them.

—*Bob Kegan*

While changing the culture of your organization, you will struggle, change your beliefs, and likely emerge a different person, with an expanded identity compared to the one you had when you began the venture. This is the clarion call to new leaders in the new world order: claim your right to develop a bigger mind.

Everybody's mind has to get bigger if the leadership culture of the organization is to change, because creating real, sustained change is a bigger challenge than your organization has probably ever faced before. The phrase *bigger mind* may not sound scientific, but we think it says what we and you are really after. Increasingly complex challenges require increasingly bigger minds. Each of the three leadership logics or mind-sets we introduced in Chapter One—Dependent-Conformer, Independent-Achiever, Interdependent-Collaborator, in that order—requires more mental depth, breadth, and ability to handle complexity. Figure 3.1 reflects that order. How big does your mind need to be to deal with your challenges? Regardless of how big, you're probably aware right now that it and you need to develop and grow. If you want to change your organization and change the ways in which people work together, you need to develop your people and yourself.

Figure 3.1 Leadership Logics: Getting a Bigger Mind

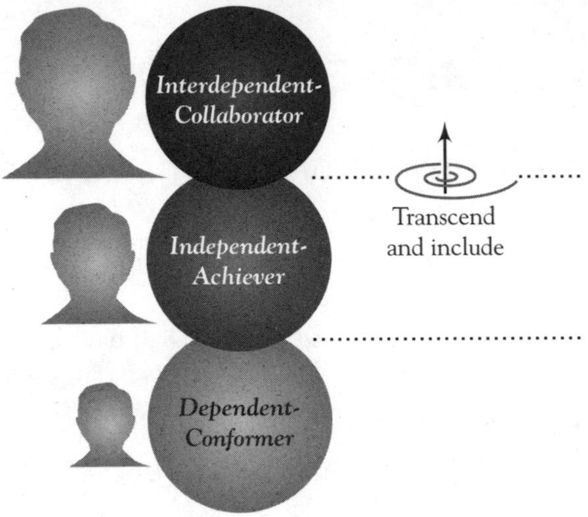

This chapter looks at the general process of developing that bigger mind from the Inside-Out. The concept applies to both individuals and groups and their organizations. In this chapter we will stay mainly at the group, cultural level. Chapter Four will immerse you more directly in the personal level, which is where you must start.

The Nature of Lifelong Development

Although grown-ups like to consider themselves, well, grown up, development really means that no matter how old we are, we still have ways in which we need to keep growing. This can mean facing up at last to grizzly challenges and attaining the wisdom needed to deal with increasing complexity.

Most of us understand development as a continuing law of life. We were all kids once. We understand from our own experience and from watching our children grow that there are stages of early development that are, beyond question, a normal and inherent part of life. But many of us are not aware that those stages or levels of development do not stop at age twenty-one.

As long as you breathe, opportunities to pursue the next stage of development never end.

Stages of human development look a lot like a staircase. We can see that clearly as children: first learn to walk, go through the "terrible twos," start school, and hit early adolescence and then coming of age. But what stair do you see yourself on at age twenty-eight, or forty-two, or fifty-five? As you think about that, consider several principles that are part of our basic understanding of stage development:

- You actively construct ways of making sense of your world, and you can find patterns of sense making that you share with others. These shared patterns are the levels or stages of development. (In leadership contexts, we are calling them *leadership logics*.)

- Stages of development emerge in a (mostly) predictable sequence, with each next stage transcending and including the previous one (Wilber, 1996). When you pass from one stage to the next, you don't lose what you've learned in the previous stages. You have access to all the knowledge and internal operating logics that inform and trigger actions of previous stages to call on when you need them.

The staircase image supports and fits these psychological developmental principles. It suggests that each stair predict-ably rests on the one below but embodies a more advanced sense-making ability, a more sophisticated internal logic and aptitude.

Higher stages are more complex than earlier stages, but they are not better in any absolute sense. Each expands the size of your mind. Developmental movement from one stage to the next is usually driven by limitations in the current stage. When you're confronted with increased complexity and challenge that can't be met with what you know and can do from your current development position, you may take the next step up.

Individuals in all kinds of societies understand this idea about development. That is why all see the potential for wisdom in their later years and why some societies elevate the social position of the wise elder. Stories from grandfathers and grandmothers shed light on current challenges. And we've never met a leader who didn't have a powerful story about someone more advanced on the developmental staircase who helped him or her take the next step toward a later stage. Regularly we see the evidence of the wisdom that comes from mentors, elders, and others who are further along life's natural developmental pathway.

There is also mounting agreement among development experts that movement from one stage to the next can be accelerated considerably when you are consciously aware and working on your development (in the zone of intentional change we described in Chapter Two) from one stage to the next. Naturally those who consciously choose to climb get there faster.

The Inside-Out of Growing Mind

In Chapter Two, we talked a good deal about the Inside-Out nature of culture. Let's say more here about the Inside-Out of personal development. It is empirically, scientifically comfortable to hold things "outside-in," at a distance, studying and analyzing their function, dealing in facts. But lifelong development requires more; it demands the attention of your innermost essential self—a self that seeks and finds meaning. The Inside-Out interprets, unravels, and deciphers a quality of experience like belief, value, and intention. Inside-Out is your essential self, and meaning is the medium. Outside-In is your functional self, and action is the medium (McGuire, Rhodes, and Palus, 2008).

For context, we need to recognize that our modern world is out of balance. For a few hundred years since the Age of Reason and the mushrooming of science, much of Western society and most organizations have tried to collapse the Inside-Out and Outside-In realities into the Outside-In scientific perspective. This is why management science gets more attention than the cultural interpretation of leadership. It is very important to re-separate these two tangled perspectives and gain back that pair of eyes that allows us to see multiple dimensions. It is safe to say this is why we are advancing through a so-called postmodern era: to regain our essential selves.

Inside-Out is a sense-making process, and because we are social creatures, that means dialogue with others. So developing from one stage to another is both an individual and to some degree a social process. And self-exploratory dialogue does entail social risk and vulnerability. Lifelong development is an ongoing journey on which you remain conscious of and pay attention to the two basic sides of your human nature: Outside-In and Inside-Out. Both are necessary and valuable, but Inside-Out may be the more interesting and necessary for sustainable development.

Voice of Change

Seven weeks into the tenure of the new director of the FBI and six weeks after the terrorist attacks of September 11, 2001, a Sunday morning U.S. network news pundit demanded: "Director Mueller, I want to know why you have failed to change the culture at the FBI!" The question itself betrays our U.S. bias for treating organizational culture as just one more thing to manage and manipulate. Void of insight that culture is an internal territory, this well-respected newscaster exposed a fault line most of us share: collapsing the Inside-Out into the Outside-In into a singularity. He considered culture just one more task to manage.

Your Outside-In perspective is full of objects or things, and you can see them all: it's all stuff you can point to, including people, and you don't have to talk to any of them. It is low-risk territory. It is a perspective that locates things, it is scientific and empirical and about surfaces, and it is personally removed.

Inside-Out is different terrain. It is a province of subjective experience and high-risk territory that requires you to talk to people and get to the bottom of things, to engage with other people and go much deeper than coffee machine chitchat or the one-way content of inspirational executive speeches. You have to dive into Inside-Out without knowing what lies under the surface. Surfaces can be seen, but depth must be interpreted. Outside-In takes you only so far, and when it comes to transformational change, that's not nearly far enough.

Development and Leadership Logics

Various researchers have categorized the individual stages by which adults tend to function. Some suggest as few as three separate stages and others as many as nine. The logics in the right-hand column of Table 3.1 were conceived by Bill Torbert, one of our closely allied learning partners (McGuire, Palus, and Torbert, 2007). Bill calls his seven adult developmental stages "action logics" because each represents a certain consistency of actions or behaviors based on the development-level mind-set by which individuals interpret their surroundings. We worked with Torbert in correlating our three stages of culture (or leadership logics) with his seven (leader) action logics. Our stages also correspond with other developmental theorists (see Appendix A). Of these logics, Rooke and Torbert say:

> Most developmental psychologists agree that what differentiates leaders is not so much their philosophy of leadership, their personality, or their style of management. Rather, it's their internal "action logic"—how they interpret their surroundings and react

Table 3.1 Leadership Logics and Leader Logics

Leadership Logics	Leader Logics
Interdependent-Collaborator	Transformer: shape-shifter, imaginer, *alchemist Collaborator: partner, both-and, *strategist
Transitional	*Freethinker Rising*
Independent-Achiever	Freethinker: initiator, nonconformist, *individualist Performer: winner, high flier, *achiever
Transitional	*Specialist Rising*
Dependent-Conformer	Specialist: technician, niche connoisseur, *expert Moderator: pleaser, conflict avoider, *diplomat Dominator: authoritarian, manipulator, *opportunist

Note: The asterisk signifies Rooke and Torbert's (2005) descriptive terms.

when their power or safety is challenged. They should, because leaders who do undertake a voyage of personal understanding and development can transform not only their own capabilities but also those of their companies [Rooke and Torbert, 2005, p. 1].

We do not mean that people perched on higher stages are more intelligent than they were at the one below or smarter than others at earlier stages. They're not inherently better or more valuable as people. Each stage serves an essential purpose for each person, and organizations almost always need a mix of leaders at different logics to do different kinds of work.

But in leadership logic development, each successive logic or stair holds greater facility for learning, complex problem solving, and the ability to set new direction and successfully lead change. People who gain another step can learn more, adapt faster, and generate more complex solutions than they could before. Those at later stages can learn more and react faster because they have a bigger mind. They can see the bigger picture with all of the complex systems connections more readily than people at earlier logics can. People at later stages are better at seeing and connecting more dots in more scenarios (which means they are better at strategy). That's all. But that's a lot.

Continuing with Table 3.1 in mind, let's look more closely at the leadership logics and their connections to what leaders do.

Leaderships and Leaders: Connected Logics

The leadership logic of a culture does not determine the stage of development of individuals within it. But it does determine the boundaries of acceptable behaviors. For that reason, many of the people in a given organization will have individual leader logics that fit (are consistent with) the cultural stage, or leadership logic. Organizations seek out individuals who are consistent with their level of beliefs and practices. While most individual leaders in any given organization likely are a logic match, it is also possible that many are not.

To stress the concepts, the three profiles that follow are written as if there were an absolute match of cultural leadership logic to individual leader logics. But in any organization, the fact that there are many individuals with logics advanced beyond an early stage of the culture is a great advantage when entering change. When a large number of individuals are at a logic that is earlier than what the organization needs, that constitutes a disadvantage.

Dependent-Conformer

If you operate within a Dependent-Conformer culture, the organization creates certain conditions for your continued inclusion. In these social systems, your sense of self is derived primarily from your connections to others. Although you can override your own needs, your social orientation derives from a drive to coordinate your needs with others. We call this the Dependent stage because of your shared dependence on and with others to understand or construct your reality. The dependence is mutual: everyone in it believes in it. Most people make the transition to this stage in late adolescence or early adulthood. In this stage, as the table says, you might be a Dominator with an extreme need for authoritarian control, or you might be a Moderator, diplomatically controlling yourself in order to get along with others through a generous kind of paternalism. Or you might be a Specialist due to technical expertise in your craft, seeking control over the things you work on or with. In any case, control is very important to you, and you don't much like public conflict.

Whether you are an official, supervisor of others, or an individual contributor, you likely have a Specialist logic. In a Dependent-Conformer culture, most individual leaders do. They may be certified (for example, as machinists, teachers, accountants, project managers, doctors, lawyers, or software engineers), or they may hold organizational affiliations, such as priest or government official. These affiliations do not, however, determine the level of a leader's logic.

From an educational perspective, a leader associated with this stage sees education as teaching and training in skills (mostly technical). For this person, the primary function of learning and development is to build competence and skills to use as mechanisms for control in meeting not only the standards of a specialty but also the top-down standards of the organization. Mastering a specialty is what learning is about, whether the leader is a machinist or physician. Dominator, Moderator, and Specialist individual logics are found in about half of all organizational leaders.

Independent-Achiever

If you're a Performer in the Independent-Achiever stage, then other people's reactions cease to be the primary way you define and understand yourself. You have become an independent, self-possessed person, and you have created your own internally generated values and standards. This sense of individual identity allows you to examine various opinions and perspectives and make your own standards-based decisions, modulated and discerned within, and yet expanding the boundaries of your organization. You are highly adaptive and are adept at continuously adjusting to your environment. You likely have mastery of technical data for analysis and make what you believe are rational, independent judgments. Your greatest drivers are success, achievement, and individual competence. You coordinate and cooperate within and between groups to advance your interests primarily and secondarily the interests of your organization. You seek to do both, but in a pinch you come first.

If you're a Freethinker (Table 3.1), then you're well positioned to make your way to the next stage. The Freethinker is an individualist who has mastered the idea that reality is constructed and is what he or she makes it from his or her own perspective. The Freethinker understands the logics of others and can be an excellent facilitator in group settings. But this person also feels free to make up new rules and construct new organizational orders—for example, actions that are good for the whole organization, even when others in earlier logics may have a hard time discerning the benefit.

About 40 percent of all organizational leaders are Performers or Freethinkers. Many (but not all) adults make the transition to this stage during their middle to later years.

From an educational perspective, people at this stage see teaching as coaching. Learning is a dialogue, a two-way street, but the coach is seen as having more expertise than the learner. However, Freethinkers are well on their way to experiencing a coach more as a guide who offers multiple alternatives to consider and discern.

Interdependent-Collaborator

In this latest stage of development, we label leaders as Collaborators or perhaps Transformers (Table 3.1). Collaborators are excellent strategists, and their strategic influencing skills are extraordinary. Those skills make them powerful change agents. They are competent at learning in complex environments because they make connections at multiple levels and across systems simultaneously. Collaborators are energized by these multiple levels of interplay at personal, organizational, interorganizational, and all other manner of intersystemic levels.

Transformers are rare. They are able to reinvent themselves and transform their organizations through an unusual capability to simultaneously deal with multiple situations at many different levels. A Transformer can take care of tactical tasks while keeping strategy (the big picture) in mind. Transformers are also truth tellers, because they have advanced beyond the common fears of personal worry and onto a plane of concern for the whole enterprise and everyone in it. A Transformer leader works as easily with the CEO as with Marti Machinist on the shop floor because he or she rewards both with equanimity.

For Collaborators and Transformers, the dichotomies of either-or thinking give way to a both-and mind-set and a search for win-win potential across and among people and systems. Leaders in these roles experience themselves as instruments of productive change for the benefit of all. They can generate new orders, processes, and systems, allowing new interorganizational realities to emerge and potential innovation to permeate both human and operational systems.

From an educational perspective, the Collaborator views teaching as guidance. What distinguishes a guide from a coach is that a guide doesn't believe that he or she knows best in any given situation. The prevailing philosophy of a guide is that people collaborate and guide each other. With this outlook, guides can potentially generate more knowledge and therefore more multiple right answers than nonmutual approaches can generate.

Go back to Table 3.1 and take an additional moment with it.

Do you see something close to your own leader logic?

Does that leader logic line up with your organization's leadership logic?

If not, is your leader logic advancing or lagging behind the majority leadership logic of your organization? Is this a source of frustration or alienation in your experience?

More broadly, do you see the connection between the leadership culture and logic in which you work and your capability as a leader?

Independent-Achievers have bigger minds than Dependent-Conformers.

Interdependent-Collaborators have the biggest minds of all. How big does your mind need to be to deal with your challenges?

Getting to the Next Leadership Logic

Leaders who come to week-long programs at the Center for Creative Leadership (CCL) often have a moving, powerful experience. It's not unusual for them to describe it as life changing. But when we follow up, we too often learn that after they went home and back to work, too little changed, because they reentered the dominance of their cultural reality. The powerful experience they had had promoted a new (temporary) state of being, but it's not the same as advancing to a new (lasting) development stage or leader logic. (We use *state* and *stage* to signal a difference in how long things last.) There is a relationship between short-lasting state and enduring stage (or logic), however, and it is a very important relationship.

Voice of Change

Leaders we work with often express confusion about the difference between a state and a stage. State precedes stage. A state is fleeting; a stage is ongoing. Perhaps a simple analogy will prove useful. The state of security that comes from being defended and cared for by your girlfriend or boyfriend is not the same as a stage of security that comes from a mature relationship you know is reliable. The state of security you feel with her or him is situational, but a stage of security (your long-term relationship) arises from that state.

It is the same in organizational culture. Imagine you have worked for some time in a dependent role. Recently you have gotten a taste of independence—you made some decisions without checking with the authorities—and it felt pretty good! That's a state: you get an experience of the new thing in the old place. That state is not a stage until you can access that state as a constant, reliable condition. You know it when your mind-set shifts from one stage to the next. Achieving a new state may be relatively easy. Achieving a new stage is harder. One way you know you're entering a new stage is that you give up old beliefs, which can make you feel confused and in the process can be disorienting and uncomfortable. Giving up a belief in the authority of others and becoming the authority of and for yourself is an example.

From States to Stages: Practice Makes Perfect

Practice does make perfect, and it is also the essential difference between short-lasting states and long-lasting stages. When you have a new breakthrough experience that raises your ceiling of awareness and expands your zone of intentional change (recall Figure 2.1), if you can trigger another occurrence of that experience or increase the rate at which it is recurring, then you can speed up the process toward attaining the next stage of development. By making yourself aware that the development process is happening, you become actively involved in it as your own personal way of operating. In other words, the more often you can achieve that alternative state of experience, the closer you get to its becoming your regular mode, and you are on the path to achieving a bigger mind.

Let's say that you are a Specialist, still deeply identified with and conforming to the group that practices your particular craft. Now let's say that you experience an extraordinary kind of individuality that frees you from the constraints of dependence on the group. Let's say this experience happens just once more, and the independence you experience really grabs your attention. Have you advanced from a Dependent-Conformer to an Independent-Achiever? No.

One or two isolated experiences don't complete advancement from one stage to the next. To step upward, you have to sustain the experience of heightened awareness long enough and often enough so that it takes over and replaces the previous stage of awareness of your world.

Voice of Change

The transformation principle: Sustain and practice a new state and you will make it to the next stage; maintain the new bigger idea long enough and you will advance to the next leadership logic.

From States to Stages: Self-Reinforcing Steps

Developing leaders often don't know what's needed or involved in a later development stage. That is bound to be hard for them to grasp when they're in an earlier stage. However, self-reinforcing, practical steps aid the process of transition from one stage or leadership logic to the next: awaken, unlearn, and advance (Kegan, 1982). In the following, we illustrate them as they apply between the dependent and independent stages. (We have applied a similar dynamic to groups, which we discuss in depth in Chapter Six.)

Step 1: Awaken. First comes the ability to perceive that a new way of making sense of your world is possible and that doing things differently is feasible. What happens in this step is that the current-stage logic battles to override the upstart newcomer (the advanced, potential logic) that enters with its new big idea. A leader in the grip of this process will experience quite a bit of emotion because the next advancing logic feels invasive. If the new experience is strong, then the new, big idea can sink some early roots. If you're in this experience, you may struggle to put the new, big idea into practice. The reason for the struggle is that the old idea works to dominate the new idea. But if you stick with the new idea and continue to create experiences in which you can try it out, you will make progress.

Step 2: Unlearn and Discern. Next comes the ability to hold the old idea of doing things up to the cold, harsh, brutal light of day. Examine it, analyze it, and grill it as if you're a bad cop in a worse precinct in a 1950s hard-boiled detective movie. Ask that old mind a lot of "why" questions: "Why not this new idea?" "Why, old idea, are you so stubborn about accepting the new idea, this new belief?"

Take the new idea out and test it. Develop it in the action of your day-to-day work, and test it with a pattern of new applications: "What we'll do and how we'll do it." When you make mistakes or when these new applications don't work out, pay attention to your feelings of disappointment and guilt—a natural reaction and a powerful learning opportunity. Don't get down on yourself or fall into a guilt trip that will drag you backward. Think of yourself as an explorer, a discoverer of new realities. Stay the course, and don't stop at the boundaries and limitations set by the old assumptions and beliefs. The old idea (built on a less advanced leadership logic) won't like being disposed of, so you'll need to hold it out at a distance as an object to view and analyze. When you can treat it as an object of your discernment, you can make value judgments for yourself about which reality—that mind or the bigger mind—is better for you.

Step 3: Advance. Advancement happens when, after some practice and effort, the new idea gets stronger and begins to make more sense to you and dominate the old idea. Your new leadership logic becomes your governing logic. It's a little like having your newer, bigger self sitting on your shoulder, telling you how this newer, bigger idea is much better than the old one. When the new logic is taking hold of you, when you can really see the earlier logic for what it is, you've achieved a bigger mind. But remember that you haven't lost your previous logic or stage; instead, you've incorporated it and transcended it. That earlier logic and stage will be there when you need it. You can depend on that.

Getting There: An Example

Technology Inc. is based in a Midwest Rust Belt state. When we first connected with it, it was a traditional, hierarchically organized manufacturing organization and the major manufacturing employer in its U.S. locations and its site in Canada. Bart, the CEO, had looked at his own experience in manufacturing and the competitive landscape and had determined that for a company the size of Technology Inc., future competitive advantage had to be about leadership.

After visiting us at CCL, Bart committed to a long-term development process that would start with individual development for the executive team, continue with a less intense individual development for managers and supervisors, and then branch out to team development for the executive team and the leadership teams in other locations. This work unfolded over six years.

Then, boldly, Bart decided in dialogue with his executive team (by this time, a third the size it had been when we had first come in contact) to move from a hierarchical to a process-centered organization (PCO). Only later did we come to understand this had been his intention all along, and that prior individual and team development was what he and we would call readiness work to lead transformation. At this point, he reengaged with us to help him and the company make the leadership transformation to support and sustain the new structure, system, and processes that came with the move from hierarchy to process centered. He had already invested heavily in the structure, system, and process work but quickly recognized that work on the culture had to be integrated with and simultaneous with it from then on.

We'll talk about Technology Inc. (and five other cases) throughout the rest of this book. Right now, we use it to illustrate what the interim steps of awaken, unlearn, and advance look like in real life. Its example will help you see what it's like to create a sustainable state that moves you and the leadership culture toward a more advanced leadership logic.

In the beginning of our work with Technology Inc., some of its leaders were trying to make sense of the organization's direction and grasp the bigger idea of how to manage in a horizontal, customer-driven PCO. As they explored the new environment and the challenges of thinking customer-first in a horizontal process, they felt confused. After all, only a few weeks earlier, they were in a regular command-and-control, top-down vertical environment where the boss said what to do and everyone did it.

One day early in the work, one of the company's managers said to another, "This is strange—a very different way of seeing things. Is it something we can put into a project plan for implementation?" They were struggling with how to make sense of a new reality, and the only way they could think of dealing with it was to use familiar tools such as project plans, Gantt charts, and spreadsheets. They were trying to put the new idea back into the box that they knew. The predominant Conformer leadership logic at Technology Inc. was to follow the rules passed down by supervisors in the hierarchy. But the new, bigger idea had to be about independent decisions and actions in order to achieve better performance results. Putting the new idea into the old box wasn't going to work because it wouldn't fit with the fact that these two managers had an Inside-Out need to develop a new leader logic into this new structure that required a new collective leadership logic.

Getting Clear, Getting Simple

What worked at Technology Inc. was a collaborative inquiry about what that new big idea needed to be. The answer was distilled into a maxim: "I am a member of my process team. My team can face problems, make decisions, and take action." It sounds incredibly simple, and you might be asking why it took a whole day of conversation to come up with such a simple, obvious statement. The short answer is that simple isn't the same as simplicity, and achieving simplicity—getting to the clear, powerful essence of an idea—isn't always obvious. What leaders do with that maxim is the important thing.

Spreading the Word

We took that maxim into the leadership culture of Technology Inc. and asked them to practice using it. We wanted them not just to repeat it like a parrot, but to apply it to their operations in action development, explore what it meant to them, and discover the beliefs needed for the new, bigger idea expressed in those simple sentences to take hold in the organization.

Prolonged use of the new logic—not just the maxim but the collective leadership logic behind it—began to take hold with several people. Those same two managers who tried to put the new idea into the old box expressed their experience after sustained practice with their new-found problem-solving ability based on their advanced Independent-Achiever leadership logic. "Now I'm beginning to see," said one, "that it's not so much about what I do about a problem. It's about how I understand it, how I see it. It's about my attitude—what I believe. My perception of how things are is shifting. It's really about who I am becoming. And now that we can see it and believe it more clearly, we're starting to apply these new insights to the work on the shop floor."

After continued use of the bigger idea, these leaders made the transformation in their beliefs system, and their leadership logic shifted to one of independent achievement. Through action development, they sustained the new big idea and the new state of awareness (they remained in a conscious zone of change) long enough to examine the old idea of being told what to do and see how the new idea made sense because it worked better for everyone—themselves and their customers. When their beliefs changed and they made that new bigger idea their own, the new idea became dominant over the old idea. They got bigger minds.

Transformation

After several quarters of practice, the leaders at Technology Inc. stood at a completely different stage. "We can't imagine going back to the way it was before, back to the supervisor decision making we had before the process teams took hold," said one leader. "We couldn't work in an environment like that anymore. We'd feel suffocated with somebody trying to tell us what to do all the time. Now we tell ourselves what to do. We look at all the possible good answers to a problem, and then we come up with the best one and put it into action. A lot of times, solutions are so obvious that one of us just goes and fixes the problem and then comes back and tells the rest of the team what he or she did. I could never go back to the old way."

At Technology Inc., individuals transformed themselves from one leader logic to the next by practicing a bigger idea—one that stretched their capabilities and created a challenge they had to sustain. By doing it together as a collective, they transformed their leadership culture to the next level. They became Independent-Achievers, producing direction, alignment, and commitment as outcomes. They expanded their leadership culture to include more people throughout the organization and to make the PCO a new reality.

Another Example: Memorial Hospital Gets a Bigger Mind and More

When Memorial Hospital's senior vice president of human resources (HR) sought us out, he said he had an organizational issue that he believed included training but that was also well beyond the scope of training in that it delved into deeper, more serious kinds of development. He said they needed deep change, maybe transformation of some kind. The hospital was doing breakthrough operational work and advancing cutting-edge operations practices in health care management, but something was missing in leadership.

A few months later, he and Glen (the CEO) visited us at CCL. Glen told us:

> Our operations are strong—the data report on strategy implementations is strong evidence—our community support is solid,

but our economic base and our competitive environment are eroding—rapidly. We're okay in the short run, but we're in trouble in the long run. Our management is very good, but our leadership is lacking, falling short; people are not engaged. I have been asking people, everyone, to be more customer focused, but they don't listen. There is no change in behavior. We are very slow to move. To survive and thrive, we have to take leadership to the next level. I don't know why or how, but I believe leadership is the answer to our problem. Can you help?

Memorial Hospital is a regional, full-services health care provider, struggling to maintain its role and identity in a rapidly changing economic environment. The fallout as a result of the North America Free Trade Agreement of the 1990s had pushed Fortune 500 companies out of the region, threatening Memorial's economic security. At the same time, niche medical services providers from national health care operators pressed into the local area and competitively undermined specialty medical functions in Memorial's well-considered strategic system. How could Memorial compete in national niche specialty markets, each requiring big investments in dollars and equipment, while also remaining compressed in a locally depressed geography with the economic base in retreat?

Memorial had created a business strategy for dealing with this. The aim was to focus on customer-friendly operations for competitive advantage. For example, single-station services in the emergency room would make the ER more customer friendly, and physical planning and reconstruction were already becoming operational.

Memorial had a broad leadership strategy in mind as well. To create a more collaborative customer focus, it needed distributed decision making in the leadership culture and throughout the organization. In other words, it needed to reach at least a stage of Independent-Achiever leadership logic. But its reality was otherwise: Memorial was a classic Conformer culture. Set in a very conventional part of the country, the "don't make waves" local society reinforced the cautious, follow-the-rules conformance to standards. And of course health care in general has low tolerance for mistakes for obvious reasons.

Glen and others at Memorial knew intuitively that what their organization needed was more than just a new way of technically managing their challenges, and CEO Glen and the senior vice president of HR came to us already believing the need related to leadership and the culture. As Glen told us, "I believe this is going to be solved through leadership, not by management. I'm just not quite sure how."

We delve into this case more deeply later in the book. As you will see, Glen's own ultimate willingness to develop his own leader logics would contribute greatly to the transformation that was achieved.

As Memorial's process of transformation unfolded, leaders were willing to give the basic process of opening up leadership culture the time that this work required. They took part in meetings lasting more than three full days in order to undertake change. Executives brought key directors into a group that became Memorial's change leadership team. In turn, members of this team took courageous risks. They were willing and able to engage in truth telling; go after root causes; endure breakthrough, confusion, and relief; and take on sacred cows. They also extended work outward from the change leadership team to other leadership teams and eventually to all managerial ranks.

In this process, of course, they encountered problems. The biggest was that one powerful member of the senior leadership team was determined to undermine change covertly. We'll say more later about how that played out for two years before it was solved.

A few years later, however, after Memorial Hospital had undergone its first-level transformation in leadership culture, we measured its stage of development. We measured the leader logics of all members of the executive team. Glen declared that he knew for certain that his own test results were more advanced than when we had started to work together. When we asked how he knew that, he replied, "How could they not be? I just see things differently now. I have a much bigger view." Others on the executive team felt the same way. And the data we gathered indicated that every individual on that team had advanced to Freethinker—toward a bigger mind.

In fact, Memorial Hospital's leadership team had measurably advanced, and in the process it created for itself a bigger mind. It had developed a new set of leadership logics that it could use to meet ongoing and emergent challenges. All members of the team were capable of more complex double-loop learning, a term Chris Argyris (1995) coined. It means going beyond just detecting and correcting a system error (single-loop learning) to also question the values, variables, and root sources of the system error. Double-loop learning not only corrects a current error but also examines the whole system simultaneously and corrects future errors by connecting the dots in potential alternative actions for better results. With double-loop learning, leaders at the hospital were capable of more complex systems thinking and more creative long-term solutions to chronic problems.

At Memorial, individuals sustained the states of making sense of the bigger idea as they practiced it with patients and then took time to make sense of their advances and mistakes. One of the stories from the work with Memorial came from Nancy, a nurse:

> I was headed to a nurses' meeting when I saw a new patient and her family, and they looked lost. So I made the decision to be late to the meeting and instead escorted the patient and family to their room. I was pretty nervous about my decision, because our norm to be on time to nursing meetings is very strict. So when I came in ten minutes late, I just told people about the decision I made and how it was in conflict with our meeting norms.

But we talked about it, and finally everyone could see it was a good decision. I learned something about the personal risk involved in making customer-focused decisions on my own that conflict with other beliefs in the culture.

By taking the risk and applying the bigger idea, Nancy sustained and extended a state with a bigger idea, and she was engaging in the zone of change. This may seem a small and not very significant decision, and yet it is a conscious one she would not have had the presence of mind to make otherwise. Change comes one conscious decision at a time, and a hundred such decisions strung together make for lasting change. In this case, her gamble paid off terrifically: the nursing team supported her decision and made sense together about how this bigger idea was going to change some things—and not just the on-time team norm. Nancy and others could see the implications of continuing with this commitment to the bigger idea. She knew it would change both her beliefs and her actions in ways she didn't yet fully understand.

We hope this example does two things for you. First, we hope it helps you see that bigger minds are possible. Second, we hope it impresses you with the need to stick with it if you want transformation to succeed. Stay the course. You can't fully understand it all ahead of becoming it and doing it. At some point you have to want to do it. You have to intend to be and do the next bigger mind. You have to wake up and pay attention to decisions you are making—all the time.

Am I There Yet? A Personal Challenge to Advancing Leadership Logics

Have you arrived? Do you think you've made it, that you pretty much know all you need to know and that it's others who need to change?

You know what we mean, and maybe you have good reason to think you're home free. Take a look at how successful you are—can't argue with success! But here's a word of warning: that's the kind of self-satisfaction and perhaps even arrogance that comes with prolonged power.

Maybe you don't think of yourself as arrogant or self-satisfied. Fair enough. But success can actually get in your way developmentally. We'd like to give you a couple of ways to think about success that illustrate its potential to derail your advancement to the next stage of leadership logics.

First, consider the personal trappings that come with your success. You have a power position in the organization, money and stock options, and a second home. You have influence and maybe you get to move in high places with other well-positioned people. Well, so do most of the celebrities featured on the cover of *People* and so do a string of ex-CEOs as long as one's arm. Can you honestly say that the logic of achievement and success is your greatest leadership aspiration—to be wealthy, famous, and influential? Don't get us wrong. We're not saying there is anything wrong with that. We're just asking if that's all there is for you.

Maybe that's all you want. If that's true, then okay; it's your choice. But here's the second challenge to your success: organizations live and die. They live if the leadership in them can create new logics and adapt, and if not, they die. At this writing, conditions in the financial industry bear out this fundamental truth. It is easy to speculate that myriad leaders without the bigger minds required for sound, long-term strategy have been cluelessly leading their organizations down dead-end roads. It's positively Darwinian. States can prop up their organizations no matter what the rest of the world is doing, but recent history in what was once the Soviet Union and the rise of competition in China are just two examples of how well that idea plays out. You may be at a point where you need to change and transform your leadership logic in order for your organization to meet rising challenges. If you're convinced that the leadership in your organization (but not *you*) needs to change, chances are that you personally won't be overseeing successful major change.

Ceilings and Floors

People for whom financial success is the primary logic behind their actions (you'll find lots of them in the Independent-Achiever stage) sooner or later hit a ceiling at which a repetitive, circular "more and more and more and more" is their only aspiration. Until that logic changes, more and bigger is all they know, and they will repeat the same unexamined routines over and over. They're not advancing; they're bouncing off the ceiling of their own reasoning, trapped in a loop closed off from alternative ideas.

We are suggesting that you raise the ceiling of your leadership logic when it has outlived its usefulness. Challenge your current thinking and aspirations and look at the potential of changing your logic and getting a bigger idea about the way the world can work for you. You have to outgrow habits and conventional thinking if you're to successfully meet the grizzly challenges that face you and your organization every new day when the sun comes up.

Whatever the ceiling is of your current leadership logic, that ceiling limits the way you think about and consider alternatives for yourself and your organization. One thing is absolutely certain: left unexamined, your ceiling will block more complex ways of understanding your situation and creating alternatives. If you can challenge your habits, raise the ceiling, and create more Headroom for your awareness, you will be able to develop to that next stage of leadership logic.

Exercises

Questions

To gain a sense of what leadership logics mean to you, consider these questions, and write your answers in your journal:

- Who is the "advanced" wise person in your life whom you aspire to be like?

- What is your highest aspiration? What more advanced value do you seek to attain?

- How do your current beliefs about development restrict your own advancement toward a bigger mind?

- What do you need to do for yourself to try out and practice risk taking and learning that advance your leader logic and get a bigger mind?

- What does your senior leadership team need to do to awaken and energize Inside-Out development in the team?

- What does your senior leadership team need to do to awaken and energize Inside-Out development in the organization?

- What does your senior leadership team need to do to awaken and energize Inside-Out development in the leadership culture?

Plot Your Leadership Logic

Locate yourself on the Leadership Logic pathway in Figure 3.1, and then respond to this question: What specific change in your belief system about development would help you move further along?

In your journal, record how your level of leadership logic is expressed in what you do and how you do it as a senior leader in your organization. As you write, address this question again: What specific developmental change would you make to help you move along and up the staircase?

Repeat this process as a personal assessment of members of your senior leadership team (pick a friendly teammate or two to play with). Then at a team meeting, share what you have learned, and engage in a conversation around implications for the current collective leadership logic and culture and what commitments the team would make to advance on the pathway.

4

ENGAGEMENT AND LEADER LOGICS

> Freethinkers are those who are willing to use their
> minds without prejudice and without fearing
> to understand things that clash with their own
> customs, privileges, or beliefs. This state of mind is
> not common, but it is essential for right thinking.
>
> —*Leo Tolstoy*

Too many change plans are downright harebrained and silly. How do they get so offtrack? It often comes down to leaders' not understanding the importance of readiness in planning and implementing change. We once worked with an organization whose future-state picture of itself was so dramatically different from its current reality that we asked its leaders how they planned to develop such new capability. In response, they showed us a spreadsheet that proved they had enough head count. Sorry. Head count does not equal talent. Availability is not a skill. Amid excitement about big stretch goals, leaders sometimes confuse aspiration and capability.

But what exactly does transformation require from you and other senior leaders?

First, as this chapter explains, it requires *you*. No change effort gets off the ground without leader engagement. By *engagement* we mean a deep Inside-Out process. Engagement is not telling; it is asking. It is including others as equal, collaborative inquirers mutually engaged in the process of figuring out how to address complex challenges. As we illustrated in Chapter Three, Inside-Out is a human experience of interpreting vagueness and ambiguities for oneself through the process of dialogue. Engagement is rarely happening when one person is talking to or at another through scripted speeches, e-mails, or training programs that merely convey information for assimilation. That's Outside-In. Although engagement can and should include Outside-In activities, those alone do not constitute it.

Second, we will explore where you are on the staircase of leadership logics that we discussed in Chapter Three relative to the level you intend to reach. If you're now at level one (Dependent-Conformer leadership logics), you are not ready to jump to level three. And if you and other leaders are still personally using individual leader logics of level one, you can't expect your next change effort to whisk you up to be a level three Transformer.

In Chapter Three, we introduced the cases of Technology Inc. and Memorial Hospital. In this chapter, we revisit those businesses and introduce several more.

Engagement

Consultants often propose a simple, step-by-step program for transformation—the recipe for the perfect cake—that any disciplined organization is supposed to be able to follow.

Cookbook approaches assume that your organization is a predictable environment. Don't believe it. Organizations are composed of people, and people are complex. The world surrounding your organization is also complex. Transformation is therefore also complex. Formulas sell books and fuel uncounted seminars, but they never provide reliable pathways of organizational transformation.

Don't get us wrong: some research-based, step-by-step process advice draws attention to things that need to be done. Paying attention to those is necessary, but it is not sufficient to bring about change. For that, you need to be engaged and truly ready to change. No matter how appealing in simplicity and design, a step-by-step process doesn't give you the multidimensional engagement and discovery-based learning you'll need to leverage in transforming your organization.

Nor can step-by-step processes anticipate the kind or level of engagement you need. By *engagement*, we mean the connectedness that determines how people interact with each other, how people learn or don't learn together, and whether there is mutuality in defining and solving problems that are both ambiguous and uncertain. Using both Inside-Out and Outside-In perspectives is required, but the Inside-Out perspective is the essence of engagement. Engagement is genuine, creative, authentic, multilateral, and multilevel. When the whole group is engaged, interactions are both personal and public. They support speaking from one's inner core, and they welcome sharing from the wellspring of the spirit—the group's hopes, aspirations, fears, values, and beliefs. Engagement is the process by which leaders work with leaders, leadership teams work as teams, and the leadership community connects to advance mutual learning as a central dimension of the change process. At the core, engagement is how direction gets set, alignment occurs, and organizational commitment is achieved.

Levels of engagement tend to vary with levels of leader logics. The earlier the stage of logic, the less engagement is likely to occur, and the later the stage of leader logic, the more engagement is likely to occur. Dominators and Moderators are

Voice of Change

Engagement matters. People do not like being manipulated by sheer force. They prefer to be engaged. Would you rather be engaged in a participative human process or manipulated like a cog in the wheel? As a learner, do you prefer to participate in the process or have it dictated to you? Do you value learning in a mutually supportive environment or being told what to get done? There is power in engagement. It invites curiosity, imagination, possibility, and the potential for new belief.

mainly concerned with control over others and self and therefore less likely to share deeper Inside-Out thoughts and feelings,
doubts and concerns, especially multilaterally. Collaborators and
Transformers are concerned with the advancement and good
of the human system and operational systems overall. And since
they also possess high levels of self-awareness and tolerance for
ambiguity, they are much more likely to engage multilaterally
with others in Inside-Out work.

Your challenge is unique to your organization. You're going to
have to learn and discover your own way to lead change. Unpre-
dictability means that your and your other leaders' engagement is
key. But ultimately what is essential is the engagement of folks who
carry no management title but are nevertheless much involved in
creating the outcomes of direction, alignment, and commitment.

Consider the following two moments from the case of
Technology Inc. Technology's general challenge was to change
from a traditional hierarchical manufacturing environment
to a flat, process-centered organization (PCO). Its long-term
goal was to develop a leadership culture to support transformation from a primarily Dependent-Conformer leadership culture
to one that was more Independent-Achiever, with pockets of
Interdependent-Collaborator. Technology's leaders anticipated
that ultimately the pockets of Interdependent-Collaborator culture could be leveraged to move the whole PCO into a mostly
Interdependent-Collaborator leadership logic.

"I Do My Eight"

It is now the third day of a Technology Inc. retreat, and twenty
people sit in a circle in the anteroom of a golf club. Collectively,
we and they have already talked about the difference between
leading and managing and have spent a lot of time defining the
new roles that would be required to transform the company into
a PCO. The conversation has been difficult, but everyone has
gotten through it so far with a lot of urging, coaching, coddling,

Photo 4.1 How a Group at Technology Inc. Defined Differences Between "Lead" and "Manage"

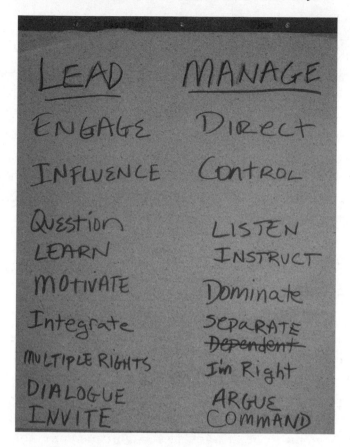

persuading, inviting, and a little pushing. Photo 4.1 captures the group's many hours of figuring out new roles and working hard to understand how much would be required of people to shift those roles from less managing to more leading.

Everyone in the organization who had gathered in this circle had been steeped for years in a traditional manufacturing shop floor role. One machinist, whom we affectionately dubbed Joe Sixpack, summed up the culture: "I do my eight, and I hit the gate." Joe said he did what he was told to do. He was a fine machinist, but he had no interest in participating in a customer-centered process that required his active engagement with others.

Like Joe, every other company person in the room worked in a hierarchical organization in which the senior team set direction and supervisors told shop floor employees what to do. To them, we looked like supervisors too, even though we were there to facilitate conversation. True to form, they all waited anxiously for us to tell them what to do. But we weren't telling; we were asking. We wanted them to talk to each other.

To get everyone involved and thinking about the organization's change initiative, we introduced the idea of role play. We planned to play one part and asked for volunteers to play another. We expected some reluctance, but we didn't expect an excruciating delay while people "tied their shoes with their eyes." No one said a word for a full five minutes! No one wanted to connect with us and engage.

Connectedness

Fast-forward several quarters to a later Technology Inc. retreat. Most of the same people are in the room, and there are a few new faces. On everyone's mind is the absence of a former key player, Jim. Everyone knows Jim is gone, but no one is saying what happened to him.

Finally, Kim asks. At first, the group turns its back on her, a common group tactic. It wants to avoid an uncomfortable topic. But Kim is having none of that: "I want to know what happened to Jim, why he's not here, if he's been fired or if he quit, and I want to know why."

Bart, the company owner, slides off his chair and sits on the floor in the middle of the circle. "Kim," he says, "I'll tell you what you can know and what you cannot know about Jim. Jim left the company in a way that binds us by law to keep confidential. Exactly why and how he left, we do not have a legal right to discuss. Period."

"But," Bart continues, "we can talk about anything else you want to discuss about Jim. We can talk about why you think he's gone, what you and we observed about his work performance while he was here, and what you think and feel about him not being here. So we can talk about anything that has to do with Jim leaving except for that which is restricted by law—the purpose of which is to protect Jim and the company."

Kim then spoke about how Jim had seemed unplugged, not really showing up fully at work. At that point, Frank and Susan entered the conversation, saying how Jim's disengagement affected them. Soon the door opened on a lively group dialogue about learning—how one person can disrupt the flow of learning and how important it is for everyone to be as connected to the learning process because it has become core to the company's manufacturing process. Almost everyone was in on the dialogue, heads were nodding when others were talking, and body language conveyed openness and a feeling of shared understanding.

As the talk died down, a new group member who hadn't attended the first retreat said, "Kim, when you first brought that up—that Jim had left and no one was talking about it—that really scared me. I don't know why, but it did. Then, when we all started to make it okay to talk about, I was really relieved that we could discuss tough things without freaking out. It may still be a tough issue, but that it's okay to inquire almost about anything—that's pretty amazing."

As we defined it earlier, in a leadership culture, engagement is the connectedness that determines whether and how people learn or don't learn together. The kinds of connections leaders make as they lead groups shape the kinds of leadership practices that others in the organization will value and engage in too. How that engagement or connection between individual leaders works in the leadership collective is the function of a leadership culture.

Engagement and Leadership Logic

Take a moment to think about the degree of engagement you are most comfortable with at work.

Do you seek a formal, professional environment with strict protocols?

Or do you prefer a more open environment where people let their guard down and go into depth about issues?

These differences correspond to different styles of engagement. Each of the three leadership logics or cultures we have introduced also implies its own kind of engagement and its own kind of distribution of power. Table 4.1 (which builds on Table 3.1) should be a useful reference for you as we discuss the engagement style of each.

Dependent-Conformer Engagement

In the first Technology Inc. retreat we described, the individuals were following Conformer norms. They were embedded in honoring a code of dependent and predictable conduct. Members of a union shop or military or law enforcement personnel generally engage in this way. Belonging, maintaining order, and respecting the command-and-control hierarchy are earmarks of such leadership cultures, and this kind of engagement can create close cohesion (giving you protection in a firefight, for example).

Table 4.1 Leadership Logics (Cultures), Leader Logics, and Organization Roles

Leadership Logics	Leader Logics	Organization Roles
Interdependent-Collaborator	Transformer Collaborator	Future Generator Big-Medium
Transitional	*Freethinker Rising*	
Independent-Achiever	Freethinker Performer	Innovative Facilitator Practical Adapter
Transitional	*Specialist Rising*	
Dependent-Conformer	Specialist Moderator Dominator	Supervisor Paternalist Authoritarian

On the negative side, it can also raise fears of being excluded from the pack when you do not conform. In Conformer organizations, mistakes can get you punished or excluded, and so covering them up becomes important. People in these cultures avoid risk. Knowledge is held by those at the top, who can be secretive about what they know and closed to sharing it with others.

When boundaries are strictly drawn between what is okay to do and what is not, then mutual, balanced engagement isn't possible. People may appear to be engaged in a flurry of activity like constant reactive fire drills or reorganizing business functions, for example. But do not confuse lively activity with significant engagement. Engagement leads to change, but mere continued amplification of activity usually does not produce much real change in ideas or outcomes. Open arguments and expressions of conflict can also look like engagement, but that's not what they really reflect unless there is the actual possibility of dissent that leads to some mutual learning and new outcome. The use of force is not engagement either. In a Conformer leadership culture, engagement is mostly restricted to the avoidance of deeper contact and fosters the appearance of engagement. The top leadership structures engagement to control it and focus on predictability of behavior in the rank and file and the maintenance of power in the hands of the few. Expectations for secrecy, loyalty, and obedience shape engagement in a Conformer culture.

Independent-Achiever Engagement

In a leadership culture of Independent-Achievement, engagement looks like success on steroids. Leaders can be obsessed with execution; every action is honed to a competitive edge. Winning doesn't just matter; winning is all there is. In an Achiever culture, in order for the team to win, there is mutual engagement, and Inside-Out learning can occur because it is good for me and the team. Engagement focuses on performance. When legendary football coach Vince Lombardi famously said, "Winning isn't everything, it's the only thing," he exemplified engagement in an Achiever culture. Risks are commensurate with rewards, and knowledge is power. There can be a lot of internal competition, but there can also be a fair amount of cooperation when it is mutually beneficial. The atmosphere is entrepreneurial. Jack Welch's GE had a look and feel of an extreme form of this kind of engagement. Execute, win, share learning, cut the deadwood, expand the opportunities, and succeed. Period.

Achiever engagement centers on individuals. Unlike the Conformer who is embedded in the code of the group, Achiever culture individuals push deeply into themselves. They explore and expand their own space and time to prove themselves and succeed personally. Their Inside-Out leadership logics are about competing and winning, while their Outside-In interpretation is about execution and calculated risks. Engagement between such individuals yields a range of behaviors and outcomes. On one end of this range, goals may be limited to individual success, and friendly foes may abound. Closer to the middle of the range, cross-functional teams often find it hard to make progress because members carry the independent agendas of their primary group. At the other end of the range, successful teams form and begin to cooperate with other teams for their mutual benefit. Engagement in this culture is largely motivated by self-interest of self and a primary group.

Interdependent-Collaborator Engagement

Interdependent-Collaborative engagement gets beyond individual achievement to a point where both successes and failures are shared because both are equally regarded as knowledge. Collective learning is highly valued, and mistakes are regarded as opportunities from which to learn. An individual's competency is viewed as talent, skills, knowledge, and behaviors that make the individual and the organization successful simultaneously. Win-win is the mind-set. Mutual assistance is valued. Collaborative engagement means exploring how you, I, and the whole organization and its partners can win.

Collaborative engagement is complex. Many agendas are operating simultaneously, yet they are seeking mutual integration. Individuals are engaged in their own deeper cycles of learning. And at the same time, group interaction centers on opening up the subject at hand and reaching multiple right answers that can be advocated, integrated, and prioritized.

Our CCL colleagues speak of "putting something in the middle" as part of collaborative process. This is a method of turning a problem into an opportunity by placing the subject of discord or confusion in the middle of a dialogue and therefore objectifying the inquiry for a more conscious, reflective result. Signaling that the subject is being put in the middle indicates that the interchange will be one of sharing and inquiry rather than debate and advocacy. Our colleagues also see the value of striving for an emergent, interdependent leadership logic even while the overall organizational culture is in a Conformer-to-Achiever transformation (Palus and Drath, 2001).

As we said earlier, you don't necessarily need to be at the top Interdependent-Collaborator level of leadership logics. But your leadership culture and logic does need to be at whatever level is right for implementing your new business strategy. A leadership culture can't pull off a strategy that is beyond its level of ability to engage and learn.

Engagement and a Leader's Logic

The second column in Table 4.1 lists the logics that individual leaders can adopt and groups them in the three broad cultures and the transitional stages between them. The seven leader logics are Dominator, Moderator, Specialist, Performer, Freethinker, Collaborator, and Transformer. A good way to see how these leader logics connect to engagement is by considering a few examples, mainly drawn from other cases we have studied and will be introducing here. We gratefully acknowledge the work of Rooke and Torbert (2005), reflected throughout this section on the seven leader logics.

The Dominator

Although Dominators are a small percentage of all leaders, they are common in many organizations. Think about the "kiss up and kick down" leader, or the one whose only style is command and control. These leaders are opportunists; their primary motivation is their own advancement and retention of power. They often espouse ideology and usually demand strict secrecy, loyalty, and obedience from others. At the core, they are authoritarian. There are many such leaders in governments today from which you can choose your own example. One will also show up below as a problematic character in our discussion of the Freethinker.

Dominators engage from a perspective of demonstrating and protecting their position to get others to perform in a predictable, determinate way. Engagement is very rare, always in private, and shared with only a select few with whom they share power or with those few who are doing their bidding.

The Moderator

Global Electronics is a worldwide electronics design, development, manufacturing, sales, and service company with billions of dollars in revenues. For six years, the business strategy called for the double-double (a doubling of revenues every two years)—and for six straight years, revenue had stayed flat as a pancake. Although the business gave an appearance of powerful activity, with boundless hustle and bustle and responses to one serial crisis after another, in fact it was lifeless.

The CEO of Global Electronics, Dawson, is a prototypical Moderator. Dawson was extremely animated and interested in meeting and solving the challenges facing Global Electronics. He said that he really wanted to launch an effective change initiative and was going to lead a transformation. For Dawson, engagement was all about appearances and pleasing others as a technique to legitimate his power and influence. He assured us he wanted to engage with us and with his team and the larger community of workers to make a difference. His modus operandi, however, was all about maintaining his position through the approval of others.

In getting to know members of the senior team, we found several disturbing signs. There was a vice president of strategy on the senior team, but by all accounts, there was no coherent business or organization strategy. A new corporate university was being designed and launched, but we saw no evidence of any commitment to organizational learning. There was no organizational vision. Fear in the rank and file was high, trust and morale low. According to Dawson, although the annual layoffs were cranking up again and there was rampant dissatisfaction among the senior team with the results of multiple interventions with Dawson and the team by some well-known consulting firms, this change effort was going to be different.

The day after Dawson agreed with us on a planned pathway for transformation, we received word (from someone two layers beneath him) that he was no longer interested. Apparently one or two members of the senior leadership team had approached Dawson with misgivings about the arrangement, and he had cancelled the plan on the spot. He had waffled under the influence of the last person to see him. His internal motivation to appear a good listener, a good leader, and a team player had led to yet another false agreement to engage.

As a Moderator, Dawson had no strong commitments to real engagement within the organization beyond his own diplomacy to maintain his position. The logic driving his actions was to please others in the moment, for which he needed only the appearance of engagement and activity. Our brief experience with Dawson and Global Electronics only hinted at what it must be like to work where constant crisis management replaces strategy and credibility is often absent. From an engagement perspective, members of this leadership culture were constantly wondering which was the real Dawson. Others expressed concern about leadership that put pleasing colleagues ahead of achieving business goals. The importance of being just one of the gang was seen as disingenuous by others who shared their experience of this culture as being one of continually asking, "What is real?" "What is my role?" and "What are the real values, beliefs, and assumptions held by leadership?"

The Specialist

Liam was the senior leader of NuSystems, a public service institution. Telephone inquiries revealed that Liam and the NuSystems leadership culture epitomized Specialist logic. Over the years, their pattern had been to approach the subject of organizational leadership development and then inevitably avoid deeper engagement. But according to Liam, this time seemed different. In the midst of a changing industry, succession management at NuSystems had become a big problem—because it had none. Years of insular freedom from significant external competition had left the company without development systems. Now competition was pressing in, NuSystems' leaders felt confused, and the organization's influence seemed to be waning.

In conversations, Liam freely confessed needing help because talent systems and culture were not in the organization's expertise. He said that its leaders were very hard working and extraordinarily dedicated, but he acknowledged that was not enough. His board of directors agreed with him and shared a sense that a crisis was brewing.

As a generally conservative, bureaucratic research organization, NuSystems was prone to analysis paralysis. Its leaders approached every problem with a study and then championed the findings of the study as though the study itself was an organizational outcome. Consequently, the company's leaders rarely made any decisions of any import other than to delay serious action for seriously mounting problems.

In NuSystems' Specialist culture, experts were lauded. Being right was often more important than being successful. Conflict was avoided, and both disagreements and genuine dialogue were forced underground. A large and disgruntled underground of employees said that appearance was deemed more important than results and that a corporate trust had been broken. In general, employees had diminishing confidence that their leaders could meet emerging challenges.

When Liam brought us in, he pledged that he and his team would support the culture work. As the process unfolded, however, there were warning signs that Liam was not entirely ready to be the instrument of change. For example, he insisted that all ideas pass through him before they were explored with others. The effect was to narrow the issues that could be explored within the executive team and beyond with the leadership culture in general. Moreover, the executive team frequently took significant issues and their pursuant questions off the table as undiscussable. There were few indications that Liam and his team were open to developing bigger minds and advancing beyond the Specialist logic dominating the leadership culture.

As we continued to use discovery information from internal sources, Liam increased his concern that messages be nonthreatening and noncontroversial. Liam needed to be assured that he was in control of the organizational messages. When we indicated that leadership culture change work was not amenable to risk-free guarantees, he asked for "no surprises." Liam's Specialist leader logic, which often displayed Moderator elements, drove his actions related to engagement, even though he frequently cloaked his aspirations for engagement in the language of a Performer and Freethinker.

NuSystems formed a change leadership team from across its operations. The team convened a series of meetings to cultivate exploration, and it identified several sources of the organization's difficulties. A series of action development teams formed, and the change work proceeded.

We noticed a great deal of interpersonal contact and willingness for interaction, so we thought NuSystems was advancing toward significant progress. We were wrong. Following the deep analysis and discovery work, the team abandoned the powerful groundwork it had completed, and the change platform it had assembled evaporated. The team's analysis of the issues met the focus of this particular Specialist logic, but advancing into the actual work of change did not inspire the same collective interest.

Eventually we disengaged, since it was clear that there was no commitment to real engagement on the part of Liam and several of his key supporters. Rather, they would encourage vigorous exchanges among experts with competing points of view without demanding authentic mutuality in goals, Inside-Out disclosure, or public learning. The team was active, creating the appearance of progress, but it hardly engaged around outcomes of substantial change and development. Such as it was, the engagement showcased only actions that would mollify the various constituencies through an appearance that good-faith efforts were being made.

Our brief experience with the organization only hinted at what it must be like to be an employee where appearance trumps substance and activity replaces strategic priority. The Specialist logic limits the degree of engagement to the nature of its specialty. In this example, the specialization of analysis limited advancement to surface expressions of commitment where appearance triumphs over in-depth, Inside-Out exploration. Any hints of deeper questions raised of the Specialist's direction, alignment, and commitment are either suppressed or dismissed as the mutterings of a few unhappy, untrustworthy outliers.

The Performer

Recall from Chapter Three that Performer logic is that of independent, self-possessed leaders who have generated their own values and standards. A Performer likely has mastered technical skills and can make what appear to be rational, independent judgments. His or her drivers are success, achievement, and individual competence. Thus, the Performer's mode of engagement is to connect around issues of execution and outcomes driven by the application of expert knowledge. Performers emphasize a technical Outside-In approach—a powerful, necessary, compelling, data-driven method.

As an example, consider Adam, the CEO of Professional Services Inc. (PSI), a company with roots in media management. When Adam came to us, he had been at PSI about a year. PSI was a century-old company with a strong culture of entitlement. Its market approach was, "If we build it, they will come." It emphasized internal harmony in relationships and relied on control systems to drive the business. But with Adam, all that was going to change, as "execution" became the focus and the word. With Adam at the helm, one might even say PSI was now obsessed with operational execution: it ate accomplishment for breakfast, thought accomplishment all morning, breathed it all afternoon, and slept with it all night.

PSI certainly faced a challenge. Through mergers and acquisitions, it had expanded into multiple product lines, but in a dynamic industry environment, its own results had been stagnant for a number of years. Changes at the board level had led to Adam's hiring, and the new board had empowered him to lead the company in a new direction, competing more aggressively. The business strategy was to integrate divisions, create efficiencies through shared systems, and differentiate in each of PSI's markets. The leaders would execute this strategy flawlessly even if success in one segment undercut success in another.

PSI executives had gone through a senior leader development program. We were called in to help them discuss and focus on the collective leadership culture, but whenever we introduced the subject, executives immediately refocused on operational execution within each division. Every instinct was to "make it happen" in their own divisions, whatever the costs. The leaders were absolutely engaged, but only to drive the success of their own divisions. And learning to increase their leadership logics together was not on their agenda; nor was there any sustainable sense of collective will to advance in such a way. Expertise ruled over innovation in their interactions, and independence over-ruled all. Each division leader was expected to use that expertise to pull off victory for that division. There were exceptions—a few Freethinker team members who tried to influence the group toward a healthy, cohesive company.

In the end, the Freethinker voices were drowned out, suc-cumbing to the driving Outside-In perspective on execution, market pressures, and financial performance. The goals expressed were very effective in PSI's near-term operations. But ultimately these performer orientations resulted in selling off business units in order to sustain the one unit in which Adam had the greatest personal investment.

As we suggested, Adam was a Performer; for him, it was all about achievement and financial success. He knew what he wanted to be (the CEO), but he wasn't sure what he wanted to do beyond make each division's numbers and return shareholder value—an important part of the game, but not the whole game. The logic behind his actions was to please Wall Street, but he was not strategic in his long-term plans. He looked little beyond quarterly results. In other words, like many other performers, Adam's engagement was limited to success in the short term.

The Freethinker

A Freethinker knows that reality can be constructed from one's own perspective. He or she understands the logics of others and knows how to facilitate groups, but can also make up new rules and organizational orders.

As an example, recall Glen, the CEO of Memorial Hospital. Glen knew his leadership needed deep change and to become more customer friendly if it had any hope of making and keep-ing the hospital's services competitive.

He was unsure exactly how to proceed, but he was certain the solution was going to be in organizational leadership, and he was committed to following through. More than anyone else at Memorial, Glen had called for change, had invited it, had pushed for it, and had summoned others to take risks and change their beliefs toward a more customer-focused hospital. But he had a tough call to make. A strong and powerful member of his team was actively undermining the change progress. This vice president was a Dominator who intimidated the people below him, knowing that others would not follow if he did not change as well. As a result they were reluctant to participate in the transformation efforts. Clearly Glen had to step up and do something about this vice president.

Glen was steadfast in a way that wasn't always obvious to others, some of whom thought he was dragging his feet regarding the disrupter. He remained stalwart in his support of Memorial's change leadership team. He remained devoted to the work with us and said so repeatedly in public. And when it came time for him finally to deal with the problem on his team, he was firm and swift. As a Freethinker, Glen was well aware of the problem vice president's leader logic; still it was a tough political problem for him to solve. He needed and took time to disentangle the myriad issues that needed to be addressed in order for his decision to have the impact it needed.

When he did make the decision, Glen engaged the hospital's entire leadership culture, calling it together to make sense of the damage done by this disruptive figure and inviting them to engage fully in the journey going forward. His demonstration of personal vulnerability and public learning was not only courageous but also highly effective for the long run. His engagement with the leadership culture created credibility, collective learning, and an undeniable foundation of trust. Everyone there honored his lead and stood up with him.

The logic behind his actions was to initiate change and construct new orders of health care with benefit to all. He knew how to communicate that in words that people with other logics would comprehend. He knew that operational achievement was only a step toward the next phase of work and stage of excellence for the organization. His deep and abiding purpose was customer-focused care. As a Freethinker, he assumed that to overcome the arbitrary constraints in an environment with many Specialists and Performers, he needed to fully engage all of these logic holders in an active dialogue and in action development with each other and with him. He knew that achieving DAC was not going to be easy and was going to take time.

The Collaborator

Whereas the Freethinker can master multilateral communications required for engagement, the Collaborator takes engagement to the next level and continuously takes actions and forms agreements that bring about continuous organizational change. Collaborators have their heads in the clouds and their feet on the ground. Both visionary and practical, they see organizational walls as building materials that can be disassembled, discussed, and rebuilt in new forms that serve the organization's future.

We use Bart at Technology Inc. as an example of Collaborator because of his deep intentionality (which we discuss in Chapter Five) to advance the development of his company, his leadership culture, and himself toward that level. The process-centered organization that he envisioned and is still engaged in creating is the ultimate Collaborator environment. Interdependent collaboration initially exceeded his own capability, and so he set about to advance toward it collectively with the leadership culture.

At least as much as any other senior leader we've worked with, Bart is simultaneously visionary and practical, and so he has a range of leader logics to draw on as situations require. (Recall that each stage both includes and transcends previous stages.) Bart can move across Specialist, Performer, and Freethinker logics with ease, and his extraordinary strategic vision supports his rise up into the Collaborator logic that he practices. Although he would never say this of himself, he creates recurring states in which he expects to rise into advanced stages of fulfillment, which he then translates into new organizational realities. Since we have worked with him, he has taken on increasingly personal Inside-Out risks, and his openly public learning has disassembled barriers and created an environment of experimentation with new human systems and operational practices. Practice makes perfect, and Bart practices with clarity of direction, courage, and commitment to advancing potential through human ingenuity and spirit.

The Transformer

Whereas the Collaborator can generate many possibilities and outcomes as an effective agent of change, Transformers go beyond that with an ability to consistently explore, learn from, and integrate multiple perspectives into ever unfolding and increasingly bold transformations. They have the extraordinary ability to reinvent themselves and their organizations in breakthrough, and sometimes historic, ways. They are, in effect, organizational wizards. We found an example of one in Roger, the CEO of Credlow, who told us he wanted to develop his culture and individual leaders simultaneously.

Credlow finances the purchase of used cars, specializing in doing business with North American car buyers with bad credit. Credlow intentionally broke old stereotypes about used car dealers preying on customers. Selling and financing used cars in an underserved market that was viewed by most as an economic cesspool required both the right business model and the right culture.

The change drivers for Credlow were dissatisfied customers and increased competition for clientele. Roger was committed to leading a transformation. To that end, he and his senior leadership team went through a leadership culture workshop together. The collective learning from this workshop was that interdependence at Credlow had to build from a foundation of independence (Performer plus Freethinker logic). The senior leaders committed to deliberately pursuing both independence (up from dependence) and interdependence as a way of moving the whole organization and its culture forward.

But Roger himself was a Transformer, dedicated to the idea of Credlow's building a nationwide network of local service agencies. He was constantly switched on. Business meetings seemed chaotic. He would require a profit report from Region A, interrupt the presentation when his cell phone rang, then return his attention to the reporting out. As he did so, he might transform that moment into a learning event, calling his chief information officer willingly front and center for groupwide, Inside-Out learning.

In typical Transformer style, Roger was a ringmaster, orchestrating all three rings of the circus and yet not really in charge of any. He was taking on one hell of a challenge: raising the leadership logic of his leadership collective to his own. A straightforward truth teller, he expected and got the same treatment from his company managers. The engagement of most Transformers is like that of Roger. They are alchemist-like, constantly transforming opportunities, situations, conflicts, and people from one form of system and business and consciousness to another. Their imagination knows few boundaries. Like Roger, they have very big minds. At the same time, they are just as vulnerable to feelings and experiences as anyone else in the organization, and they know that these experiences are the essence of life as they have come to know it. They see everything as development, and they construct new orders of being and doing in constant motion.

Moving Forward

In this chapter, we've fleshed out the meaning of engagement as it applies to leadership logics and the leader logics that tend to go with them. Engagement is about your willingness to accept your current leader logic and the leader logics of the senior team members and to set course for developing the leader logics appropriate to achieving your business strategy. Now let's connect engagement to overall readiness for cultural change by attending to some critical personal factors in leader readiness to drive change and transformation. This is the focus in Chapter Five.

Exercises

Questions

- What kind of engagement is required for your organization's future?

- What one or two beliefs does your senior leadership team need to hold in order to change?

- As a senior leader, why do you have to stand up first to yourself and then to your team's culture in a change process?

- Review the seven leader logics and supporting case materials. Which seem most like your own?

- Using this same reflection, what leader logics are present in your senior team?

- What are the implications for engagement within the team and between the team and the larger community of workers in your organization?

- What ideas do you have on where you need to develop?

5

PERSONAL READINESS AND LEADING TRANSFORMATION

> Your vision will become clear only when you can
> look into your own heart. Who looks outside
> dreams; who looks inside awakens.
>
> —*Carl Jung*

"Fire . . . ready . . . aim!" is the wrong sequence for strategic action. *Ready* needs to come first. When it comes to leading transformation, it is critical that you consider your own personal readiness first. Throughout the first four chapters, we have called attention to the personal dilemmas of change and transformation. Our intent has been to prepare you for your own degree of challenge in stepping up to issues of strategy, leadership culture, and leader logics. In so doing, we have sought to demonstrate that change is more than an outside-in intellectual exercise, that it is intensely personal and inside-out, and that it involves cognitive intelligence, emotional intelligence, and a deep awareness of values and beliefs. In this chapter, we invite you to explore your personal readiness to guide transformation.

Personal Readiness

The senior leaders we have worked with embody Jung's insight to varying degrees—some more successfully than others. From our research and learning with organizations, it is clear to us that senior executives who have been able to move the needle toward sustainable organizational transformation have also experienced a significant personal transformation. That commitment to personal change is a fundamental part of their readiness to take on the leadership and management challenges of change.

Intentional, strategic change requires developing the human system in concert with operational systems. For successful, sustainable cultural transformation, members of the change leadership team must be collectively and personally ready. The readiness starts with you as the leader of that collective. The collective must also be deeply aware of the connections between personal development and team and leadership culture development. Without that awareness, any approach to organizational change will likely devolve into a random series of trial-and-error events, that is, disconnected attempts.

Readiness depends ultimately on a balance of several broad factors that we call the balance wheel of readiness, which is the focus of this chapter. Understanding those factors will equip you to judge your own and your leadership's collective readiness to transform.

The awareness and understanding of what it takes to develop and connect business strategy with leadership strategy, and to move the leadership culture toward a development stage consistent with those strategies, evolves from a process of personal readiness that leads from ideas to action. In our experience, even the less successful senior change leaders come to understand the imperative for committing themselves to their individual development and to collective development—even those who finally decide not to do it.

Readiness for the Role of Guide

The rightmost column in Table 5.1 shows a progression of educational roles that climb the logics ladder from controller to coach to guide. Over the past twenty years, much progress has been made on the role of coach in organizations, and most organizations we work with use coaching to develop senior leaders. In this chapter we introduce the educational role of guide for

Table 5.1 Leadership Logics (Cultures), Leader Logics, and Educational Roles

Leadership Logics	Leader Logics	Educational Roles
Interdependent-Collaborator	Transformer Collaborator	Guide
Transitional	*Freethinker Rising*	
Independent-Achiever	Freethinker Performer	Coach
Transitional	*Specialist Rising*	
Dependent-Conformer	Specialist Moderator Dominator	Controller

post-Achiever leaders. By *guide*, we mean people who are at the Freethinker leader logic or beyond and who simultaneously are aware of their own development and take responsibility for the development of others. From our experience, it is clear that a leader's personal readiness to pursue an advanced independent or interdependent leadership culture must include a capacity to both guide and be guided in the journey toward organizational change.

We've observed leaders who have become comfortable with the role of guide. In each case, the organization affords a clear base of power and influence from which a guide can lead or drive change. But differences exist in what roles and practices the guide leaders choose to exercise from one organization to another. To judge your own readiness in this regard, spend some time with this question:

Do I tend to reflect, act, and reflect again? Or do I tend to act, react, and act?

A tendency to reflect, act, and reflect will serve you better than a tendency to act, react, and act.

Those who guide a learning process must be open to giving feedback and receiving it from others. Think of yourself as the guide on a trek. Trek guides and participants set out on a journey together, often through unknown or unmapped territory, in uncertain weather, and without much collective knowledge of the strengths and weaknesses of each member in the party. So guides are leaders but not directors in full control. The group depends on everyone's efforts, talents, and contributions; risks and rewards are shared. The same is true in your journey of change.

As a guide, you also commit to handling polarities of confidence versus anxiety, uncertainty versus stability, cognitive versus emotional processes, and short-term versus long-term views. You must also find balance between Inside-Out and Outside-In and uncover the deep roots of intention and impact.

Two Ways to Discern Readiness

One way to discern readiness is to examine the leader logics among the members of your senior leadership (see Figure 5.1).

Figure 5.1 Discerning Readiness for Change

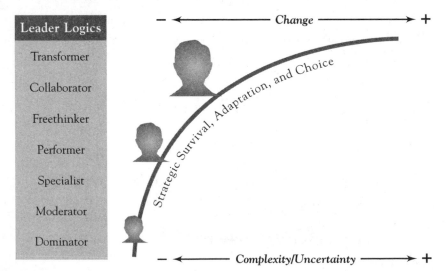

Leadership mind-sets change and shift and require different levels of logics based on the amount of change and the amount of uncertainty. Stay aware that how big a mind you need, how big a mind your team needs, and how big a mind an organization must develop to change do vary across functions, divisions, and subcultures.

The Balance Wheel of Personal Readiness

Another way to visualize readiness is to think of a wheel on which are balanced three qualities or forces of readiness: intentionality, control source, and time sense. (See Illustration 5.1.)

Illustration 5.1 The Balance Wheel of Personal Readiness

Source: Bruce Flye. Used with permission.

Grasping each of these practical factors will help you lead and manage change. For example, it will help you create the space required for culture transformation.

Intentionality

Intentionality is a measure of three things: your perceivable clarity about the rightness of a cause that is of a higher order than self-interest, the perceivable connection of your own human spirit and passion to that cause, and the perceivable strength of your courage and commitment to stick with that cause.

Here, engagement reenters the picture. Recall that in Chapter Four, we defined engagement as a deep Inside-Out process for collective learning and achieving direction, alignment, and commitment. Intentionality we define as actively using the zone of intentional change by bringing the unconscious into conscious expression of values, beliefs, assumptions, and aspirations, which are then translated into strategic actions for change. In this way the Inside-Out of the leader becomes an element of the Outside-In, ever-present reality for the senior leadership team and leadership community. Engagement and intentionality are inevitably coupled because appealing reasons to engage create strong engagement. Deep and compelling engagement starts with asking, "Why?" Intentionality embodies the answer and the reality that the leader is fully committed. In this sense, intentionality is more than the Outside-In intention of creating value for shareholders in that it encompasses the Inside-Out qualities of heart and soul.

Being a change guide involves deeply knowing why you want to be one. Robert Haas, CEO of Levi Strauss, remarked, "You can't energize people or earn their support unless the organization they are committing to has soul" (O'Reilly and Pfeffer, 2000, p. 251). Personal readiness for change leadership calls for the Inside-Out powers of vision, hope, and belief. It calls on soul and spirit. If you are really just in it for position, money, and power, then you're not ready for this work. If you think you're the expert and you are going to show everyone else how to change, then you are not ready. If you think you can delegate this, then you are dreaming. It is never just others who need to change. Think about that for a moment.

> To what extent are you clear about your own vision, aspirations, and motivations to be an intentional guide of change in your own leadership culture?

The question of intentionality is that of your own level of clarity and conviction about why others should pay attention to your guidance as a senior leader. The authentic change leader is a masterful designer of the future, out to change the world in some significant way that far exceeds his or her ego. Jack Welch's black belt, martial arts metaphor, popularly known as Six Sigma, made quality a dominant differentiator for GE by raising the Six Sigma process to the same level of focus, dedication, and continuous learning that is required to become a certified black belt. The Six Sigma process arose from Welch's intentionality at GE and has become the standard for quality around the globe.

Other examples are Jimmy Carter's intentionality, which helped change the relationship between Egypt and Israel and altered the future of the Middle East. In practical terms, his faith, dedication, and strength of conviction enabled him to stay the course until a peace treaty was agreed on. One of Steven Jobs's intended successes was changing the relationship between computer technology and the home and family environment. Andrea Jung transformed Avon from a door-to-door cosmetics company into "The Company for Women," with a culture that enables its sales representatives to achieve economic self-sufficiency.

You don't have to be a famous "great person" to lead change and transformation, but you do need to have and convey intentionality. That comes from your inner wellspring of hopes, desires, and visionary beliefs. As a change guide, you have to tap into spirit, lend it to others, and put heart and soul into your organization.

Changing a leadership culture is risky. Intentionality dwells in your beliefs and values. Courageous acts flow from beliefs. What you believe to be true either is true or is becoming truer as conscious awareness increases. Therefore, it's a personal imperative for you to be clear about your deep intent regarding the breadth and depth of change you seek. This is a no-kidding matter.

The leadership culture that you form either creates transformation or fails to make change. You have the ultimate responsibility for the design of that leadership culture—its rules, moral code, supporting organizational structures, rituals, information flows, and decision processes. Together with leadership, you will determine what is legitimate and desirable in the leadership beliefs and practices on which the organizational culture will depend.

Beyond your operations mode, in articulating intention, you need to stretch your comfort zone into the emotional and the relational. You must find your voice that speaks to the heart and spirit of your colleagues. Intentionality is a matter of deep conviction that surpasses mere necessity. You must examine the degree to which you are ready to go deep inside to understand and then to go public well beyond some general notion that change is good.

You must speak to the spirit of making a unifying difference that is good for all. That difference may unfold in the workplace, the market, or the world, but it has to be deeply compelling. Intentionality can be a deeply personal, resonant driver for us as role models for an alternative future that brings our personal lives, our work lives, and our community (in whatever scope or sphere we conceive it) together in an integral holistic living system.

Finally, you need to know the trajectory of your intentionality and how you balance competing commitments between your internal organizational forces and the external competitive forces, all with their own commitments and intentions. It's not about right or wrong, but it may be about finding win-win zones. It's about being cognizant of how you can positively influence others who do not yet share your degree of intentionality.

Your intentions, clearly and passionately expressed, are or can become a call to create and make use of Headroom, joining others in social discourse. Your intentionality needs to speak to everyone's inner self. In his inaugural speech, John F. Kennedy brilliantly declared, "The torch is passed to a new generation." This simple phrase of intentionality became the rallying cry for expanded participation in the political process. Martin Luther King Jr. expressed his intentionality regarding civil rights by saying, "I have been to the mountain top and have seen the other side." His was another spirit-driven clarion call to set off together toward a more inclusive culture. In both instances, subsequent actions were consistent with the concept of leader as guide.

In short, intentionality holds and extends three essential human qualities:

- Clarity about the rightness of a mission coupled with a high-level vision that sets the strategic direction for the sustainable long-term future of the organization
- An internal compass that navigates true to the course the organization has struck and the individual courage and commitment to stay the course
- Connection of human spirit to the work through passion, persistence, and the long-term pursuit of visions and connections that are of an order higher than oneself

Where do we see strong intentionality in the cases we've introduced so far? Here are three telling examples.

Intentionality at Professional Services Inc. and NuSystems. Personal transformation is critical to Inside-Out awareness, but if there is no engagement to expand and share the personal with the leadership collective, then the Outside-In forces that are so familiar to us will likely take over and win out over culture transformation.

In our discussion of leader logics, our example of a Performer was CEO Adam at Professional Services Inc. (PSI), where everything was translated into the terms of divisional operational execution. Adam was desperate to change the old Dependent culture to one of Achiever, but he lacked the Inside-Out intentionality needed to be a successful instrument for change and transformation. For Adam personally, the clear and singular goal was profit, no matter what it took. His Outside-In perspective became dominant within PSI's senior leadership and obfuscated any real intentions for sustainable transformation.

Adam himself believed he had been through a personal transformative experience. But his view that his inner transformation was unique and mattered only to himself meant that he did not think a similar breakthrough experience needed to be spread wider or shared with others. He did invest in seminars for the company's top and midlevel leaders, exposing them to gurus in market mind share, execution, and change management. However, members of the senior team reported that although they gained new knowledge, their leadership practices didn't really change much; overall, change and transformation never came about at PSI.

Why not? Adam had no intention that went beyond the market-driven culture of action and achievement. His intentionality had little power because it reflected no clear, sustainable, long-term vision beyond execution and creating shareholder value. The excitement was all his—it did not inspire anyone else—because the extent of his vision was meeting divisional goals as defined by Wall Street.

Our earlier example of a Moderator-Specialist was Liam, the CEO of NuSystems. He is also an example of a leader who lacked intentionality. His Moderator-Specialist logic inclined him to let expert-based Specialist groups within his organization fight things out—but not while he was around. As a Moderator, he appeared to have intent, but that appearance masked a lack of deep clarity about direction and courage to stay the course. Wherever he went, he quenched the sparks of creative passion by not dealing with conflict.

Intentionality at Technology Inc. Now consider Bart of Technology Inc., where Joe Sixpack's "doing my eight" yielded to people like Kim, who opened up to collaborative processes and goals. Bart's intentions were ambitious for the organization in a broader, collective sense: satisfied customers, economic longevity, healthy and happy workers, and emotional and spiritual wholeness (though he seldom used these words). His aims and logic were expansive and developmental, and they crossed organizational lines and categories. He was able and willing to range across different logics as situations required.

Achievement and collaborative engagement are Bart's modus operandi. Technology Inc. continues to perform in the market and maintain its premier market niche positions. Our experience with the organization reflects what it must be like to be an employee where a creative tension exists between the enjoyment of learning and expectation of achievement.

At the base of Bart's inspiring intentionality are intentions and engagement that could and did inspire and became shared throughout his company's leadership culture. All compasses were set in the same direction and with absolute commitment. Although the way was often foggy, the way-finders were unbendable and steadfast in purpose, and they followed through.

Bart believed there had to be a better, more human way to operate than the one that had characterized his company historically. Recently he told us that people have a natural striving to achieve and succeed: "It's the organization that gets in the way." At Technology Inc., he envisioned and intended an organization that would provide a more civilized, enriching environment. Maintaining a lead in market position was a motivator for change, but not number one. Number one was providing good jobs at good pay (for people with mostly high school educations) in a learning environment that made great products with an entrepreneurial spirit.

Bart's intentionality brought real change at Technology Inc. because he was willing and able to share it with others. At one point, he stood in front of hundreds of employees and appealed to their hearts and minds by speaking of their value to the company and to him personally. Lots of leaders say this sort of thing. What is exceptional about Bart is that he was credible, so everyone believed him. In front of key leaders, he showed his vulnerability and humanness, admitting what he feared in the change, what made him uncomfortable about it, and what he thought about his own level of readiness. By acknowledging his discomfort, he allowed the acceptance of others' feelings of fear and uncertainty about impending changes. This supportiveness helped to alleviate those feelings so that they had less power to obscure the promise of continued prosperity and vitality for the company. Bart conveyed his deep belief that all members of the company were critical participants in the organization change process. Furthermore, people knew he meant it. They believed in his intentionality.

Sharing Faith and Becoming an Instrument. We could also expand on CEO Glen at Memorial Hospital as an example of a leader with powerful intentionality based on a purpose of benefiting all, his deepest, most abiding purpose being customer-focused care—and on his organization's cultural change as an example of success. But what would we say that he and Bart, and many others like them, have in common?

The main thing is that they all exhibit faith in a better future. It is more than vision. Their intentionality allows them to find and foster engagement in themselves and in others. These stories of engaged leaders reveal experiences of commitment to personal and collective learning; development as an individual, team member, and part of an organization; and advancement of the team and organization through difficult changes.

As a leader with faith in the possibility of transformation, your intentionality becomes a conscious instrument for change and transformation. When you become that instrument, you amplify and resonate with the work others are doing. It's much more than activity and much more than just what you do. It's about who and what you are. Intentionality helps to make you an influencer in implementing the company's strategic direction as you learn to assert your personal power in the operations of your organization and your leadership culture.

When intentionality becomes your strength, you'll no longer use words or phrases like *can't*, *won't*, or *don't want to*. Nor will you need words of the opposite extreme, like *gung-ho* or *can-do*. This is because you'll be able to present a deeply held sense of sureness in direction, even without the clarity of knowing exactly how to get to the destination amid complex situations. It is this sureness of direction, combined with modesty about the best way for your organization to proceed in specific circumstances, that fuels ongoing demand for collective cultural learning and continuous potential for alignment and realignment in your operations.

Control Source

By control source, we mean your personal belief system about choices available to you in taking actions for change. The choices are an extension of your awareness and understanding of the dynamic interplay between Inside-Out and Outside-In forces. Different leader logics reflect needs for differing levels of control and different notions of what needs to be controlled. For example, within the Dependent-Conformer leadership logic, the Specialist feels he must control things (such as the production environment) and exerts control through expertise and being right; the Moderator feels she must control herself and exerts control by appeasement and diplomacy; and the Dominator feels he must control others' behaviors and norms and exerts authoritarian control through the organization's governing institutions.

Problems of control reflect competing interests. And as Philip Selznick pointed out in his 1957 book, *Leadership in Administration*:

> The struggle among competing interests always has a high claim on the attention of leadership. . . . In exercising control, leadership has a dual task. It must win the consent of constituent units, in order to maximize voluntary cooperation, and, therefore, must permit emergent interest blocs a wide degree of representation. At the same time, in order to hold the helm, it must [maintain] a balance of power appropriate to the fulfillment of key commitments [p. 75].

Leading change means advancing into unknown territory. You and each of your senior leaders will need to assess and measure your comfort with the change process against your need to control the uncertain, unexpected, and unpredictable. Individually and as a group, you will need to find an internal compass whose needle points the way between your own needs for control and control that is shared by others in the interests of cultural transformation. In the process, you may recognize a tension between what your organization expects of you for the sake of stability and what you expect from yourself for the sake of a different future. Of course, you didn't get where you are without satisfying both external and internal demands. To succeed at guiding organizational change, you will certainly need to be able to balance adequate management control with the demands of evolving, leadership-based, change-guidance processes.

The organizations we have worked with are no different from yours; all deal with conditions and needs that are in some ways relatively certain and stable, and others that are ambiguous and require flexibility. Successful change guides accept the responsibility to recognize the difference between what can be controlled and what will need to be openly addressed in an emerging, dynamic change process. They understand that leading change often involves loosening up on their personal needs for control; it means they will need to share control, along with sharing their anxieties and worries about that loosening with others on the change leadership team. To a greater or lesser extent, depending on the breadth and depth of the organization's change initiative, assisting the whole leadership culture in sharing control *is* the work of change. It is also the concept we aim at more squarely in Chapter Six.

Leading change means assisting others to accept and use the control that you lend them in order to make change happen. At the Specialist or Performer logic where you are now, or through which you may have passed, you settled into a certain comfort zone about control. That's a boundary you need to cross as you expand into Freethinker logic. As you move from your old zone of comfort, you begin to regard yourself as the progenitor of new beliefs: you loosen your own need for and practice of control, extending powers of control to others who are not accustomed to having it. You extend engagement and help them learn to use it for the greater good.

Control Source at Technology Inc. Bart's success didn't arrive without control struggles. Bart has an entrepreneurial bent and a practical need for profit. Lending control to others cost a lot of money on several occasions. How did Bart deal with the challenge? He started by sending a message to himself: it was absolutely up to him to model a future way of living and working the no-man's-land between certainty and ambiguity. He took on the need to evaluate and guide people along the tightrope between driving for results and experimenting with new degrees of freedom as the organization changed. In the course of that change, he reframed his philosophy from a somewhat individualistic "results-oriented work" to a more collaborative "results-oriented work environment."

To change the business's operational approach to a process-centered one, Bart articulated a three-year plan with annual recalibration. Bart also consistently demonstrated one of the key balancing aspects of personal readiness: an internally grounded self-awareness and openness to others about his own levels of comfort with the unknowns of the shared journey—a dynamic integration of control source and intentionality. This openness fueled his own development of a bigger mind, making him more adept in a Freethinker leader logic. In expanding his own leader logic, he created an environment for other senior leaders and the process for team leaders to do the same. He admits he was challenged by the need to release control, especially in areas where he did not have the knowledge or experience to make control viable, but he made a personal commitment to model an alternative mind-set of control source in order to enact change leadership.

Control Source at Global Electronics. In contrast, issues of control were Dawson's Achilles' heel at Global Electronics. Recall that for half a dozen years, this worldwide enterprise had, at least nominally, aspired to grow its annual revenues.

Dawson had skillfully suggested a general "big hairy audacious goal" for change (Collins and Porras, 1997). Outwardly he also expressed comfort with ambiguity and uncertainty. However, as he and we discussed the change process with his team, his ability to act as a guide was consistently thwarted by his strong need for predictability—for being perceived as in control and having answers. His private claims of self-confidence and comfort with flexibility and ambiguity quickly faded in the presence of his team and other constituents; there, his words and actions showed him unable to let go of the status quo. He conveyed the sense that a need for change did not apply to his own role as a leader, and this attitude was reflected by members of his leadership team in their interactions with the workforce. He couldn't reach the bigger mind that would help move him from his safe zone.

Although Dawson was an avid reader in the field of leadership and change, his internal compass kept him focused solely on externalized, Outside-In, serial operational moves (all of them failures). He couldn't find the Inside-Out courage for risk and reward. These limits also thoroughly undermined his credibility. In the end, he attributed the lack of change in the organization to factors beyond his control. Those who were a few levels down in his organization viewed him as untrustworthy and incompetent. His need to control the status quo and his tendency to duck accountability locked him into a game of corporate hide and seek, avoiding responsibility for one failure after another. As a Moderator, Dawson could see change as desirable only as long as it wasn't precarious, risky, or unsettling to anyone. Like Liam, the Specialist leader at NuSystems, Dawson avoided conflict, which further weakened his ability to face the issues of control. These problems left him personally unready to lead a cultural change.

Control Source at Credlow. Roger, the Transformer CEO of Credlow who was guiding his senior leaders and company culture up from a Dependent-Conformer level, also has a story illustrative of control source.

Here is an excerpt from one of Roger's speeches to a group of his managers-in-training in 2004, at the end of another year of restructuring, rebranding, and expansion:

- How Are You—working for a company that could give a "rat's ass" about what the industry thinks, says, or stands for?
- How Are You—in the area of self-discipline?
- How Are You—in understanding what a "privilege" it is to manage the lives of others?
- How Are You—in understanding the connection between body, mind, and spirit?
- How Are You—in fighting complacency?
- How Are You—in regard to empathy and understanding what it is like to be in the shoes of others?
- How Are You—at understanding YOU?

- How Are You—at handling change and more change and more change until it's not change, it's a way of life?

Note that Roger inquires about how people are feeling at this point, after all the change the year entailed. From there he went on to acknowledge that culture is a hard thing to grasp and to list all that they had been working on: growth, accountability, business challenges, respect, trust, bonuses, customer service, humor, independence, interdependence, bias for action, bias against complacency, constructive debate, fully engaging people in dialogue, no fear of change, financial bottom-line orientations, and the beginning of some love. Imagine a CEO talking about love.

But other than that, Roger wasn't expecting much.

Can you see how the speech reflects his willingness to keep control away from the center of his concerns?

Can you see how, by pushing the boundaries of engagement and what is open for dialogue and making multiple connections of potential culture issues, Roger has put his own need for certainty and control aside?

This is how Transformers operate in multiple planes and dimensions simultaneously.

Time Sense

"Set not your loaf in until the oven's hot." So the English proverb has it. Internally for each of us, the pressures of time raise constant anxiety: we never believe we have enough time. Stewart Brand (1999) laments that contemporary societies are increasingly shortsighted in time frame and attention span and suggests we need to correct that: "The trend might be coming from the acceleration of technology, the short horizon perspective of market-driven economies, the next political election, or the distractions of personal multi-tasking" (p. 2). Whatever the root causes, the impact is a lack of responsible, long-term, in-depth thinking on behalf of business and society, and their institutions. This is a particular problem in American corporations, largely because top managers often get paid off with lucrative profit-sharing options for maximizing only their company's short-term value. But what about the company's responsibility and long-term position in the community, the industry, the economy, and society? The turbulence in the housing and financial markets and the banking industry in late 2008 bears witness to the negative impact of this narrowly self-serving time sense on communities, nations, and the global economy.

Is Time a Constraint or a Resource? So many prospective clients want to know of us, "How long will this change take?" It's not an unreasonable question, but it reveals a major concern of executives. Senior change leaders acting as guides to others need to be able to convey that time can be reserved for change instead of being a limiting factor. It's all in how you perceive it.

Time sense is a key differentiator of personal readiness for leading organization change. The question is whether you experience time as a constraint to be handled with the usual time management skills, or if you see it as a resource to be leveraged for the greater good of the organization and its constituents. Since organizational change is typically a long-term journey, leaders who see time as a constraint often also believe that sustainable change is impossible because there is not enough time. They are victims of what one of our clients referred to as the "thirteen-week clock"—that is, a focus on this quarter's earnings, the report to the investment community, and the feedback from that community (plus, minus, or neutral). This snap sense of time ("Three-ball in the side pocket!" Whack!) shows little appreciation for how long it took the organization to develop its current systems, structures, processes, and culture in the first place. Impatience with time tends to grow when intentionality is weak and leaders are reticent to challenge the conventional wisdom that accompanies Moderator, Specialist, and Performer leader logics.

An alternative longer-term framing of time does not rule out quickness. It can embrace the "ten-minute team" and metaphors like, "Now is all there is, so use it well" and "the eternal right now." But to develop a bigger mind and model readiness for change, you will need to explore and practice using and living in different kinds of time. For example, different meetings you attend can be based on differing senses of time, from the no-sitting operations meeting, to a multiday retreat, to engaging in serious play to deliberately forget about time in order for brains to storm. The personal challenge for leaders is to recognize that it's important to use time in ways other than obsessing about the bottom line.

Time to Execute and Transform. From the 1980s into the mid-1990s, senior leaders were surrounded by management frameworks focusing on operating plans, managing by objectives, time management tools, and a suggestion that good leaders carefully limited their daily number of interactions with others (Kotter, 1999). The premise was that time was only a constraint to be managed. While all of us work under pressures of deadlines, effective change leaders demonstrate a readiness to both execute and leverage time as a resource in guiding change. In such leaders, we observe openness to staying the course toward change rather than darting away in expedient, speedy short-cuts from thoroughness, ownership, and the need to embed each change in the culture. Research and the experience of others confirm that forcing change too quickly can backfire. Transformation is not a proposition of either execute *or* change. It has to find the time for both (Beer and Nohria, 2000).

Slow Down to Speed Up: Examples from Memorial Hospital, Technology Inc., and Credlow. At Memorial Hospital, CEO Glen endured strong demands on his time from the board, community groups, medical schools, nursing schools, patient advocacy groups, volunteer organizations, his own team, and his workforce. It would have been easy for him to say that he didn't have time to be an active guide in the organization's change efforts and to expect others to take up the slack. Instead, he spent time every day walking down corridors, conversing spontaneously with staff, volunteers, patients, and families. He turned himself into a model of how to change toward a culture that provided exquisite patient experience and placed himself on that front line. He used time to informally create an environment that recognized the importance of relationships, feedback, active listening, and constant communication in promoting change. Through his willingness to model intentionality and engagement, he also created the space and time for the development of a bigger mind and the accompanying leader logic, moving from Performer toward Freethinker and Collaborator.

"All this change in the leadership culture is so we can respond fast," he told us recently. "Every CEO wants that. But you've got to slow down all the time to keep learning and maintain that edge." He also revealed his orientation when reminding us, "All we have is time—you never run out of time."

Bart acted similarly in the manufacturing plant at Technology Inc. He found time to walk the floor daily, engaging work associates by name, asking for their perspective on becoming a process-centered organization, and getting them to share stories of successes, fears, and uncertainties. He communicated his own sense of the known and the unknowns in the journey and consistently communicated his support for a collective journey from the traditional, hierarchical, dependent organization culture toward one of greater independent decision making. Always he was able to maintain a focus on the ultimate goal of Interdependent-Collaborator processes to drive the work and produce results. At no time did he retreat from the importance of results and customer satisfaction, but neither did he criticize in a negative manner when a new approach did not produce great immediate results.

At Credlow, CEO Roger considered various issues, including that of time, openly in his speeches. In one he asked, "How are you going to handle it when the only really important bell to ring signals from 'birth to death,' and what you do in between is up to you?" Following is an excerpt from Roger's journal:

> Development (people, the organization, the business) is mixed with some very interesting success and some disappointing setbacks. Of course, it's not all struggle. There is always a silver lining. It's the timing that is key. Without the struggle, there is no silver lining to take advantage of. Timing, timing, timing. Rallying Credlow people is never an issue. They are the most achievement oriented group I've assembled. Focusing the rally and energy when many things are coming at you at once is the challenge and the beauty when done properly.

> What's it like for me? It is what the core of leadership is all about. It is the test of the culture and the test of our growth. I find it very challenging but it can be exhausting at times. Anything done well can be exhausting. The key with timing . . . is the endurance of leadership. Many understand timing and adversity but underestimate the endurance aspect.

> What's next? We continue to walk on. We continue to connect. We continue to fight gravity and inch away from the norm. We continue to grow a bit and look for silver linings with the development of our people and the economic landscape. We walk on.

These examples point up a time sense that is unusual for someone at Roger's level of leadership, and they show how passionately and powerfully he expresses it.

The examples are also consistent with how Credlow leaders actually use their time. Operations-based discussions in senior team meetings are constantly interrupted with developmental conversations about the culture and the people. In fact, the concern is so ongoing that taking time out for learning has become a continuous part of business meetings. The values and belief systems about the relativity of time are so consistently integrated that it is sometimes difficult for Credlow leaders to keep track of the hour in a conventional sense. Into his organization's culture Roger inculcates the sense that the work of the organization reaches beyond next calendar quarter.

What might look like a poor use of time to others is actually just what is necessary for organizational transformation. This element of personal readiness is critical because it sends a clear message to fellow trekkers that they can and should use time for learning and for the advancement of the group, beyond the daily execution. By leveraging your personal time resources of informal, face-to-face contact, you draw more people onto the path with less effort than you would have expended arranging, convening, and conducting formal meetings of your various constituent groups.

Striking a Balance

In our observations, the combination of intentionality, keen understanding of control source, and great time sense turns skeptics and nonbelievers into people willing to take more responsibility, make decisions, and work fast and effectively beyond directives from above. We began the three with intentionality because expressing intentionality and inviting engagement early helps leaders to develop the Headroom (the topic of Chapter Six) that is so important in a collaborative organizational culture. But you can probably see how good time sense and making time for informal interactions stimulate engagement and also enlarge Headroom.

Exercises

Questions

What will your clarion call be? How will you convey your intentionality in words and actions to energize engagement, explore control source and time sense, and make a difference in leadership and organization culture that produces the effective leadership outcomes of direction, alignment, and commitment?

Write your response in your journal. Create a visual image of it in your mind or sketch one in your journal.

Write a paragraph that describes your leadership profile, including your current leader logic, intentionality, control source, and time sense. Return to your journal periodically to reflect on your time sense and control center, and write your responses.

Exercises for Self and Others

Choose a member of your senior team, and have a discussion about the main points and implications of this chapter for both of you and for each other.

Questions for Dialogue

At the next team meeting, have each team member individually complete the scaled questions that follow. Then have them explore together the meaning of the results and the requirements for increasing the change readiness of the team and the organization if there is to be a transformation of the leadership culture.

To what extent is the executive team clear about its intentionality to change the leadership culture in order to achieve sustainable direction, alignment, and commitment?

1	2	3	4	5	6	7	8	9
Team is not very intentional about change			Team vacillates about why change is necessary			Team is very clear and explicit about intentions for change		

To what extent is leadership capable of effectively addressing ambiguity and uncertainty associated with complex challenges?

1	2	3	4	5	6	7	8	9
Leadership is very cautious in dealing with ambiguity and uncertainty			Capability exists in some but not all			Leadership uses ambiguity and uncertainty as a driver for change		

To what extent have prior change initiatives been hampered by competing time pressures?

1	2	3	4	5	6	7	8	9
Time pressures have not been a barrier			Time pressures have been used as an excuse not to change			Time pressures are always a major constraint		

To what extent is the executive team willing to engage in the uncertain, ambiguous process of guiding organization change, not suppressing or controlling it?

1	2	3	4	5	6	7	8	9
Team is not currently willing			Team vacillates between exploration and suppression			Team actively engages uncertainty and demonstrates capability to share control		

To what extent does the senior leadership demonstrate behavior consistent with sharing power and influence in creating collective leadership?

1	2	3	4	5	6	7	8	9
Leadership is heavily siloed and turf protective			Support for power and influence sharing ebbs and flows			Sharing power and influence with the leadership collective is expected and rewarded		

To what extent do members of the senior team trust the intentions of others in changing the leadership culture?

1	2	3	4	5	6	7	8	9
Absence of trust			Some trust among some members			A lot of trust among most members		

6

HEADROOM

Standing Up for Change

He not busy being born is busy dying.
—*Bob Dylan, "It's Alright, Ma (I'm Only Bleeding)"*

Production has never worked right at this plant. No one on the shop floor has ever taken a share of the company's performance-based bonus system, and every one of them could use the extra money. But money is the least of it. The front office people don't like the shop-floor people. Ethnic groups cluster and work separately. The executives are pushing something called a process-centered organization, which threatens to lay tracks right through the middle of a lot of well-placed barriers. Look around the room. Nobody is going to let that happen.

But wait. The senior leaders at the front of the room are saying something new. They are not ordering compliance; they are asking for community and collaboration and commitment. "We believe this process-centered organization will benefit all of us," they say. "But we don't really know how to do it. We need your help to figure it out. We need for you to believe in it too. The days of telling you what to do are over. There are no more supervisors. We are asking for your participation. We want you to figure out better ways for this to work, and we want you and your process teams to make decisions and take actions. We want you to believe us, to test this—to take a risk and try this new thing."

Minutes pass in silence. Then, like a loose rock tumbling downhill becomes an avalanche, a small murmur breaks into challenges and questions. A Russian-speaking worker turns to a Portuguese-speaking worker and says, "You've never even said hello to me." And then he teaches him to say "hello" in Russian. Then he teaches the whole room how to say "hello" in Russian—and everyone does. People hoot and howl, and then they all learn to say hello in Spanish, in Portuguese, and in Polish, and they hoot and howl and laugh some more.

Then things get serious. Manuel, clearly one of the informal leaders of the Puerto Rican American contingent, stands up and directly asks one of the organization's senior leaders: "Do you mean to say that I can change how we do this part of the process just because I think it's better?"

"Yes," Mitch says, "we do mean that. If you believe it's better and want to take the risk. But it would be even better if you got your team members involved."

"What happens if it's a mistake?" Manuel asks.

Mitch replies, "Geez, we're already making a lot of mistakes every day. Wouldn't it be good if we made one we all learned something from?"

The room laughs. And then the questions and responses go deep and then deeper into the operational complexity and how to understand how to fix it. There are more questions than answers. Big questions spawn bigger minds, barriers break down, and ceilings lift. People stand and challenge each other and start making sense together: front office and shop-floor people, process engineers and senior strategy team people. Everyone is playing at the same table, and no one is allowed to play the "I've got the power" card. And while some of the buzz is social and some of the challenges raise past conflicts, most of the time it is the din of people telling their truths and trying to see an alternate way of doing things.

A few weeks later, the plant made the bonus list for the first time. It has never missed making it since. For the first time, people in the plant believe senior leadership, and they believe each other a little bit more too. Out of new beliefs came new practices. When something new worked, it remained in practice. Together the people in this plant, at all levels and under all titles, created the space to show up, stand up, and grow up into bigger minds. We call that space, and the energy needed to keep it going, *Headroom*.

In Chapters Three and Five, we explored an Inside-Out approach and Readiness—two of the three basic frameworks underlying transformation. This chapter enlarges on the third, Headroom. Headroom means supporting growing, bigger minds in yourself and others in order to face and unravel big organizational puzzles. In Headroom, individuals, groups, and the leadership culture systematically and intentionally develop toward an interdependent collective leadership logic.

Let us stand beside you right now and say that we are in it too. We've often put ourselves in the middle of change and transformation during our work with leaders and their organizations. Headroom is about our own learning alongside yours, and it rises out of several years of intense learning alongside our clients, paying attention to what was happening in their organizations.

The concept of Headroom came to us as a discovery in our action development practice. By *action development*, we mean the process of helping clients to implement key organizational strategies while simultaneously transforming their leadership culture. Action development initiatives are broad in scope, ongoing, and focused on big changes in both the operations and the culture simultaneously.

In experimenting with and crafting the Headroom process, we've combined theories and methods from many sources, applying them in rapid prototypes, learning what combinations worked best. We acknowledge our main sources and mentors in Appendix B. Our own contribution has been to apply combinations of interventions toward changing leadership culture over the long run.

The Basic Concept

In March 2007, the *Atlanta Constitution* relayed an Associated Press report of an e-mail sent by Chrysler Group chief executive

Tom LaSorda to Chrysler employees in an effort to "rally the troops." According to the paper, LaSorda told employees "that the company's 'future is in our hands' and urged them to redouble their efforts to improve the automaker's fortunes. 'We need to rededicate ourselves to taking waste out of our business while providing great vehicles and an ownership experience that will attract customers and keep them coming back'" ("Chrysler Chief," p. G2). About two weeks later, according to the *New York Times*, the head of Chrysler's parent company Daimler confirmed that talks were well underway to sell it off (Landler, 2007).

Obviously the earlier e-mail from the CEO directly to employees had not reflected what things really looked like from the executive suite. We mention this disheartening example in order to say that in our work, we see many more examples of ineffective change leadership than we do the effective sort; many ineffective efforts involve similar vague electronic urgings to get involved. Senior-leader events featuring inspirational speeches and two days of golf often amount to much the same empty gesture, as if a social atmosphere with Outside-In change messages were going to foster organizational change.

Organizational development specialists have said, and senior leaders have known, for years that you have to be involved in change for it to be successful. But what does that mean? Does an annual retreat assembling the top leaders count? What about speeches in large forums followed by Q&A sessions and celebrative kickoff events? No. There is nothing wrong with those forums for sharing information, clarifying new direction, and celebrating. But significantly more is needed to create change, and we call that "more" Headroom.

Principles of Headroom

In our work with leaders, leadership teams, and the organizations they seek to transform, we keep three principles of Headroom at the front of our minds:

- It is a systemic approach to development that occurs while achieving the business's strategic challenges.

- It contains and enables forces that fuel and energize transformation of the organization's unified leadership culture.

- It accumulates across multiple spaces and forces that connect and gain momentum in the organization.

We also try to hold a particular image in our minds to remind us of the basic problem that Headroom aims to solve (see Photo 6.1).

As we said briefly in Chapter One, creating Headroom means raising the leadership culture's ceiling for development. Headroom assists everyone in advancing together and getting the bigger minds required by the organization's challenges. Creating it is a social process. A shared Inside-Out experience is an interpretive process that requires dialogue among people, and Headroom is a particular form of engagement.

Photo 6.1 The Basic Problem That Headroom Tries to Solve

Source: © iStock Photo 2007 Viorika Prikhodko, from istockphoto.com.

Headroom means making time and places for exploring the future and figuring out the leadership beliefs and practices needed to get there. It's also about having genuine and creative multilateral connections with others about the work that transformation really requires and specifying and committing to whatever new agreements are required to change the way things are.

Creating Headroom means raising ceilings of expectations and hopes, thus creating an upward draft of energy, just as a rising plane creates an updraft beneath it. That updraft invites other people to stand up and use more of themselves to build new beliefs in the possibilities and potential in their work. Creating Headroom is an act in which you literally stand up for and grow up into change. Headroom creates a space in which your mind expands as you imagine, explore, and create a different future. It creates room for others to stand up to and provides different states of experience for all involved.

Headroom alters the forces of social reality in the leadership culture. It gives space for internal and group dialogue, authentic public engagement, and collective learning.

Methods and Tools

There are some reinforcing mechanisms for Headroom: speeches, videos, and e-mail communications can all contribute to that collective engagement. But they are not the basic methods. They are ancillary. There is nothing scripted or canned about the process of creating Headroom. Recall how Liam at NuSystems wanted his remarks at his change forum scripted? Headroom won't come about like that. Scripts and speeches, no matter how charismatic, are one-way and Outside-In. Headroom is socially multidirectional and Inside-Out.

Effective Headroom methods and tools trigger and accelerate development. One of our basic methods is to help leaders access their preverbal level of images, triggering creative resonance. The concept behind our approach is based on the concept of aesthetic competencies for creative leadership described in *The Leader's Edge* (Palus and Horth, 2002). Palus and Horth use visual images, metaphors, and other devices for reaching Inside-Out states of advanced awareness. For example, putting something in the middle of a circle of people to ponder (a symbolic image or object) can center their focus and their reflections around a core question on an organizational issue or opportunity.

Such methods and tools help to create states of openness within people by tapping deeply into the human spirit and imagination. Another core methodology we use is dialogue: the verbal meaning-making part of Headroom that follows the preverbal loosening of normal boundaries of thought. We often refer to dialogue as collaborative inquiry (co-inquiry) because we focus more on asking questions than on advocating a direction.

We have a suite of action-development-focused quick tools that are portable and pragmatic, and they all reflect group self-perceptions providing immediate access to leadership logics from a variety of viewpoints such as team, functions, subcultures, and alliance partners. We also have a suite of scored tools that provide validated measures of various aspects of culture and climate. Both types of tools help clients align feasible strategies with ways to develop capabilities that the strategies require.

Voice of Change

Creating Headroom can be a one-time event, but that won't take you very far. The key to its successful use is to commit to practicing it. You want to move from being consciously incompetent to unconsciously competent—as you might be when shooting a basketball or using a word processor. When you first try out Headroom, you may need to experiment with it for several days. With practice, you can cut that time to several hours. After extended practice time, you can get it going in just minutes.

We also make use of Bill Torbert and Associates' *Action Inquiry* tools (2004) to provide organizations with several transformational learning pathways. The methods, tools, and mechanics of creating Headroom are fairly easy to learn. (See Appendix B for a sample list.) Most of our clients find freedom in their use—the process is energizing. But there are also personal risks and rewards. It is very important to commit to and sustain the practice in order to realize the rewards.

What Headroom Can Do

We had a small argument with our editor as we were writing this part of the book. He insisted we use the word *Headroom* only as a noun and not as the name of a process. He said that words denoting process usually have verbs as their roots. But in our practice, we do refer to Headroom as a process and practically as a verb itself, and we persuaded our editor to loosen up a bit and go along. The Headroom process is like a fractal's self-replication. Just as awaken, unlearn and discern, and advance (see Chapter Three) operate at the individual level of transformation, the three parts of Headroom operate at the collective level. Each experience expands the state of being for everyone included. The three parts of Headroom are Inside-Out discovery, action development of new beliefs and practices, and advancement of leadership logics and culture. Once you begin to explore its power to change things, you too may find yourself saying to someone, "Let's Headroom!"

> The three steps of personal transformation presented in Chapter Three—awaken, unlearn and discern, and advance—are paralleled when applied to groups as Headroom. Although there are many differences between the transformation of an individual and that of a group or culture, the core principles with the three steps are the same.

Inside-Out Discovery

In the space and time of Headroom, people come together to engage in the development process, making sense of the transformation and becoming intentional about what it requires. They become skilled in the use of tools that expand their Inside-Out range of cognitive and emotive conscious awareness to meet the organizational realities of the challenges they face. Headroom encourages authentic, transparent, personal willingness to engage in truth telling and public learning; it allows people to say the truth as they see it, exposing what before couldn't be discussed and so covertly threatened change.

Core outcomes include both individual and collective unlearning and new learning. People coldly analyze assumptions about the way things are and warmly imagine what could be with renewed energy and advanced perspective. They engage through deep discovery and exploration down to levels where dialogue promotes more questions than answers. They dive deep into imagination and problem solving, exploring root causes and revealing future options and resources. This takes place simultaneously for each person and the group.

Action Development of New Beliefs and Practices

Because Headroom is an alteration of the forces of social discourse and social agreements, it allows new, multilateral connections between people across divisions and levels, as well as new unions of leadership culture beliefs and practices. This process of social discourse and agreements is like creating a new national constitution and then engaging in making sense of how to live up to the new agreement in moving forward.

This enables individuals and groups within the leadership culture to take on new perspectives, question current beliefs, and develop new ways of working in operations. Headroom can be used for forums on sense making and for renegotiating the social rules of engagement. People figure out together how to put a new idea to work. The process is exhilarating, confusing, confounding, and liberating as they "unlearn and churn" and "relearn and discern." The agreements and experiments are voluntary forms of risk taking, which can be entered by people from the top, middle, and bottom. When repeated, experiments that work become ritualized, and the new rituals embed themselves in the leadership culture as beliefs and practices. As Headroom experiences are used more frequently, they become zones of intentional change where leaders can practice action development and where isolated, subjective notions can turn into objective, shared alternatives.

Advancement of Leadership Logics and Culture

In discussing movement to a new leadership logic in Chapter Three, we described a necessary progress from short-lasting states and long-lasting stages. Headroom is a state that allows people to hold and incubate individual inspirations and organizational aspirations. In that sense, Headroom itself is transformative. It creates and strengthens experiences of thought and mode of engagement during intentional group states that the next stage will require. It grows organizational soul. It encapsulates the experience with and advancement of leader and leadership logics, both during "time-out for learning" practice sessions and also when applied through action development initiatives directly in the operational work. In the freedom of Headroom, leaders can do serious play, engaging each other in new ways, taking on new leader and leadership logics, and experimenting with bigger minds.

A leader has to create Headroom in which people can learn, grow, and develop their capabilities. Initially, developing in this way requires that people take time out for learning together in a safe, separate space that is independent from the usual grind of operations.

Figure 6.1 Headroom: Growing Bigger Minds

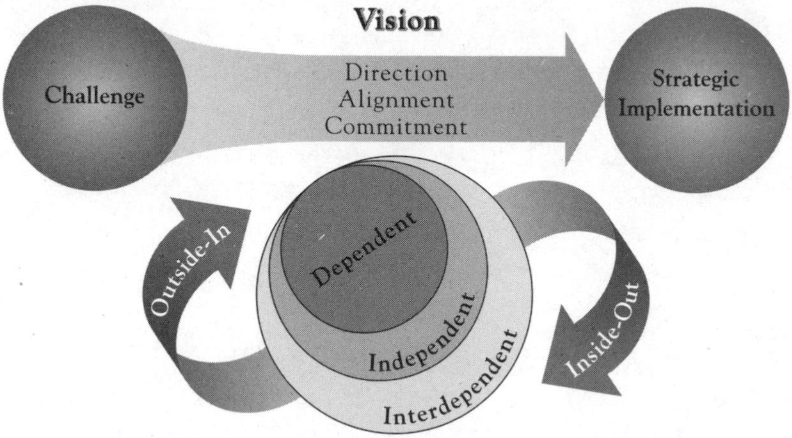

Thus, Headroom moves individuals and advances the collective toward later stages in the leadership culture. In fact, if sustained, Headroom is the major process that advances the collective leadership logic, culture, and new organizational capability. When a leadership culture creates and uses Headroom, its learning and its collective mind expand toward a more complex logic. Figure 6.1 revisits the overall view.

Courage, Commitment, and . . . What Else It Takes

As a leader creating Headroom space, you'll face some of the same challenges we discussed in Chapter Three when we described the Inside-Out versus the Outside-In approach to leading and managing change. You'll need to drop your guard, build trust, and dig deep into beliefs and assumptions.

As a process of constantly, relentlessly, unnervingly seeking alignment in the leadership culture, creating Headroom takes courage and commitment. It takes guts to believe deeply in a new vision or strategy and to stick with it. You will have to stand up and be seen, actively challenge the status quo, and stand up to peers who will undermine change if you do not bring them along.

Voice of Change

In the summer of 1776, at the Continental Congress in Philadelphia, men committed to a new course of action. They did so aspiring to a higher leadership logic—from the lowest level of Dependent-Conformer up to an independent logic. Their Declaration of Independence documented this collective commitment, and its words must have gripped those who deeply pledged its adoption. It is not far-fetched to imagine that those men at that time were experimenting with some form of Headroom for a nascent nation. They were certainly shifting their beliefs, based on a new vision and direction, about what the new direction and new practices would require of them and the new capability they would have to develop in order to realize that strategic vision. Imagine the depth of commitment such an endeavor required.

A change guide's commitment to Headroom implies an undistracted focus on change and determination to follow through. Involvement is comparatively easy. You can be involved through showing up at occasional events or writing e-mails. Commitment doesn't stop and start. It is more like an obsession, and it gets under your skin so that you never quite get completely away from it. Change is right here and right now, applying the new. Involvement may contain some measure of association or participation that largely remains at the surface of things, but commitment is gripping and engrossing. One becomes immersed in the heart of the matter.

Headroom as Process

Headroom is a No-BS zone where people tell the truth and believe each other because people are genuine and authentic when they are there. It is a space and time in which the rank and status of individuals are secondary and the future of the organization is primary. The essence of Headroom is social, although it requires specific space and time in initial phases to take root and to practice. People explore multiple right answers together and choose the best ones and agree to try them out in action development.

People change the rules. They make new agreements and go off and change the way things are. Headroom is a process that alters not only experience in your society but also outcomes in your operations.

Headroom experiences are reinforced by repetition. Repeating the process allows you to practice new beliefs and new practices together and alter them until they fit.

Headroom isn't the beginning and the end of culture transformation. There are conditions that must be present in order to create it, such as the three elements of personal readiness we described in Chapter Four (intentionality, control source, and time sense) and the willingness to take on the investment, risk, and vulnerability. You need to have the right mix of people and the right timing with regard to the organization's ability to face its future. But creating Headroom can be the key to the kind of engagement and commitment required to make real change.

"Upping" Headroom

It's not hard to experiment with Headroom. The leaders, teams, and organizations we have worked with have found it a practical way to discover and transform. You can sum up our admittedly elaborate explanation of the Headroom process with this simple phrase: *Show Up, Stand Up, Own Up, and Grow Up.*

Show Up. Engage directly with others in the change effort. Be genuine and authentic. Think about how much of your time you spend in leading the change using face-to-face encounters with others. Look to generate more questions than you have answers to give. When you become the model of how it can be, and in fact how it is right now, you become the change before their very eyes. Seeing is believing, and a change in beliefs is what you are after.

Stand Up. Stand up first and be seen. Go into the public forum, along with others, to say how serious you are about the change. Describe what you personally and professionally are willing to risk.

You have to stand up to the status quo and challenge it actively. Stand up to peers who may undermine Headroom. Stand up to and with the leadership community specifically about creating new space for people to learn, grow, and develop together. Stand up about the ambiguity that significant change stirs up, and for the time it takes to make real change.

Own Up. Say in public you don't know all the answers; then ask for others' help to figure things out and follow through. Stand physically and emotionally in front of and genuinely with others, and be clear about what is certain and what is not. Acknowledge your place in the culture. Owning up to these things will create the trust your people need to explore a common future together. When you own up to others, the majority will engage and own up too.

Owning up requires a willingness to expose one's genuine uncertainties, and so it can't be scripted. Scripting is a way of avoiding accidentally saying what you didn't mean to say, and if you're deliberately not saying things that some part of you urges you to say, you're not really owning up at all. A cautious instinct for careful planning is the opposite of what is required in creating Headroom. If you, as a senior leader, aren't willing to show up fully and genuinely, with your own personal questions and

Voice of Change

You cannot delegate culture change. The culture is not "out there" somewhere; it is in you—in your gut, your heart, and your mind. You can no more have someone else change the culture for you than you can have someone else change your mind. It is that fundamental. If you want others to commit, then you commit first. If you want others to adapt and change, then take the lead. It's yours, and you have to deal with it first. It is difficult to quantify the enormous level of trust and credibility you will generate. That is why you need the space and time of Headroom.

uncertainty about the future, then how do you expect others (who need to trust you) to deal with their uncertainty?

Grow Up. Big questions spawn bigger minds. To create Headroom, you must be certain and confident about the direction your organization must take, but you will be continuously uncertain about exactly how to get there. That is why you need the energy of everyone involved in figuring it out as you go. This is the kernel of collective learning and a key to a learning organization.

Reflect for a moment on the change challenge you're facing. How much do you really believe, deep down in yourself, that the change required in the organization is really only all about others? Are you frustrated that your change management programs aren't working very well even after they've been well planned and staffed, led by expert consultant teams, and after you've written all those great memos, and invested in leadership retreats that set the new vision of organizational imperatives?

Does management success in your organization require a lot of answers? Are you supposed to be the expert with all the answers? Will you be making yourself personally vulnerable and risking your position if you publicly profess that you do not have all the answers? How much, in short, do you believe in this change—and how feasible is it?

How Headroom Gets Going

With the right conditions, Headroom emerges naturally. We've seen it many times in our experience, but never in quite the same way twice. We believe this is so because of Headroom's expressly developmental nature. It doesn't start by setting "stretch goals" or "raising the bar." It does, however, almost always stem from someone's engaging himself and others in a process of changing, in real time, live and face-to-face. And there are other general patterns.

New Social Discourse—New Social Contracts

Sometimes Headroom starts in the middle of an organization and then gets higher executives' attention. More often, it appears during planned events among executives and senior leaders as they struggle with vision and strategic imperatives— sometimes about organizational survival. Then, when the heat in the system urges executives to really take it on, they form and practice Headroom in action during their shared operations work as they focus on newly created leadership practices— practical matters that must get done in operations.

In such cases, executives have already made what they believe are imperative changes in systems and structure, but the changes aren't yet working right. Headroom arises as senior leaders engage to learn collectively about why changes aren't working. The leaders call on each other to face up and engage. Those actions require a new social contract and agreement to create new beliefs and to try new practices. Leaders and groups employ Headroom-creating tools; action development occurs between events; and prototypes spawn new behavior, beliefs, and culture. Leaders at the top develop clarity about direction, culture, and operations requirements to face up to future challenges. There's a movement in methods from safe, to not so safe, to risk and vulnerability, and from learn and practice to new social contracts for change.

When they're ready, senior leadership expands direction setting to the middle of operations and seeks alignment in core systems and processes. The top levels of the organization serve as architects for the whole organization, inviting, demonstrating, and expecting. Mechanisms emerge for reinforcing change, such as culture leadership teams, measures, scorecards, and stories and powerful artifacts of change. Headroom becomes practiced, viral, self-perpetuating, evolutionary, and revolutionary throughout the organization.

Fundamental social principles and dynamics of social contracting and social discourse are at work today in your organization.

All you have to do as leader is harness them. What's the greatest team you ever played on? Do you want to re-create that experience in your organization's culture? When social contracting sets the parameters for change and social discourse is the process for change, then people will respond well to measurement practices that invite them to face the challenges alongside you.

Headroom in Action

Following are a few observations of Headroom in action. Wherever it starts, it must eventually penetrate the entire leadership culture:

- *Resistance evaporates because change is a pull, not a push.* As people say their truth about how they see things, exposing what before couldn't be discussed, the underground resentments are transferred to above-ground declarations and new directions. Negative energy that covertly threatened change is transformed into positive energy that fosters change.

- *People engage through multilateral connections, and anyone can engage with everyone, across all levels and for the mutual benefit of all.* The intern can engage with the president. Headroom structures the potential for participative social agreements that intentionally shift the beliefs and norms of the leadership culture toward interdependence. Its intent is to be fully egalitarian and fully connected in intentionality for the benefit of all— individuals as well as the organizational whole. Self-aggrandizement yields to collective discovery.

- *People enter and reenter a third space of collective learning.* Formerly they occupied two spaces unconsciously: one "mine," the other "yours." The third space, Headroom, is a more conscious, anticipated, ritualistic space set aside for our creative ventures. As people's intentionality grows, Headroom becomes a space for taking time out for collective learning. People learn to slow down in order to speed up and power up as Headroom alters and advances time sense.

- *Headroom gradually becomes more and more systemic and developmental.* Whatever development occurs in Headroom is injected into at least some part of the organizational system. The more strategic it is, the more effective it is. Events are vehicles to moving into Headroom; they aren't the territory of Headroom. In Headroom, when a mistake or an organizational fault line is uncovered and owned by the collective, the learning event moves people into action development initiatives. The group makes a contract to alter the way things will be done, and operations change.

- *Headroom is the catalyzing source of a united force for change through the leadership culture.* It triggers and fosters achievement of direction, alignment, and commitment (DAC) in the culture. Effective DAC outcomes expand and extend the ranks of the leadership culture. Headroom's power far exceeds that of issue-based problem-solving behaviors, motivational speakers, empowerment, and any number of single-focus interventions.

- *Headroom extends the leadership culture through invitation and celebration.* Although it is noncoercive, open human interaction, the process creates a draft of peer pressure that moves some people along for a while in passive compliance. Clients have called this the "fake it 'til you make it" quality of Headroom. This functions to convert negative energy forces to neutral ones.

Playing over Your Head

What forms initially out of Headroom is a small, critical mass of leaders networking on their shared new beliefs and behaviors. How many are needed for that critical mass? What about others who don't believe in the change?

We can't put a number on critical mass, but to reach it, you need to strategically select and recruit leaders for early inclusion who have the most influence in the organization and then enable those leaders to get others to "play over their heads." Most people want to succeed. The more they see risk rewarded with success, the more they want to join in with a winning team. To create that playing field of success, senior leaders must work out the social aspects of Headroom.

A kind of social contracting, or recontracting, occurs. When senior leaders show up and stand up in an organizational operation that has been slogging along (from an entire manufacturing plant to a single department), their actions rekindle hope in the rank and file. People stir toward commitment because they want to believe. They seek a core of people to engage with who are embedded in common purpose and values. Their thoughts and feelings are often experienced as a breakthrough, and you may hear some say, "Thank goodness! Finally something is going to happen that can make a difference."

From that contracting, leaders can strike new agreements. They do not have to be formal; they can be verbal or written, a document that everyone signs and shares, or a dialogue in which all say "aye" to some consensus. However cast, the agreement publicly declares an intent to change something together. As a loose social contract, it shares permission to try new ways of working; it can also recognize limits to risks that people need to take and can guarantee zones of safety. Risks aren't eliminated, however, and there must be honor within the boundaries set by agreement.

Surrounding an agreement itself—the basic shared understanding—is a social discourse that reinforces and tests any practical boundary the agreement implies. For example, the U.S. Constitution was developed as a shared social contract. First came the drafting of agreements for a new country. Following came the testing of those new national boundaries of principle and law. Through an ongoing process of testing and reinforcing those boundaries through the courts, town meetings, and all manner of public forums, Americans continuously interpret and reinterpret their social agreement. The social contract provides the structures and rules; social discourse leads to understanding how they work.

Headroom, Learning, and the Elusive Learning Organization

Does success in your organization require a lot of right answers? Are you supposed to have them all? If so, you're a million miles from being a learning organization. Our experience is that big change challenges require shared, collective learning. Facing new and significant challenges simply means that you don't know, exactly or certainly, how to get this big-bad-challenge thing done. Not knowing in a public way is usually uncomfortable for executives. You didn't get to your position by not knowing the answers. And you're probably a high achiever who has relied on expert knowledge to get you where you are. In 1991, Chris Argyris wrote an article titled "Teaching Smart People to Learn." In this piece, and in his work more broadly, he says that successful individuals don't know how to deal with failure, its consequent embarrassment, and the defensiveness that follows—all of which prevent senior leaders from learning from mistakes. He writes, "Because many professionals are almost always successful at what they do, they rarely experience failure. And because they have rarely failed, they have never learned how to learn from failure" (p. 2).

It is easy to agree with Argyris's insights, yet more than two decades after the advent of the learning organization era, many senior leaders experience significant ongoing failure with organizational learning and change initiatives. Still, we find that more senior leaders today than ever before are willing to experiment with culture transformation, including dealing with their own vulnerability in the learning process.

After all that has been made of organizational learning in the past several years, we believe that Headroom is a practical approach to achieving it. We call it collective learning—that's what we see happen in Headroom. Not only have we experienced it firsthand with clients, we have also conducted evaluation studies that demonstrate those clients are achieving a core capability in collective learning. With Headroom, learning becomes collective. It happens when enough leaders in an organization can manage their collective control sources, time sense, and intentionality to allow themselves to come together. Such learning itself is risky, especially if you're in a Specialist culture not known for rewarding mistakes. But learning advantages come from mistakes—*new* mistakes. Learning publicly with others, taking risks, and making yourself socially vulnerable during the learning process are the way through significant cultural change.

We believe that Headroom is a practical approach to creating a learning organization. It isn't always the entire process of advancing from one stage or logic to the next, but it's an essential component. When Headroom is sustained, it supports the advancement of Inside-Out capability, appropriate control, and good time sense—the three main aspects of transformation readiness we discussed in Chapter Four. In the presence of Headroom, collective learning takes place openly, honestly, courageously, and collaboratively. The process acknowledges that taking risks and making mistakes are essential to public learning. Learning from them keeps the momentum for organizational change moving in a positive direction.

Headroom at Technology Inc.

We used a story from our work with Technology Inc. to open this chapter because it illustrates the power of Headroom. Technology Inc. has a sophisticated, performance-based shared compensation system, but because of relatively low productivity, one of its plants had never shared in the wealth—until Bart and members of the senior team showed up at the plant and demonstrated their willingness and ability to engage in processes of change, including the process of Headroom. They believably demonstrated raising the ceiling and in doing so drafted the engagement of people in the plant. The key idea became, "I am a member of my process team, and my team can solve problems and take action." It wasn't so much the maxim itself that mattered as that it summed up something that the people in that plant could believe in and use to open out to bigger minds.

A couple of weeks after that demonstration, Bart called us. "It's a miracle," he said. The plant had earned its way into the compensation plan for the first time in its history. We don't think it's a miracle. We think it's Headroom at work.

Risk and Resolve

Not all transformation efforts work. There is risk in Headroom. You will need to face the question of how much change you, your team, and your organization can tolerate. Discerning how far you should take your change initiative may be the most important skill of all. Unrealistic goals are divisive, and failing to reach them creates cynicism. Aim toward feasible strategic goals combined with Headroom, and you will exponentially increase your chances for successful and sustainable change.

In their play *Inherit the Wind* (2007), authors Lawrence and Lee recount the 1920s "Scopes Monkey Trial" in Tennessee. The case was about teaching evolution in public schools, and somewhat ironically was offered as an allegory for transformation. In the following scene, Drummond, the defense attorney, and Cates, the young teacher standing trial, are left to speak in the courtroom after the jury has returned a verdict in favor of the prosecution:

Drummond: You won.
Cates: But the jury found me—
Drummond: What jury? Twelve men? Millions of people will say you won. They'll read in their papers tonight that you smashed a bad law. You made it a joke!
Cates: Yeah, but what's going to happen now? I haven't got a job. I'll bet they won't even let me back in the boarding house.

Drummond: Sure, it's going to be tough. It's not going to be any church social for a while. But you'll live. And while they're making you sweat, remember—you've helped the next fella.
Cates: What do you mean?
Drummond: You don't suppose this kind of thing is ever finished, do you? Tomorrow it'll be something else—and another fella will have to stand up. And you've helped give him the guts to do it!

Inherit the Wind takes its title from Proverbs 11:29: "He that troubleth his own house shall inherit the wind." It's not inaccurate to say that creating Headroom for organizational and cultural transformation will trouble your organizational house. Risk is inherent, and the work is not for the faint-of-heart.

Exercises

Questions

- Where is a third space that you can secure for your team to experiment with Headroom?

- What can you do to get your team to exceed its current restrictions in control source and time sense in order to play with Headroom?

Scale, Journal, and Dialogue

Respond to each question that follows using the rating scale provided. Then write a reflection in your journal, and outline the role you are willing to play in creating or improving the conditions for expanded and extended Headroom in your organization.

To what extent do senior leaders intentionally engage others in the team in public learning that is developmental for the leadership team culture?

1	2	3	4	5	6	7	8	9
	Little			Somewhat			Substantially	

To what extent are there face-to-face encounters in open social discourse between senior leadership team members and other leaders that focus on change through a process of developing bigger minds?

1	2	3	4	5	6	7	8	9
	Little			Somewhat			Substantially	

To what extent have you and your colleagues engaged in questioning and reflecting on values, beliefs, and assumptions about management and leadership in the context of change?

1	2	3	4	5	6	7	8	9
	Little			Somewhat			Substantially	

To what extent are senior leaders openly engaging with each other and the larger community of workers in the organization around cultural beliefs and practices and how these affect the changeability of the organization?

1	2	3	4	5	6	7	8	9
	Little			Somewhat			Substantially	

Get together with your team or another group of colleagues, and facilitate a dialogue around the concept of Headroom and the implications for change in terms of leader behavior, group and team behavior, and the creation of a bigger mind and an emergent leadership culture that more effectively connects leadership practices with the business strategy.

7

ENGAGING YOUR SENIOR TEAM

Eventually, all things merge into one.

—Norman Maclean

We'll bet you have inside you a personal and revealing story about a team that you were on that continues to inspire you about the potential for excellence when people are in sync and working together. Your story may have involved family, sports, military duty, a crisis, or some kind of organizational work.

What is that story?

We ask you to remember your team story because you're going to need your own personal inspiration to build organizational aspiration among your senior team.

So, what is that story? Stop a moment or two to reflect on it.

You'll also need vitality, verve, and a line of sight from vision to strategy and outward to fields of potential as you build one tactical, operational step on another. And as we've been saying, you and your team will need to keep your whole selves—all of you together—focused on strategy and the big picture of vision.

This chapter is about involving your senior team from the outset in transformational change. Is that feasible? If it is, how best to proceed? What challenges are likely, and how will you deal with them?

We're still building here on three basic lessons that we've learned from experience and that you've been absorbing from the previous chapters:

1. You can drive new product development, software installation, quarterly reporting, and other management functions.

But you can't drive culture change. For new beliefs and Inside-Out work, you have to participate and demonstrate your own willingness and ability to adapt and change. And in playing your part, you become an instrument of change.

2. The whole senior team must be willing to engage in the cultural change it professes for the organization. If the team is ready to do the work, then feasibility for change is high. If it's not ready, then substantial, lasting change is unlikely. Ultimately people in key roles must act and be the change they expect from the organization.

3. The team must raise its leadership logic to the level required by your organization's vision and strategy. If your strategy requires an independent leadership logic and your senior team has a Conformer logic, then its collective mind-set needs to grow. This may require some sizable, serious cultural and development work for the team.

Factors in Senior Team Readiness

Our work across years, industries, borders, and many different senior teams reveals five factors that indicate a senior team's readiness to work on cultural change:

1. The executive team is engaged as both enabler and participant.

You've seen this happen: executive teams at the top decree the change and enthusiastically rally and invite everyone to get on board, but they themselves don't jump on the train—and the train never leaves the station. When executives don't change, no one else will.

In the Introduction, we recounted how one big change in human resource (HR) operations failed the day it began. In that case, there was actually no HR executive at the senior table. Nor was there significant engagement by the executive team about the change in direction of HR services. Instead, there were dozens of adults colluding in a passive-aggressive stance while an entire department went up in flames. That kind of behavior destroys a culture and damages credibility. It's better not to go through the motions at all if your team has little intentionality and no commitment to outcomes. Dismal change efforts breed cynicism and are counterproductive to future attempts.

The team that succeeds is one that understands it cannot make change "over there." It must lead the change, engage the organization, and participate in developing change leadership capability.

In all of our client work where change was progressive and successful, the executives actively participated. Even in the most conservative, traditional, Conformer organizations we worked with, change success comes because executives declare, "If we don't do this first, then why would others be willing to do it?" Sounds like common sense to us.

2. Leadership development is part of the organization's cultural history.

The organization has experience with and appreciation for leadership development as a means of building organizational capability. The leadership culture has seen the effects of its previous leader development efforts.

3. In struggling to implement change, senior leaders know that the missing piece is change in the leadership culture.

The team sees compelling reasons for change. It is clear on the need to improve operations but sees that the strategy for improvement lies in leadership's focused effort to work through the human system, building aligned talent as an organizational capability.

4. The senior team is willing to engage in emergent work.

It sees that organizational cultural change is not a management program with guaranteed deliverables; rather, it's a trail that leaders blaze as they go forward. The key to success is the senior team's willingness to develop their ability to tolerate uncertainty and ambiguity.

Voice of Change

Pool hall principles apply to strategy work in change teams. Any numbskull can make a straight shot of the three ball in the side pocket, but the question is, Can you play the game? Can you read the table and set up the next shot and the next? Can you run the table? Likewise, making the numbers quarter by quarter is necessary but not nearly sufficient when it comes to strategic responsibility for the future. Doing what you always did and getting what you always got stops working when markets change, because you will stop getting what you got. Shooting pool requires a big mind capable of looking at interconnecting systems and anticipating scenarios and alternatives in an unfolding, hard-to-predict future. You need to connect the best and brightest players on your change team and get them working together strategically in order to maximize your potential. Two heads are better than one when you have a healthy mix of leader logics and skills on a team that challenge each other and extend the leadership logic of the whole to face the future together.

5. The senior team recognizes the need for cross-boundary work.

The senior team sees that cross-boundary work is essential. That appreciation is often expressed as horizontal process work where peer-like relationships are required to cooperate and collaborate. Processes can include crossing the boundaries of functions, alliances, agencies, suppliers, and other entities throughout supply chains and networks.

Strategies for Change

Here is some essential strategic advice. You'll see that we are continuing the theme of collective learning throughout.

Don't Hand It Off to HR

If your team shifts this work over to HR to plan and implement, or turns it into a "program" for someone to manage, then your feasibility for change drops several points. Culture change, just like talent development, belongs to the whole organization, not to a function of it. For sure, HR can help secure some expert resources, provide project management help, or even supply advisory consulting. But don't think "they" (meaning really any function or individual outside the leadership team) can create change for you. No one, no group, can do this for the team. No proxy can carry the senior team's responsibility.

Begin Privately Within the Team

Jump-start the change work behind closed doors with just your team. Try the changes; practice playing your part in the team's culture. Learn a few things about change within the team, and think about how sharing those lessons beyond the team might play out. After some practice, you can be more public with the work and use it to create the Headroom necessary for people to participate in public learning and social recontracting.

Be Willing to Give the Time

We talked about time sense in Chapter Four using Technology Inc. as an example. When first discussed at that company, the idea of "taking time out for learning" in the middle of a concentrated, uninterrupted manufacturing process seemed inane to many on the leadership team for whom a steady, continuously urgent pace was sacrosanct. "Take time out to do what? To talk? That's nuts!" a few leaders said. Changing that belief on that team was a huge undertaking with a big payoff.

Practice Strategic Leadership

Inherent in the readiness factors stated above is an eye for feasibility, and this requires continuous learning. Think of strategy building as a learning process. This kind of strategic planning is different from the planning you do every three to five years that yields a strategic plan for stuffing a three-ring binder. As you make progress in change, you learn, and as you learn, your perspective on the territory changes, so your strategy adjusts and shifts according to what you are learning. As creating strategy is a learning process for strategic leaders, so feasibility analysis and discernment is an ongoing process of collective learning (Hughes and Beatty, 2005).

Locate the Team's Core Leadership Logic

At this point in the game, you need to figure out where your leadership team actually is in terms of its leadership logics. Use the language in Table 7.1 to describe in general your leadership team. Is it conformist and molded into the hierarchy, or is it a pack of mad-dog competitive achievers who will do almost anything to win? Or where else is it on the continuum?

The leadership culture in your organization will not rise above or grow bigger minds than the leadership logic and culture that the senior team holds in common. Leaders everywhere exhibit the King-and-I syndrome: "No head shall be higher than *my* head!"

Separate Strategy from Operations

In team meetings, figure out a simple way to conduct regular operational business management separate from the organization's more complex strategic leadership issues of change. Carve out separate recurring Headroom time and space to talk about the most challenging of the latter.

Operations and change require different modes of discussion. For operations, you can use the centrally controlled approach of a team leader who manages an agenda based on deliverables and disseminates information for programmatic rollout (essential facts about the company's new health

Table 7.1 Team Leadership Logics, Leader Logics, and Focus and Beliefs

Leadership Logics	Leader Logics	Focus and Beliefs
Interdependent-Collaborator	Transformer	Organizational wizardry, transformation
		"Advancement for common good."
	Collaborator	Synthesizers, strategic influencers, complexity, systems thinking
		"We are collectively capable."
Independent-Achiever	Freethinker	Innovation, unconventional, new organizational orders in construction
		"I determine value with you."
	Performer	Winning, adaptive achievement, technical reason and mastery for my benefit
		"We compete to win."
Dependent-Conformer	Specialist	Control things, being right, technical expertise
		"Personal competence is our highest value."
	Moderator	Control self, go along to get along, paternalism, conflict intolerant, diplomacy
		"Appearances matter."
	Dominator	Control others, loyalty, obedience, my power, honor the code, respect authority
		"I have the control."

insurance plan, for example). For dialogues-of-change work, you need to open up Headroom and alter the time sense of the team. These can be liberating rituals that the team eagerly anticipates. Discussions can also be sparked by action development agendas. For example, the team can review actions and outcomes of the new leadership logic it's trying out, gleaning lessons of change experience for anticipating and planning the next round of actions.

Identify Sails and Anchors

Based on where your team is centered right now in regard to its culture and logics, which team members are likely to push for change, and which ones are likely to resist? Where are the extremes? For example, if you have an essentially Independent-Achiever senior team, which members may be Dominators or Moderators, Collaborators or Transformers? What strategic influence can you bring to assist lifting anchors and setting sails?

Have Tough, Difficult Conversations

You can't get around them. All that stuff the team hasn't been talking about undermines progress and gets in the way. Put those issues out in front, in the open, and then deal with them. A steady diet of difficult conversations isn't fun; a little can go a long way. Those difficult dialogues can open the forum for many other topics that were previously out of bounds. These difficult conversations are crucial (Patterson, Grenny, McMillan, and Switzler, 2002).

Balance Questions of "What" and "How" with Those of "Why" and "What If"

Establish and encourage dialogue that consists mostly of questions; you want collaborative inquiry (McGuire and Palus, 2003). In the course of that dialogue, make sure you or others are asking plenty of "whys" and "what-ifs," which will take you closer to root causes and bring up more alternatives for addressing systemic causes of repeating problems.

"What" and "how" are helpful too, of course, keeping you practical and the team's feet on firm operational ground. Strike a balance of questions. If your team tends to lapse into the what and how, push it back toward why and what-if. Pressing against boundaries is developmental and a good source of learning (McCarthy, 2000).

Make Strategy Conscious

In Chapter One, we defined leadership strategy as the organization's approach to advancing the leadership culture, practices, and people systems necessary for future success. It's about what leadership needs to look like and be collectively capable of doing and how it will be developed in an organization.

We've said that leadership strategy shows up, consciously or not, in the organization's choices about leadership culture and in its beliefs and practices (see Illustration 7.1). The strategy also shows up in the kind of people, or talent, systems the senior team chooses to manage leadership development. This all has tremendous implications for your leadership development systems and programs—but it is much more than that.

Illustration 7.1 Culture Is the Elephant in the Room

Source: Bruce Flye. Used with permission.

Leadership strategy is about the strategic intent of and for leadership as a collective and what it needs to be and do as capability for the whole organization.

Executive and leadership teams bear a responsibility to make the organization's leadership strategy conscious and explicit. They need to be as aware and diligent about the leadership strategy as they are about the business or operations strategy. Moving the choices that are the expression of strategy into the team's zone of intentional change can vastly increase the feasibility of change.

The future lies in leadership practices that align vision, strategic drivers, and core capabilities. First, get the business strategy right; then work on the leadership strategy. Then get both to operate as one, and your chance for success accelerates tremendously.

Lift to the Level That Strategy Requires

We can't imagine any individual or team wanting to take on the work of transformation unless that amount of change is clearly needed for the long-term sustainability of the organization. In reshaping your leadership strategy, figure out point A (what you have today) and point B (required for tomorrow). Become clear and honest about the gap in your leadership culture between points A and B. Define it, describe it, and discuss it with team members. Determine what beliefs and behaviors have to change to cross that gap. Then decide what level or type of leadership logic is necessary to implement your organization's strategy, and make the changes the level requires. The match isn't merely nice to have; it's a must. Your organization's future depends on it.

Create Safety with Numbers

There are more and less safe ways to start or leverage public learning within the senior team. One safe way to start is by locating a few others on the team who are willing to join you in a conversation about future possibilities. Your answers to the questions we pose in the "Identify Sails and Anchors" section above will help you identify likely partners.

Can you identify three or four other people on the team who likely believe the organization has to move from point A to point B? Do they also practice leader logics in line with or in advance of the team's general leadership logic? At one of our clients, for example, three people from the executive team listed others they thought they could count on in a change effort. That analysis became their first assay of the feasibility of culture change.

It's often all right to identify just enough people to start. But be realistic: some of them will also need to be the right people. They will need to possess some organizational influence or power. So don't start unless you have enough of the right players in your selected start-up group. You need the CEO or the chief operating officer or, even better, both. If people in key positions are strategic, complex thinkers and have proven their ability to tell the truth, deal with conflict, and take risks, then your chances are pretty good.

Aim at "Good Enough"

There is no perfect team.

Think of cultural change in your senior team as a game of chess and each team member as a piece. Then visualize a match in which your new selves are playing your old selves. Your new team positions its strengths and intentionality in order to triumph over its worn-out identity and its current shortcomings in relation to emerging challenges.

Do your new selves have enough of the right pieces in the right positions on the board to mount a sound offense? What are the strengths and weaknesses on each end of the board?

And what about "civilians"? If some people haven't enlisted on your side yet, you can ask them directly to withhold their judgment for a while and not align against you. Sometimes it's fine if certain senior team members are neutral to the change. You can gain advantage by convincing potential detractors to sit on the fence and keep an open mind. You'll be surprised how many people will comply with such a request because you respected them enough to be straight and include them. If they're not yet believers, then openness and "doing no harm" are the most you can expect of them. They have to be authentic. If they're open to new possibilities but not actively setting anchors, that's a positive state. It's enough.

Change Leadership Teams

Change becomes less likely if your CEO, COO, or other major power broker is authoritarian, a controlnik, a conflict avoider, or a pleaser. The same is true if, outside the team's immediate sphere of influence, there sits another key player in a powerful and influential position who opposes leadership culture change. On the senior team itself, it takes only one detractor to seriously damage or even sink the ship of change. If people in a key line of business, an important geographical area, or an essential function see their executive vice president, for example, defying the announced change in direction in word or deed, then they won't support the change and may actively work against it too.

There is a way to mitigate these problems: create what we call a change leadership team (CLT). The CLT is a special team made up of key executive team members (not tokens), influential leaders across and down a few layers into the organization, a company folk-hero maven or two, members of the board, and representatives from the supply chain or client and constituent groups (or both of these). The CLT is an extension of the senior team, not a replacement for it. By creating a CLT, you can build a powerful set of stakeholders with a collective, cross-boundary voice for change. Using a CLT has several advantages over relying solely on an existing senior leader team. A CLT can strengthen a weak core leadership logic on the executive team, and its members can be advocates on behalf of the organization and so extend the developing leadership logic base. It can extend progress on change work when significant turnover on the senior team is anticipated due to restructuring or retirements or when key players are not yet fully accepting of the change work. A CLT can speed up and extend the change work of a strong, ready executive team.

Voice of Change

Recall from Chapter Two Mike's story about the maintenance staff who replaced the executive suite chairs with seating more suitable for vice presidents. Mike's organization, a government agency, faced a series of forced retirements of executives, including the president, and no one was ready for the succession challenge they faced. They were the most conscientious public servants we've ever met—they cared deeply about their responsibility. Developing the senior team's leadership logic alone was not a feasible plan because half of the team would be gone in two years. The more workable solution came in the form of a CLT, commissioned by the president, which served in an advisory capacity and addressed the major change issues facing the agency and the leadership development capability required to address them. A few key team members assembled to strategize about the right mix of players and made some brilliant choices in selecting players who could come together as a CLT for a strategic interim passage during this tumult of turnover. The CLT was remarkably successful, creating a leadership strategy and executing its development toward a more independent coaching culture (their term for advancement through shared learning). The lesson: Just because the executive team is not ready doesn't mean you can't make progress toward change.

The CLT also provides a broad base for stakeholder representation, which means political power. A few advocates well placed across the political landscape can unblock resources and lever alignments when needed. CLTs are also good for staying the course for a long period of time, and they can even become part of the institution. A benefit to CLT members is that they can be recognized for their significant, influential, long-term contributions to the organization's transformation. You can even use CLT assignments as part of your succession system for high potentials because in a change environment, they'll learn valuable lessons about the extended cross-boundary organizational systems.

Challenges to Teams at Different Logics

Depending at what level of logics your team and its members are starting out, you will face different challenges. Here we discuss a few of them.

Dependent-Conformer Team Challenges

Left unsupported and unchecked, senior team leaders with a center of gravity in the Dependent-Conformer range of logics will likely attempt to sink the ship of change—some passively and some actively—because issues of maintaining control are so prominent for them. That can include the Specialist-logic members who are at the upper, transitional end of the Conformer range. But keep in mind that Specialist leader logic doesn't refer to the same thing as an expert or specialist leader role. It's not the job or role that defines leader logic. Experts in terms of job or training (doctor, lawyer, investment banker) can have Transformer, Specialist, or Dominator leader logic. What determines leader logic is how you interpret your surroundings, make decisions, and react, especially when your power or safety is challenged.

Transformation may be hardest for a Dependent-Conformer culture. To advance such a culture, you hope to identify as many post-Specialist logic members as you can on the senior team. It's common to find a number of Achiever-oriented people. However, most senior leaders in a Conformer culture may be specialists by role who straddle the boundary between Conformer and Achiever logics, one foot in each world. From there they can shift either way. In that light, their potential is awesome.

Nearly 40 percent of all leaders have a Specialist leader logic. Most Specialist senior team members rose to senior positions because they were the best technical experts in their department earlier in their careers. Usually their self-confidence is high and well earned, and they believe they have a lock on their discipline (medicine, the law, stock brokering, software architecture, nursing, investment, or something else). They see their own watertight expert thinking and thorough knowledge as the vehicles of their mastery and control. Data and logic are their primary tools. Most have been valued because of their pursuit of perfection on their way to becoming senior leaders, and they are still highly valued for past or recent expert contributions.

As part of a leadership team for change, these specialists can be tough to deal with. They like to be right. We mean, they *really* like to be right. A lot. They often think that collaborating on imagining a future is a waste of time. They often think, "Not all meetings are a waste of time. Some are cancelled." Not uncommonly, they condescend to those whom they perceive as having less expertise than they. But one thing they *do* respect is—you guessed it—other experts. For this reason, when Specialists become problematic, it can be a big help to bring outside experts in change to the change team. If Specialists believe there is a change expert in front of them, they will respect that and pay attention (Rooke and Torbert, 2005).

In addition to members with Specialist logic, Conformer leadership teams may also contain Dominators and Moderators, though together they comprise less than 20 percent of all leaders. Both types pretty much hate dealing with emotions publicly at work. By behaving in self-absorbed, intolerant, aggressive ways (fueled mainly by fear), Dominators can stultify entire divisions and sometimes whole companies. But the passiveness of Moderators is no less of an obstacle to organizational change. Executives can rise pretty high in organizations, sometimes to the top, using passive diplomacy as their significant major skill. (It's amazing how often smart people simply avoid making the wrong enemies and wind up at the top without having accomplished all that much.) Dominator and Moderator logics are both extreme logics, and both lack receptors for feedback and change.

In our practice, we never advise succession or termination. We do, however, see clients struggle with resistance from a few people at the top during transformation efforts. When we do, our own conclusion is that you can either change the people or exchange the people. We believe every effort should be offered for development, and we know that sometimes the CEO has to decide that someone needs to go, and that sometimes that someone decides to go.

Independent-Achiever Team Challenges

An Independent-Achiever team culture has a bigger collective mind than a Dependent-Conformer team and a more complex, integrated understanding of the world. It welcomes feedback that helps members learn to deal effectively with ambiguities and be successful. After all, the main Independent-Achiever leader logic is that of Performer (about 30 percent of all leaders). Unlike Specialists, Performers are skilled at interpersonal relationships and are very good at positively influencing others. They also really like to win. So if change is commensurate with winning, then they are in. They're also good at teamwork and in implementing strategy.

What's not to like about the Independent-Achiever team culture? It's not about liking or not, actually. It's about capability. An Achiever culture (short on Freethinkers) isn't very good at innovation and can lose out in a competitive market because it's not keeping up. Performers are great at implementing strategy, but for creating new strategy in the heat of battle, they are not so good. For that kind of creative work, the team needs Freethinkers, Collaborators, and Transformers.

About 15 percent of all leaders command Freethinker, Collaborator, or Transformer logics (Rooke and Torbert, 2005). Freethinker logic is at a stage of development where leaders begin to get a really big mind. Like others with leader logics in the Collaborator culture range, Freethinkers can discern the difference between principles and actions; their insights, born of truth telling, can lead to nimble course corrections. They know that they are in charge of constructing their own reality and take charge of putting new orders of things in place to respond to the challenges they face. For Achiever teams that are developing toward Collaborator leadership logics, this means they just get better and better at systemic, strategic capability in dealing with change.

Shaking Up Senior Teams: Two Examples

It goes without saying that if your organization's business strategy is wrong, no kind of change will help. In that case, transforming a senior team or a culture simply doesn't matter (except perhaps to develop greater strategic leadership to get future strategies right). But when the business strategy is right, leadership culture change can matter hugely. The two must align. You're probably already familiar with the classic stories of Digital Equipment Corporation (DEC) and IBM in the 1990s, but we think they are worth repeating here as ways of observing how strategy, culture, and level of the latter make differences between success and failure.

In the 1980s, computer manufacturing industry leaders had shaken out of a competitive pack by owning and providing vertically integrated systems. Companies like DEC and IBM made products, installed them, and serviced them. But in the 1990s, open software and systems and the rise of personal computers and distributed networks created a new market in which customers demanded integrated systems made up of the best computer hardware, software, and network components, no matter how many different vendors were involved.

Industry leaders fell hard during the 1987 stock market fall, and after a year or two they had not rebounded to previous levels. Growth had slowed, and the market demand had changed. Layoffs and other cost-cutting measures became necessary, but the real challenge was to strike out in a new, feasible strategic direction that accounted for customers' future needs.

Digital Equipment Corporation

One of this book's authors was at DEC when that company came apart, and the lessons have never been forgotten. In the early 1990s, DEC was the number two computer company in the world, behind only IBM. Its phenomenal growth was due to the founder and CEO, Ken Olsen, who had literally created the minicomputer market. DEC was a classic Independent-Achiever culture that had grown out of a Specialist logic base of engineers. Its entrepreneurial beliefs were pervasive, and its matrix management system provided a lot of flexibility. Good ideas had room for testing, proving, and implementing. Internal competition was common, and every business line had its own information technology (IT) and HR operations. This was an expensive business model to maintain, but it was also a fast, furious, and exciting place to work—while the money rolled in.

By 1993, however, product revenue and profit had gone flat, and services brought in almost all of DEC's profit. What is interesting historically is that DEC invested nothing to create or maintain its services business. It invested only in the product business. Services were seen as an aftermarket business rather than integral to the core business. As a result, the services side of DEC had to bootstrap itself by borrowing from its annual profits to fund its future growth strategies, a practice that placed a continuous strain on business profits. Many of the leaders on the services side of DEC believed that the company needed to make a significant shift toward a services-led business strategy.

At one point, the number two executive at DEC brought together several other DEC executives and services managers to discuss how the company could double revenue from its services business in two to three years. This wasn't idle brainstorming. The company was casting about for potential future fiscal solvency. During that series of meetings, the worldwide manager of DEC's services division made a compelling pitch about how to double that business in two years with modest investment. Number two declared the manager's investment idea a "no-brainer" and said that DEC needed to implement this services-led business strategy right away. He then turned to the company's chief financial officer (CFO) and asked, "We can find the money to do this, can't we?"

Without hesitation, the CFO simply said no. (It's difficult to fathom the absolute absence of thought or consideration given to the idea in the midst of a fiscal crisis.) A discussion ensued, punctuated by the worldwide service manager's pushing his chair back hard from the table, banging it into the wall behind him, and hurling a barrage of cogent points across the table, addressed to Number Two and the CFO about how DEC's product-led mind-set would be its demise.

To no avail. There was no executive Headroom around the table that day at DEC. The executives present were incapable of creating it, incapable of lifting their ceiling of awareness in order to consider feasible responses to the changes in their market and business. As a group, they were incapable of standing up to the challenge that day. However much the evidence contradicted their prevailing beliefs in a product-led business, the beliefs held out, and no new direction was imaginable. The service manager's new strategic proposal had pointed to a shifting market in which services were becoming more valued than products and that a services-led strategy could offer customers solutions to their business problems—but that position fell on deaf ears and was ignored by the corporation.

A year later, a new CEO (an engineer by background, with a product-manufacturing mind-set) convened a team from across the enterprise and commissioned it to draft a strategic plan based on reengineering. This group's proposal again reflected the need for a services-led solutions business strategy. The new CEO was surrounded by many of the same executives whose leadership logic still clung to the past successful tradition of a product-led company, so he too ignored the proposal to shift strategy toward services. He continued down the same doomed path.

At DEC, a dozen people at the top had failed to escape their restrictive product-business mind-set; they failed to see and understand the change that surrounded them. They were smart people but blinded by the beliefs that had made them successful and unable to get a bigger mind. Although DEC had an Achiever culture, the senior team was weighted more toward the Specialist logic by executives who had grown up in products divisions. They didn't command the Freethinker logics they needed. (This wasn't DEC's first big strategic mistake, by the way; it had bungled its personal computer strategy some years before as well.)

Strategy is hard—anybody can get it wrong—but anyone doing it needs to be able to rise to a level of leader logic that's able to consider all reasonable alternatives.

The result at DEC was that 120,000 employees became 60,000, and the company eventually went on the block. Ironically the buyer wanted what was arguably DEC's most valuable asset: its services capability.

IBM

In 1993, Louis Gerstner became CEO at IBM. His tenure and the successful change he led offer an informative contrast to the DEC story. Having been in other industries prior to coming to IBM, Gerstner wasn't predisposed to the product-business mindset that characterized both IBM and DEC. "Big Blue" IT shops were the result of a core business strategy for decades, but the market had changed.

Based on Gerstner's account, we would describe IBM at this time as a classic Dependent-Conformer culture. According to Gerstner, IBM's management committee operated under centralized control that diffused responsibility and leadership. A bureaucratic mind-set caused its officials to rubber-stamp project investments without much rigor or accountability. Debate and contention were sucked out of decision-making processes by an institutionalized form of compromise based on prearranging consensus. A system of entitlement had crept into the organization. As Gerstner himself describes in his book *Who Says Elephants Can't Dance?* (2002), IBM so dominated the market that it had little sense of competitive threat. High margins and deep market share don't inspire risk taking and aggressive competitive behavior.

Despite these obstacles, Gerstner set out to change key organizational elements. First, he challenged the company's top two hundred executives to each reach out to at least five customers for face-to-face problem-solving visits. Each visit generated a report that Gerstner was involved in. Gerstner describes these visits as IBM's start toward changing its culture, and he used them to create a new orientation in which the customer would drive what IBM did. Gerstner raised the ceiling of expectation by creating new space in which previously insulated executives were exposed directly to customers. This kind of exposure created vulnerability for executives who had formerly been allowed to remain comfortable themselves as long as problems belonged to someone else. It's a lot easier to sit at the top and manage than it is to step into the discomfort and vulnerability of direct contact with customers—but the latter is full of developmental possibilities.

But Gerstner did much more than this, according to his book. He dissolved the powerful management committee and created a new leadership team. He reengineered IBM's business processes and changed the business model to focus more on the customer. He established leadership competencies in customer insight, breakthrough thinking, straight talk, and teamwork. And he built all this around a services-led model in which he saw a future where services solutions companies, not hardware factories, would rule.

Gerstner describes in his book how he first had to rise to the challenge for himself in order to learn what new strategy was needed. As he began to understand the possibilities in restructuring around solutions, he recalls his confusion: "My mind was afire . . . this is what I wanted when I was a customer. . . . [I was] thrilled and depressed, thrilled that I had discovered a capability our customers so desperately needed, and depressed to realize that the culture of IBM would fight it" (2002, p. 129).

Gerstner allowed himself to be the practice field for a shift in a corporate identity. He took on the uncertainty that change demands of leadership. By allowing himself the vulnerability of his confusion, Gerstner was able to create Headroom first for himself and then for his team and company. Deep and transformational learning was the result.

At the end, this hard-nosed businessman who had gone to IBM to pull off a turnaround said, "I came to see in my time at IBM that culture wasn't just one aspect of the game—it is the game" (2002 p. 182). By all appearances, Gerstner transformed not only IBM but himself in the process.

Learnings

One global corporation's top team fails to grow and get bigger minds, and the company fails as a whole. Another global corporation's team succeeds and transforms its culture. The teams don't do it alone, but the organization can't do it without them. DEC didn't have a leadership logic at the top that was capable of mastering a complex new world. Its leadership culture's beliefs and practices couldn't, and didn't, advance. At IBM, key people's leader logics could advance and handle the complexity of the challenge, and therefore they were capable of setting out to change beliefs and practices in the leadership culture, however difficult that effort might be.

Where Are We Now?

In Part One of this book—the seven chapters you have almost finished—you have seen how leadership cultural change can begin with you and spread to other members of a change-leading senior team.

In Part Two, you will see how much of what you have read fits together in a cycle of leadership culture transformation, and we'll share with you more about our cases where change worked and where it failed—and why. Then we'll assist you further in assessing your organization's level of feasibility for change so that you might create a plan of action for initiating change in your leadership culture.

Exercises

Questions
- What is the leadership logic of your senior team?
- What one or two beliefs do you think the senior leadership team will need to change?
- As a senior leader, why do you have to stand up first to yourself and then to your team's culture in a change process?
- Why is it essential to create Headroom in your executive team before or simultaneous with creating it in the broader organizational culture?

- What does your senior leadership team need to do to awaken and then energize Inside-Out development in the team and leadership culture?

Scales and Dialogue

At the next team meeting, have each team member individually complete the scaled questions that follow. Then have them talk about the meaning of the results and the requirements for increasing the change readiness of the team and the organization if there is to be a transformation of the leadership culture.

To what extent is the executive team engaged as both an enabler and a participant in the change process?

1	2	3	4	5	6	7	8	9
Team is not actively engaged			Team vacillates between enabling and participating			Team is enabling and participating actively and energetically		

To what extent is leadership development part of the organization's cultural history?

1	2	3	4	5	6	7	8	9
Weak history of development			Some history of development			Strong history of development		

Have prior change initiatives raised awareness that leadership through culture has been the primary shortcoming in making change?

1	2	3	4	5	6	7	8	9
Current barrier to change			Ambiguous support for change			Current support for change		

To what extent is the executive team willing to engage in the uncertain, ambiguous process of developing leadership culture and guiding organization change?

1	2	3	4	5	6	7	8	9
Team is not currently willing			Team vacillates between exploratory and formulaic approach			Team is accepting and supportive of uncertainty		

To what extent is multilateral engagement deemed essential?

1	2	3	4	5	6	7	8	9
Organization is heavily siloed and turf protective			Support for multilateral engagement ebbs and flows			Multilateral engagement is expected		

How much trust is there within the senior team?

1	2	3	4	5	6	7	8	9
Absence of trust			Some trust among some members			A lot of trust among most members		

Part Two

LEADERSHIP CULTURE AND ORGANIZATIONAL TRANSFORMATION

8

THE CULTURE DEVELOPMENT CYCLE

> We should always have in our heads one free and
> open corner, where we can give place, or lodging
> as they pass, to the ideas of our friends. It really
> becomes unbearable to converse with men whose
> brains are divided up into well-filled pigeon-holes,
> where nothing can enter from the outside. Let us
> have hospitable hearts and minds.
>
> —*Joseph Joubert*

Warren Bennis defines leadership as a tripod made up of a leader, followers, and a common goal (2007). We find this definition inadequate. True, leadership sometimes involves a leader and followers and their shared goals, but Bennis's tripod does not seem to allow the kind of collective leadership we need to deal with increasingly complex situations. For that reason, at the outset of this book, we defined leadership in terms of its outcomes: direction, alignment, and commitment (DAC). We think this more encompassing view is more helpful in understanding the practice of leadership as it relates to change. Shared direction implies that each member of the collective knows the aims and goals of the collective; each member also knows that the other members know those aims and goals as well. Alignment is the coordination of knowledge and work in the collective. Commitment is the willingness of members of the collective to expend effort toward the needs of the collective over and above the effort needed to meet their individual needs. High-functioning DAC indicates the presence of an effectively functioning leadership culture of beliefs and practices.

With DAC in mind, you can easily see how leadership development relates to:

- Individual development
- Relationship development
- Team development
- Organizational development
- Changes in patterns of beliefs and behavior in the collective
- Changes in systems and processes

DAC allows us all to see the trajectory and engage in more participative and interdependent ways of leadership, with everyone potentially able to join in shaping new beliefs, behaviors, and practices. Perhaps you can also see how thinking in terms of DAC means that an organization's leadership culture can potentially encompass everyone. Not by coincidence, that is truest for leadership cultures that have reached a collaborative level of leadership logic.

The DAC perspective is part of what led us to see Inside-Out, Readiness, and Headroom in the broader context of an ongoing organizational leadership change, which is part and parcel of the organizational cycle of planning and execution. We call that broader leadership context or model the Culture Development Cycle (CDC). The model attempts to capture how culture transformation occurs beyond the largely personal and senior team work we described in Chapters One through Seven.

The Culture Development Cycle

The CDC is an organizational learning and development framework devised to represent our grounded theory and case study research findings in transforming leadership culture. Figure 8.1 describes the cycle perhaps as well as can be done on paper—which is somewhat limited. In it you see six divisions, which we

Figure 8.1 Culture Development Cycle: A Learning Cycle for Leadership Culture

Focus here is implementation of change, integration and refinement of system, structure, and process; learning communities emerging triggers: **What if?**

Focus here is gut-level experience, personal connection to change; grassroots, truth-telling triggers: **Why change?**

Leadership Transformation

Inside-Out as Role Shift Experience

Collaborator

Achiever

Conformer

Structure, Systems, and Business Processes

Readiness for Risk and Vulnerability

Focus here is experimenting, application, and evolving strategy into action and learning; elevating ideas of leadership triggers: **Change how?**

Innovation

Headroom as Engagement

Focus here is making sense of dilemmas, imagining and defining future; public dialog in search of root causes triggers: **Change what?**

refer to at times as "dimensions" or "phases." Why not "steps"? Because we want to avoid reinforcing the idea that the cycle must begin at one place, or that one can simply move in order from one phase or dimension to the other. Inevitably you begin wherever you are on the cycle right now. But also inevitably, you must engage in all six phases in order to transform leadership culture.

A transforming organization evolves through all six phases as a collective, organizational learning cycle in order to achieve an advance in culture stage. Simultaneously, within the cycle, continuous interactions between the six dimensions of work also occur. The CDC represents the dynamic phenomenon of collective learning and culture advancement to bigger minds.

Moving clockwise from the upper right in Figure 8.1, the first three dimensions relate the personal dimensions of transformation (Inside-Out, Readiness, and Headroom) to the collective experience and engagement of leadership. Continuing clockwise from the lower left, the model also brings in the practical, external, action development–based manifestations of change as organizational innovation and adds its expression in organizational structures, systems, and processes. At the top left, the cycle includes the transformation of leadership culture and its elevation to a higher logic and bigger collective mind.

This chapter discusses each phase or dimension and how they interrelate. It also says more about the four types of questions you see on the periphery of the figure: "Why change?" "Change what?" "Change how?" and "What if?" As you will see, the nature of specific questions depends in part on the leadership logic that currently characterizes your leadership culture.

Reading this chapter (and the following two) will prepare you for Chapter Eleven, in which you will get the information you need to map your organization's actions at the individual, senior team, and leadership culture levels so that you can create a gap analysis of what needs to be done in your company to make real change happen.

Do keep in mind that our experience with clients has been stark: in the six cases we have followed most closely, the three organizations that completed major work in the Inside-Out, Readiness, and Headroom phases went on to transform their leadership culture. By contrast, the three organizations that did not work through these phases failed to achieve broader leadership change.

Six Phases of the CDC

As you read about the six phases, remember that culture change is about the interplay of leadership development and organizational development. As we've noted, big change necessitates individual, team, and organization movement toward a different, expanded way of thinking about complexity in order to make it an opportunity to embrace rather than a problem to avoid. Each phase of the CDC is another opportunity to grow into larger ways of thinking about, feeling about, and seeing the organization and the world.

The Inside-Out, Role-Shifting Experience Phase

In the context of the CDC, Inside-Out connects to shifts in the roles leaders play. We don't mean changes of title, but shifting perceptions of identity (who we are) and what we are actually doing. As a leader shifts to a new role almost imperceptibly and nonverbally, he or she often senses external, incremental changes in the environment that trigger internal shifts. A new role, especially that of guide, will upset old identities.

Voice of Change

Joubert exhorts us to have hospitable hearts and minds, suggesting to us that the imperative for transformation is "listening to your inner voice." As a developing change guide intentionally getting in touch with your inner self, you may raise to consciousness previously unexplored dreams about the cyclical possibilities for bigger minds, bigger hearts, and a bigger universe of possibilities for your organization and the world. By listening to your heart and your mind, you will become more attuned to reflecting, thinking, feeling, and acting transformatively in your daily life. As your individual leadership sustains Headroom, it continues processes of reengagement with your developing self, your developing colleagues, and your developing leadership culture. Over time these learning and development cycles must become a natural experience, continuously reinforced by the engagements that occur with Headroom. Only by opening your heart and your mind to these energizing, continuing cycles of developing a bigger mind, a bigger leadership logic, and a higher state leadership culture will you build an organizational culture of sustainable, meaningful change.

Role experience is likely to be a cultural phenomenon you have encountered in your professional life. You may recognize role experience and role shift issues in terms of organization charts, job titles, job expansion, job enrichment, role descriptions, and accountabilities. In our experience, consciously attending to role experience and role shifts contributes greatly to individual awareness and to a leader's willingness to create the conditions for Headroom and then to stand up and step forth as a role model for others.

Most organizations, most leaders, and most employees operate with explicit or implicit expectations around roles and responsibilities. Given the hierarchy effect that is present in most organizations, it is not atypical to see power and influence concentrated in the upper levels of management and reward systems that clearly articulate the managerial aspects of the job but are often murky in terms of leadership competencies. The net effect of those expectations is to set up norms about what kind of things a person can and should do, what a person can't or shouldn't do, who is in charge, what is expected and by whom, and a differential sense of responsibility and control, depending on one's level in the organization. As we have noted, to do something different, you must be something different, and role shift is central to your leading change in the leadership culture.

Identity Consciousness and the Role of Guide. Identity is an essential developmental construct. Whether that of an individual or an organization, identity speaks to what makes each unique and fuels passion and commitment to doing the right thing, making a contribution, making a difference. As you learned from earlier chapters, the significance lies in bringing internal identity concepts forward to conscious expression. Identity informs intentionality, influences leadership practices, and is instrumental in both readiness and the experience of Headroom and engagement.

Look back at Table 5.1 in Chapter Five. The right-hand column lists educational roles associated with leadership logics. Transformation to any new leadership logic requires senior leaders to take on the educational role of guide. We use that word to identify senior leaders who model new ways of being and doing, find pathways through unexplored territory, have the trust and respect of others, and take people at varying levels of capability and work with them to accomplish success.

To become a guide, you need to raise your own conscious awareness of who you are and what you stand for. You need to declare the business the organization is in and explore where you and others fit in regard to change and culture stage development. As we have said, you need to make time to stop and reflect, digging into your unconscious in order to make conscious your core values and beliefs about yourself, people in the organization, the organization's culture, and the organization's broader surroundings for change and transformation.

Think of the guides on a mountain ascent. They do everything they can to create conditions of maximum readiness on the part of climbers. They share information about the terrain *as it usually is*. They are honest about the dangers and the potential for the unexpected, and they don't typically guarantee that every climber will summit. And they are not only guides but climbers too. During the ascent, they create their own version of Headroom that allows appreciation of individual differences, consensus about dealing with differences in endurance, tolerance for the unexpected, and individual choice within a group context.

We have observed these same guiding habits in senior leaders who are able to facilitate the movement of the organization and its members toward sustainable change and organization culture transformation. Guides in transformation create Headroom to explore leadership and organization capabilities, acknowledge the unknown, and test individual and collective endurance. They keep in their mind a vision of the journey ahead without determining first how much time it will take or planning to change the route when required to sustain forward movement. In organizations, such leaders not only guide but also scout emerging horizons of bigger mind, leadership logic, and leadership culture.

As you consider your challenges and opportunities as a change guide, reflect on your comfort in letting go of formally designated job titles and role descriptions, and the entitlements that accompany them. This is a challenge. As a CEO, vice president, or senior director, you can imagine encouraging others to stand up and respond, "Tell us how, and tell us when," because that is how they have learned to respond to traditional figures of power. You'll have to rely on alternative, empowering behaviors to depict your guide role, as well as the roles of those you are inviting along on the trek.

Two other points are also good to keep in mind. First, whatever you attend to becomes part of the conscious domain for yourself and others. What you do and how you do it creates reality for others (Goldsmith, 2007). Second, as a guide, you now distribute accountability for various initiatives along the journey of change, but you do so in an environment for learning in which you are open and direct about what you know from experience and what you are experimenting with in the face of ambiguous, heretofore unexplored territory of change and transformation. In this respect, you change your leadership culture practices regarding roles and responsibilities. By starting with yourself as the model of a guide, you alter the social expectations for yourself and others, and over time you plant the seeds for the blossoming of many other guides to work with you along the trek toward a different stage of leadership culture.

An Example of Shifting Roles and Identities. At Technology Inc., where transformation efforts have been successful, senior leaders took the initiative to explore identity issues with peers and the workforce. They actively explored the identity aspiration for their organization in the future. They also actively explored what was changing about how each leader saw himself. As Technology Inc.'s CEO, Bart, declared publicly, "We are all one in creating the future of this organization. I believe in a different identity for this organization, but I do not have a proven, guaranteed method for getting us there. I believe in each one of you and your potential to create and make this a new and different organization, one that is process oriented and where each of us is accountable to collaborate, innovate, make decisions, and move forward."

The perspective among plant workers evolved from, "I do my eight, and hit the gate," to, "If I put the organization and my team first, then both will better meet my needs and support me in becoming a better contributor." Coupled with a more conscious recognition of "Who I am," "What I stand for," and "How I fit in with the changing organization," their shift to a group and organizational identity resulted in increased productivity and progress from a highly dependent Conformer culture to a more independent one. That shift was reflected in how decisions were made and how people and groups were held accountable.

However, early in the change effort at Technology Inc., employees said, "There is lots of communication and action around changing the organization and the culture, including job titles, but we still know that we have bosses and that they have bosses, so what has really changed?" In this instance, an organization rooted in a Dependent-Conformer culture and intentionally seeking to move toward a more collaborative culture had not yet fully capitalized on the imperative for role shift in creating the Headroom necessary to move the culture toward the Independent-Achiever stage of development. Movement occurred as Headroom became more widespread and more time was devoted to exploring and experimenting with small steps in shifting roles and identity.

Thinking and acting as "we," not just "me," is an early driver of collective leadership. It also promotes acceptance of the role of guide and helps seed group formation and team-oriented culture. The Inside-Out, identity, role-shifting phase work of the CDC helps to break down territoriality and to meaningfully redistribute responsibility and authority.

The Readiness for Risk and Vulnerability Phase

Leaders need to take risks and make themselves vulnerable in the course of developing skills and personal readiness. This means that senior leaders take risks with others in some public ways—at least "public" to the team. Clearly this needs to proceed in a way that increases traction for shifting roles and clarifying identities, a significant departure from conventional management and leadership practices in most organizations we know about from firsthand experience.

To increase willingness to take risks and be vulnerable, change guides need to identify and encourage openness, trust, and challenges as positive forces for change.

Guides must also continually assess the risks they and others face and immerse themselves internally in the organization to know its tolerance for risk and vulnerability. Indicators include:

- The degree of trust within your change leadership group
- Tolerance for and frequency of open, honest, direct, developmental feedback at all levels of the organization
- Expressions of emotion in response to changing roles and responsibilities
- Degree of commitment to making the unconscious conscious in identity work and psychological comfort with the unknown, the different, and the unconventional

Collaborative work on Headroom, the next phase of the CDC, depends on dealing well with risk and vulnerabilities. It requires guides to openly acknowledge their own experiences with risk and vulnerability inside the organization: how they faced embarrassment when they didn't have a right answer or how they took some heat publicly from someone several levels down. This acknowledgment is even more of a force for Headroom when guides share stories of their own personal transitions in taking risk and being vulnerable during organizational change. This includes acknowledging that mistakes will happen (since the way ahead is uncharted), that such mistakes will be treated as opportunities to learn rather than opportunities for negative feedback or punishment, and that the only definitive failure is a failure to acknowledge and learn from mistakes.

Recent brain research suggests that we rely on emotion over intellect when making decisions that involve risk and vulnerability. (We provide a sample of sources in Appendix C.) We all have emotional blind spots. Leaders emphasize and pride themselves on the use of rational decision processes to drive business strategy; their attitude is endemic to management science. Likewise, we have seen examples of emotional paralysis in executives who were unable to guide successful culture transformation as reflected in lack of self-awareness or overt suppression of emotional intelligence in problem solving.

Overlooked is the emotional side in making and reacting to decisions, often the least developed of our human abilities. We tend to see the rationality in our own decisions and the irrationality in the decisions of others, especially when we disagree or feel threatened.

As it turns out, reason is not nearly as reasonable or accessible as we thought. Research in the cognitive sciences and studies of brain activity reveal to what degree our decisions are mostly unconscious. Our brains use the logic of frames, prototypes, and metaphors. Emotion does not stand in the way of reason, but emotions influence conscious reasoning and overt decisions. For example, empathy (an emotion) is built into our brains.

Roger, the CEO of Credlow (possessor of a Transformer leader logic), embraces the emotional side of reasoning when he inquires, "How are you? No, how are you really?" and when he invokes the emotion of love as an influence on workplace behavior. Similarly, other advanced leaders see the problem and address it, as do Glen (Freethinker leader logic) and Bart (Collaborator leader logic). Each of them demonstrates the power of engagement and Headroom to bring the Inside-Out emotional components of readiness for change together with the Outside-In rational demands of the business strategy.

Our emotions often shape our messages in ways that do not match our rational intentions (Kegan and Lahey, 2001). If we do not stop and reflect or invite our audience to give us feedback, we can create reactions and engagements opposite to what we expect. Adam, Dawson, and Liam, as we have seen in earlier discussions, fell prey to the unconscious inner voice trumping the external language in their communications. If you are unaware of the emotional triggers embedded in the language you use, you may contradict your messages about change (Gardner, 2004). The fact that the rational is not the dominant or the primary human ability is another reason that we use the methods and tools we referred to in Chapter Six. The least you should ask of yourself and your colleagues is to consciously explore the connects or disconnects between Inside-Out and Outside-In before going public with expressions about change and transformation.

Example of the Effects of Risk Taking. At Memorial Hospital, the CEO's decision to remove one of the most powerful and influential members of the executive team for openly resisting change and punishing those who made mistakes created positive turbulence throughout the organization. The turbulence not only enlarged the Headroom space (our next phase) but profoundly changed the level of engagement and collective learning in that space.

Voice of Change

Heads up! We're talking here about the feasibility of change. If you and your culture spend almost all of your time in the managing part of change—systems, structure, and processes—and precious little time in the human system, then look out. If you can't risk public learning and create Headroom, your chances for creating lasting change are slim. Our clients who make it into and through those two phases of the CDC achieve powerful and lasting transformation from one leadership logic to another. Clients who do not make it into those dimensions remain at the starting gate. Make sure you factor personal willingness to risk into your feasibility analysis of change for your organization.

The Headroom and Widening Engagement Phase

We discussed personal engagement in Chapter Four. At the organizational level, engagement is the active involvement of all levels of the workforce in the public exploration of role and identity shifts, risk and vulnerability, hopes and fears, operating assumptions and norms, and current culture experience. Engagement also provides the opportunity and process for the initial forecasting by the collective of what they might be able to do to transform the desired leadership culture toward the desired future state. Through engagement, people become more conscious about the dynamics of change, their feelings about relinquishing control, their feelings about taking charge of time rather than being controlled by time, and how much they honor spirit and values as compared with dollars and cents only. At this phase in the CDC, we see senior leaders engaging others (peers, change leadership team members, employees) in developmental public learning.

If senior leaders are committed to change but recognize that either it's not happening or is haphazard and not yet working right, they can guide people toward engagement by planning an event or series of events to deal with change. As we noted in Chapter Six, Headroom is the force that fuels and energizes collective learning and engagement in exploring and testing new beliefs and practices. Headroom begins to manifest through these experiences. Such events spread leaders' own strong commitment to support connectedness in the leadership culture and to model and practice public learning. In turn, the collective learning sparks advances in organization capability, reinforces shifts in role and identity, and supports publicly the rewards of taking risks and being vulnerable. These are essential for moving toward a more collaborative culture in that they nurture continuous practice and experience of the "power of us."

As change guides collectively learn more, and more engagement events (planned or otherwise) occur, they extend Headroom to more and more individuals and groups in the organization. Guides spread throughout the organization, planting the seeds for more and more groups to engage in developing alignment and commitment to the journey toward change and culture transformation. Individuals and groups commit to implementing development within a stage and preparing the ground for the next stage.

As a senior leader and change guide, you need to visibly and accessibly model your own readiness. You create the draft that raises the ceiling for Headroom. You yourself consistently stand up and step forward in order to embed Headroom as a constant in the organization culture. Your role is emotional as well as rational because people will feel different when they are fully engaged and fully present in the Headroom space. As employees from all levels risk stepping outside their traditional roles and identities, their sense of security will depend on feeling your endorsement. The degree and level of successful engagement you model as a change guide is often the tipping point for necessary and sufficient Headroom to emerge, which generates movement along the path of the other CDC dimensions.

Example of Headroom and Widening Engagement. At Technology Inc., Bart publicly acknowledged believing strongly that the company's direction would help it remain not only viable but ahead of the competition. At the same time, he admitted a heartfelt need to engage the larger community of leadership because he was uncertain about how to move the organization to generate alignment and commitment throughout the workforce. This opened up Headroom for others in the strategy process group to acknowledge their dreams, their fears, and their discomfort working with the most complexity and uncertainty they had ever experienced in their careers. Engaging with each other in Headroom supported them in admitting to not knowing the answers and was the moment of unfreezing that led this group to expand to include other leaders. The process reinforced the power of engagement and the opportunity for all to practice it in an expanding Headroom time and place.

The Innovation Phase

Headroom creates an environment for discovery and learning. In the dimension of innovation, we see clients opening up new forms of freedom, expression, design, and operational improvements. With that, innovation adds value for clients, customers, stakeholders, and people in their organizations. What's your perspective on innovation? Do you see it as the responsibility, function, and opportunity of the many, or is it only for the few (such as the people in research and development)?

We suggest that innovation isn't only about dramatic, creative, high-visibility, high-impact contributions. When innovation is recognized as a broader core value and process in an organization, learning becomes more sustained, and the culture itself develops more rapidly. From this perspective, expanding the Headroom space and the frequency of its use, developing bigger minds, and expanding leadership logic become innovations in and of themselves.

The Innovation Paradox. Paradoxically, some organizations want to be on the competitive cutting edge but also want to maintain order and control over people and processes that are the likely sources of innovation. Our experience with organizational creativity and innovation yields findings similar to those of specialists in this arena. In the CDC, innovation is advanced by risk-taking guides. They accept the necessity of trying the new and experimenting with alternatives that could move the organization up to or keep it ahead of the competition. In so doing, guides demonstrate their higher control source, as we discussed in Chapter Five. Moreover, they intentionally use time as a resource to focus attention on leadership strategy and leadership culture, not just business strategy and business results.

When we get to the leadership transformation phase of the CDC, we will speak about a leadership mind-set that, in keeping with the principle of Headroom, consistently values and rewards being on the leading edge. It recognizes mistakes as part of forward progress and learning and does not punish them as failures. The Freethinker logic that embraces the advance from Achiever to Collaborative culture is the stage where innovation begins to flourish!

Ultimately the Headroom you create for cross-process and interdisciplinary consultations and for solving problems opens the space for more creative, entrepreneurial engagement and innovations in your internal problem-solving and decision-making practices. Gratton (2007) observes that boundary-free cooperation fuels innovation, which affirms our observations of the power of Headroom.

Example of the Innovation Phase. Memorial Hospital innovated before its regional hospital competition did. The process began when the change leadership team catalyzed discussions within and across departments that supported new practices and approaches. After Memorial's executives and then its change leadership team created Headroom, it was embraced by and expanded into all of Memorial's management ranks. Early bottom-line results were quality improvement and cost savings. Other innovative processes were proposed and tested, leading to improvements in cross-shift communications in nursing, ward management, and outreach and engagement of patient families in the treatment planning process.

The outputs of Headroom by Memorial and with other organizations we have worked with are not unlike the "group genius" phenomenon described by Sawyer (2007) or the "hot groups" observed by Lipman-Blumen and Leavitt (1999). Like us, these researchers recognize that group genius is always collaborative. Research over more than fifteen years has demonstrated that collaborative groups are a key source of creative, workable ideas that can drive organization change. Like-minded team members who, through working together, experience an outpouring of creative energy can produce actionable results that transcend the organization's constraints on leading to bigger minds and transforming the leadership culture.

The Structure, Systems, and Business Processes Phase

This is our fifth dimension or phase of the CDC, although in many organizations, it's the starting point because it concerns both change management and change leadership. Change guides often feel most comfortable in this phase, but it ends in great disappointment when leaders allow the cycle to begin and end here without developing further.

In your career, you may have experienced an organization's reorganization in response to results that were below expectations, talent that was difficult to find and keep, or innovation that had ground to a halt. Restructuring is popular because although it appears risky, it doesn't require senior leaders to expose themselves to not knowing, to needing to learn, or to public reflection on the reasons for change. Seemingly they can move right on to safe, familiar territory of what changes to make and how to make them: Outside-In, operational, tactical questions of execution.

The importance of the structuring, systems phase of the leadership culture development cycle is that it holds the power to consolidate and integrate accomplishments of preceding phases in the cycle. If you've ever seen the child's game Chutes and Ladders, you know the ever-present challenge posed by the chutes, which can take you back to where you have already been. In organizational development, the structuring phase is a chance to create a new foundation or safety net that reduces the chances of sliding back down to the prior stage before the new stage has been thoroughly learned and mastered.

One aim in the phase is putting in place whatever new structures, systems, and processes will anchor and reinforce the current, perhaps recently achieved, level of Headroom. That in turn creates the basis for expanding current Headroom in order to develop toward the next higher stage of leadership culture. In our mountain trek metaphor, imagine the group is scaling a peak. The structure, systems, and process phase is akin to the climbers' making sure they have anchors in place at their current level of ascendance before stretching toward the next level. Structure, systems, and process align people, strategy, and core capabilities on the journey toward culture transformation. And it is also true that you have to have the right culture in place to ensure that these new systems and processes work.

Change guides can become frustrated by how hard it can be for other leaders throughout the organization to detach themselves from the enormous comfort and power they feel from remaining entrenched instead of pressing on, with risk and effort, to the next phase of the journey.

How to get them back on their feet and climbing again? Begin by guiding the organization in assessing the degree to which key systems and processes support change, inhibit change, or have a currently unknown effect. That assessment will enable you and the senior team to determine in which areas intervention is necessary to align systems and processes in supporting culture development.

Example of Structure, Systems, and Business Processes. Once Headroom became established at Technology Inc. as a space and process for change, the company began to hold quarterly meetings of its top twenty leaders (the process engineers). The purpose of the meetings was to explore how structure, systems, and business processes could support culture change and, in turn, support action development in operations. In addition, this group reviewed the behaviors and practices of each individual and the collective as related to serving as guides for culture development and organization transformation.

Out of this system emerged a new process of coaching to engage individual employees in more than just task work. The new process included coaching in experiencing and experimenting with Headroom to advance the practices within a process and between processes in the manufacturing environment. After creating, practicing, and generally guiding the coaching process, the coaching collective realized the importance of learning every day in the work itself. Strategy process leaders went on to declare that learning was the work and that a learning culture was the process. This further expanded Headroom for the leadership group and other employees to engage collectively in defining what it meant to learn individually and collectively in day-to-day work. Out of this Headroom experience, the CDC was reenacted in terms of the role, risk, engagement, innovation, and leadership mind-set and philosophy. Now learning *was* the work—a breakthrough into the next stage of collaboration to continue evolving from a leadership culture of independent achievement toward one of interdependent collaboration.

The Leadership Transformation Phase

Whether you regard it as the first or last phase or dimension of the CDC, leadership transformation is intimately connected to all the other dimensions of the cycle and to the core framework for organization transformation. Recall how we have determined that one main reason for failure to change is a lack of attention to how well an organization's leadership culture supports the leadership strategy and the business strategy. For many senior executives and executive leadership teams, the concept of a leadership strategy and leadership culture to drive business strategy is not part of their leadership worldview.

It should be. We challenge you and other leaders in your organization to become clear, articulate, and persuasive about a worldview that leadership is collective, that leadership is about networks of relationships, and that its ongoing responsibility is to create conditions for people and the organization to drive toward meeting the organization's challenges.

At a minimum, have an opinion on leadership and learning, leadership and change, leadership and risk or vulnerability, leadership and innovation and creativity, and leadership as both a creative and a distributive force for enacting values.

Examples of Leadership Transformation. Paralyzed leadership strategy and mind-set can completely obstruct cultural change. At Global Electronics, for example, the CEO was proud of his command of the newest thinking about leadership, culture, and organization development. He repeatedly said the company must develop a leadership strategy and culture to support the business strategy (a growth strategy that had not yet been achieved over six consecutive years). Yet he gave little thought to the potential cultural barriers (roles, identity consciousness, risk and vulnerability, engagement) to implementing the aggressive growth strategy.

This CEO espoused leadership concepts like empowerment, collaboration, strategic leadership, distributed decision making at the lowest level, inclusion, and direct and open communication. Yet each time a member of the executive team voiced an objection to advancing ideas on new leadership practices or changing leadership culture, the CEO retreated to diplomacy, disavowing the ideas and pinning them on someone else.

In so doing, he backed away from personal risk and vulnerability and so prevented Headroom. As of this writing, the company continues to set the same strategic business goal that has not been met for eight consecutive years, and it continues to fall far short of its potential. All that keeps the organization from imploding is that it represents a foothold in North America for a global company.

Affinity groups in Technology Inc., in contrast, promulgated a belief that became ingrained in the leadership mind-set and the culture of the organization as a whole: "I am a member of a team, and we can decide and take action." This set in motion

Voice of Change

Many CEOs confirm that change is one of the top three challenges they face now and into the future. They also often argue that leadership and management development are core elements in achieving their business strategy. They espouse support for empowerment, collaboration, distributing decisions to the lowest appropriate level, inclusion, diversity of perspectives, direct and open communication, and so on. So you may ask yourself: Given this awareness, why do organization change initiatives succeed only a third of the time or less? Our response is to ask you a question: In your own experience, how frequently are these comments intentionally acted on, or are they merely given lip service in the pursuit of running the business? It is unlikely that you or your change leader colleagues will succeed unless you recognize and act to address the potential barriers to development posed by cultural issues regarding the need for shifting roles and identity consciousness, risk, vulnerability, and engagement. So will you stand up and engage, or will you be MIA—missing in awareness, missing in action?

the processes related to role shift and identity consciousness in other dimensions of the CDC.

At the same time, the organization adopted a leadership practice of "Take time out for learning." In so doing, it shifted expectations for leaders and expanded the definition of work from simply fulfilling tasks to one of continuously creating and guiding the organization toward more independent achievement using collaborative methods such as dialogue.

Memorial Hospital's change leadership team, in collaboration with the executive team, evolved a leadership imperative: "Patients, their families, and our community are number one." In articulating this strategic intent as process throughout the evolving culture, Memorial further reinforced role shift awareness and identity consciousness to create closer bonds between leaders and between leadership and the broader hospital community in executing the strategy without personalizing differences. This became an antidote to a prior tendency to deflect honest differences in perspective about hospital operations and culture as personality problems or disruptive attacks. However, the team was able to do these things only after forced turnover of the hostile vice president, who had often personalized issues in order to intimidate and quiet those with a different mind-set or philosophy.

When Memorial's CEO removed this influential individual, he created momentum for authentic social discourse, expanding participation within the leadership culture to patients, their families, and the community. In the resulting Headroom, a new leadership mind-set flowed through the hospital in favor of sharing responsibility for finding and experimenting with the next good idea.

Successful change relies in great part on identity, and identity must reflect a leadership mind-set that drives profitability, effectiveness, efficiency, doing the right thing, making a difference, and finding and creating opportunity for the next good idea. In our experience, this includes leadership that is distributed in terms of responsibility and authority for decisions that support the business strategy and drive the culture development cycle. It's leadership that enables power but not force, and it legitimizes a culture founded on social discourse and social contracting.

The Four Learning Questions and Different Leadership Logics

Look back again at Figure 8.1, specifically at the four major learning questions in the four corners of the figure: "Why change?" "Change what?" "Change how?" and "What if?" (McCarthy, 2000). These questions help leaders grow bigger minds in the process of moving through the phases of the CDC. This section is about how those four questions play out depending on your organization's current leadership logic and where it is headed.

Why Change?

When faced with how hard change is to accomplish, most of us rightly ask, "Why change?" In the why change portion of the CDC, the people in organizations try to make sense. They watch others and use their connections with others to make sense of expected changes. Intentionality and engagement are critical to answering Why questions.

In a Dependent-Conformer culture, "Why change?" can lead you to explore and test shared decision-making authority and influence because it is fundamental to strategic execution. The question can also widen your focus from mastery of technical skills to learning about yourself and your colleagues as cocreators of change. The question provides an opportunity to grow beyond controller learning logic, to get beyond "my superiors want me to." And in the trenches of change, you had better know why you're doing it, or the change effort won't last.

If you are in a primarily Independent-Achiever culture, asking "Why change?" can expand your views of what is good for the team, your department, your function, and your own achievement so that all incorporate the value of change. This requires diving deep into systemic root causes driving the need for change. You will use role shift experience, identity consciousness, and risk taking to explore the benefits of change that lie within and beyond self-interest. You open yourself to exploring capabilities across teams, departments, functions, and disciplines to deliberately grow a bigger mind to advance the organization, not just yourself or your part.

In an Interdependent-Collaborator culture or in the transition zone toward such a culture, "Why change?" includes more Inside-Out seeing, thinking, and feeling that guides you toward cocreating the Outside-In of the larger world. You are learning and growing beyond the boundaries of the self, the team, and the organization into the larger world community. More of your learning involves the spirit of intentionality and an exploration of how your values can shape or shape-shift the relationships between your organization, the community, and the global society.

Change What?

If "Why change?" is about finding and making meaning, then "Change what?" is about finding order. Many leaders are relatively comfortable with this question's analytical bent. "Change what?" requires investing yourself and your time in engaging with others to sort out facts, dispel myths, and bring forth, probe, and integrate diverse perspectives. To decide what needs to change, you must listen, think, and intuit. You use your emotions as well, revisiting issues of control center, time sense, and intentionality as they connect with the business strategy, leadership strategy, leadership logics, and leadership culture.

In a Dependent-Conformer culture, "Change what?" can create dialogue about decision making, work style, the place of learning in leadership and work, and about degrees of freedom to shift relationships, work processes, and operational systems. Addressing the question pushes you to share energy and spread responsibility, with you and the organization developing toward a more Independent-Achiever culture stage.

In an Independent-Achiever culture, "Change what?" requires you to reflect on feelings that arise in a process of shifting away from work identity groups based on "we," extending that toward more global thinking about "who 'we' would be" in an Interdependent-Collaborator culture. Learning focuses on what it will take to change identity consciousness and open oneself to working in a connected process with leaders and with workers from other teams, departments, functions, and disciplines.

Thus, "Change what?" involves dialogue about Inside-Out thinking, feeling, and acting as steps toward a bigger, conscious worldview. Because the educator role in the Achiever culture is that of coach, it's likely you will want to consider bringing in trusted expert advisers and others with practices and logics of guide who can help with "Change what?" analysis and action planning.

In an Interdependent-Collaborator culture, leveraging the learning opportunities of "Change what?" takes an even broader mind-set. Inquiry is likely to be about learning orientation and sustaining a learning environment that supports bigger minds and envisions one still bigger. In the interdependent culture, "Change what?" leads to enhancing the leadership logic and the corresponding leadership culture and to exploring greater possibilities for the business strategy and leadership strategy. For example, you may ask whether to further reinvent yourselves and your organization.

Change How?

Having reached some agreement on what to change, the learning focus shifts to how. At this point in the CDC, engagement, innovation, and leadership dimensions come to the foreground as attention shifts to experimenting, testing assumptions, and expanding beliefs about leadership logic and leadership culture. This is all about practical, feet-on-the-ground, make-it-happen practices. Recall that in the work of innovating leadership mindset, you are asking each other what you can do that is creative, feasible, growth generating, and transformational. Your efforts go toward putting the bigger mind to work—developing prototypes, running pilots, implementing systems, developing processes—to put your organization's operation on the path to practicing and using an advanced leadership logic.

In a Dependent-Conformer culture, "Change how?" means attending primarily to and applying more teamwork to innovations and experiments. It means more testing of current limits on how possibilities are analyzed, making choices, and taking action. Initiating action shifts to teams, work groups, and collectives, without needing direction or orders from superiors. From the perspective of leadership and learning logics, it's a move beyond the controller mind-set and practice toward coaching and mentoring. That movement toward a coaching culture will foster active shared learning and solidify future progress toward Independent-Achiever logic.

In an Independent-Achiever culture, leaders are independent and self-assured; they and their teammates generate their own achievement values and standards. If that's where you are and you aim to make a transition to an interdependent culture, "Change how?" questions will lead you to cocreate intentional experiences that take you beyond your own values and standards to an appreciation and understanding of others. In turn, that shift will free you up to more inclusive standards and more focus on areas that benefit the whole organization. Your work to answer "Change how?" incorporates the learning of new leadership logics into the actual work of leading. For example, "Change how?" might lead you to reframe a project so that it requires cross-team, cross-functional, cross-disciplinary work.

In an Interdependent-Collaborator culture, "Change how?" implies using more of your strengths in strategizing, influencing, and contextualizing. In answering how, you will see challenges as opportunities to practice truth telling and to elevate the leadership logic and culture for productive change and the benefit of all. You will take chances in your experiments and challenge yourself and the leadership team to do more collective learning in public. Senior leaders will be interchangeably leaders and managers, validating the logic and culture of transformational thinking and feeling, being and doing. You and your team may think in terms of the legacy you leave for future generations.

What If?

When you reach this learning question, you're in rarefied air that portends newly enriched Inside-Out reflection on the nature of your organization. In "What if?" territory, looking back out over all phases of the CDC and on how you thought and acted in response to the other three learning questions, you'll glean new insights into motives, aspirations, and hidden possibilities, private and public. It's with "What if?" that you open yourself and others to original solutions and practices that further define and refine leadership culture in your context. The road ends here in the sky. Transformational streams merge at a line of collective learning, integrated leading-managing, and "change teaming" instead of tag teaming.

Our experience has been that "What if?" learning is much the same across all organizational culture stages. It is the question that triggers deeper reflection and higher creative impulses.

Ongoing Cycles and Shifts

The CDC's four learning questions lead naturally to important questions about a triple bottom line: an expansive inquiry about the possibilities for combining economic, social, and environmental goals into a winning business strategy (Savitz and Weber, 2006; Boyatzis and McKee, 2005). This is the opportunity of developing bigger minds and advanced stage leadership cultures while executing your organization's business strategy, another benefit of Inside-Out and Outside-In actions of leadership.

Exercises

Questions

Reflecting on and answering these questions can provide you with insight into steps to take in guiding other leaders through the dimensions in the CDC:

- Which of the six dimensions in the CDC keep you awake at night, and which dimensions are you ignoring or experiencing blockages in or at? What is the gap?

- What does this gap in attention suggest about what the team needs to do to move the leadership culture forward?

- What are the costs of public learning in your culture, and how can you and your team improve the three corners of readiness together as a leadership collective?

- What would becoming a change guide require of you that is different, and what will you get back in terms of your aspirations for developing yourself, your team, and the organization?

- How comfortable are you with creating a learning environment that encourages a cycle of inquiry grounded in Why? What? How? and What if? questions that inform the learning cycle?

Imagine and Write

Imagine that your leadership talent has developed to an advanced capability to execute strategy. Write a story about your experience of advancing through the dimensions to the new logic.

Discuss with Your Senior Team

After completing the previous exercise, facilitate a dialogue with your organization's senior team to explore Why? What? How? and What if? questions. As you move through the dimensions of the CDC, focus on how the dimensions are critical to executing your organization's strategy in the near and the long terms.

9

REACHING INTO THE CULTURE

Man's mind stretched to a new idea never goes back
to its original dimensions.
— *Oliver Wendell Holmes Jr.*

In Chapter Two, we explained why culture matters. We hold that culture is often viewed in either of two ways. One, a deterministic view, says culture is the collection of social beliefs that determine behavior, limit learning, and channel choice. This view prevents learning in the collective and locates the power mostly at the top. This understanding, which is held closely in conformance-based cultures, limits an organization to a steep command-and-control hierarchy that creates dependency on the leaders by the followers. As we've pointed out, a Dependent-Conformer subculture may be useful in select environments like security systems or accounting departments, but it no longer works in many organizations. We bet this is the kind of culture you wish to transform.

A second view of culture defines it as emerging social beliefs that expand behaviors and learning, extending choices by creating new tools and meaning (Bohannon, 1995). That view sees culture as adaptive and generative in dynamic, competitive environments—the environments that are now challenging most organizations. We are betting this is the kind of culture you want to attain. Such a culture can be developed and practiced through what we called DAC—a view of leadership focused on the outcomes of direction, alignment, and commitment.

Chapter Eight used the culture development cycle as a way to place your insights from Part One of this book into a broader context of organizational activities. In this chapter, we continue to broaden our discussion as we move from changing senior leadership teams themselves to transforming the organization's leadership culture. We continue to focus on leadership in terms of DAC and emphasize that as the leadership logic advances, more nonmanagement people are invited to be part of the leadership culture.

We begin with the question of how to determine if, in addition to your senior team, your leadership culture as a whole is ready for transformation to the next level. Are your people ready to be invited into wide leadership participation in order to achieve a more collective style?

Achieving DAC through participative leadership requires a new and different kind of development. Transformation in intricate and convoluted environments requires a bigger-mind understanding of how leadership culture improves bottom-line results—every CEO's goal. An organization surrounded with rapid-fire change needs a culture with exponential powers to respond—and this is what a collaborator culture with interdependent beliefs and practices looks like. A collective leadership mind must be found and stretched in order to confront big, serious change because a leader-follower-goal mind is insufficient and often hopelessly slow to respond to complexity. A leadership culture that effectively invites wide participation and then targets and develops new organization-wide capabilities that are core to its future is a viable way to face contemporary business challenges.

Readiness in the Organization

Many organization change efforts fail because they are simply unrealistic. Just as the senior leader team can't jump directly from conforming to collaborating and just as parents can't expect their children to master calculus right after learning a bit of algebra, an executive can't expect an entire organization to skip development steps or change dramatically until the culture of the organization has developed to the point where it can change. Judging its readiness involves doing many of the same things you might do in a study of feasibility for, say, a new information technology system—but in this case, the system is made up of people. In order to advance a leadership culture, it is in your best interest to be able to realistically assess your organization's requirements for new core capabilities.

Determining the levels of readiness for change in individuals, teams, and organizations requires these key steps:

1. *Discovery.* Establish a baseline of data, root cause, and readiness analysis, and create dialogue about what your discoveries mean.
2. *Diagnosis.* Determine the leadership logic your organization needs, and establish a leadership strategy to develop it.
3. *Design.* Frame the first steps in a transformation journey, and prepare to redesign repeatedly as you learn more and more with your colleagues.

Recall our definition of a leadership strategy: that it can be seen in the organization's choices, whether they are conscious or not, about the leadership culture and its beliefs and practices, and in the kind of people systems it chooses to manage the development of leadership. It is also the strategic intent for your future leadership culture and systems. This is much more than just a training and development system for leaders.

We mentioned earlier that Global Electronics repeatedly had declared a business strategy to double its revenue in two years, but it never achieved the goal. The problem was that it was a Conformer culture whose leaders were ignorant of how vast the gap was between that culture and the Collaborator culture that its strategy required. Technology Inc. leaders, in contrast, had analyzed their organization's readiness for change in six-month increments for several years. That awareness allowed them to move steadily from a Conformer to an Achiever culture, building readiness for further movement toward a Collaborator culture.

In these two examples, the difference between sustainable success and abject failure to meet strategic goals is the ability to balance and integrate change feasibility and leadership readiness. But that begs the question: What *is* feasible in the context of this specific change for this particular organization in this unique circumstance?

When you climb a set of stairs, you take them one at a time to keep from stumbling. Metaphorically we're suggesting the same thing here. In order to get clearer about what next step is feasible in your organization, let's look at the "co" words we are using so that we are all speaking the same language: the language of CQ.

Your Organization's CQ

We use the term CQ to refer to a culture quotient measurement somewhat analogous to IQ. The "C" specifically refers to three important "co" words of cultures: *coordinate, cooperate,* and *collaborate.* Too often leaders use these words interchangeably, as if they all mean the same thing. But we give them distinct uses because the amount of cowork they describe is different for each. These three words correspond to what generally happens in the three levels of leadership logic and culture:

- *Dependent.* Conformer cultures operate successfully when a hierarchy of leaders meticulously *coordinates* the work of the level beneath each leader.
- *Independent.* Achievement cultures succeed because groups within the organization often *cooperate* for mutual benefit.

- *Interdependent.* Collaborator cultures succeed because the people in them *collaborate* for the common good.

Coordinate, cooperate, and *collaborate* describe how people work together. They embody distinct, increasing levels of freedom and responsibility for everyone in the organization. They also are clear indicators of how able an organization is at any one point to pull off major change. The level at which people work together must be aligned with the culture's ability to execute that strategy.

Within each level are three factors that distinguish the differences among them: knowledge access, how decision making is distributed, and proximity to the work:

1. In coordination, corporate knowledge is held at the top, but decisions are centralized and removed in proximity from actual work sites. Work across boundaries is therefore slow to change.

2. In cooperation, corporate knowledge is sometimes distributed based on competitive needs, and decisions are decentralized and in proximity to work sites but not coordinated across work sites. Work is therefore changeable only when parts cooperate across those boundaries with other parts for mutual benefit.

3. In collaboration, knowledge and decision making are widely distributed, and the full work process and local sites are all mutually understood by all. Work is always changing and improving in an organic process that everyone in the organization owns.

Theoretically, there could be five levels of CQ, as shown in Table 9.1. We use the extremes at the high and low end as bookends to frame the three cultures we discuss. This is not to say that your entire organization will embody one culture or stand

Table 9.1 Levels of CQ

Level	"Co" Word	Typical Culture	Essence	Occurrence
Highest	Converge	Collective-Consciousness	Joint universal awareness of how all systems work together	Visionary communities, and therefore very rare
	Collaborate	Interdependent-Collaborator	Joining forces and resources in working partnerships	Small, emergent growth in breakout organizations
Middle	Cooperate	Independent-Achiever	Alignment of the work of parts of the organization	Growing base of postmodern alternative organizations
	Coordinate	Dependent-Conformer	Management and direction of the flow of work from the top	Major base of postindustrial and older institutions
Lowest	Co-opt	Despotic	Mechanistic control and manipulation of people	Uncommon in most organizations

at a specific CQ level. Part of assessing your current strengths and readiness will be noticing variations within your organization as a whole and considering how you can leverage pockets of higher CQ to bring up the CQ in other groups.

We offer the high and low ends of the spectrum as convergence versus co-optation in order to frame the extremes. Our purpose is to illustrate how human potential accelerates as you move beyond the restrictions of mere coordination in a dependent culture. As you enter into cooperation (see Table 9.1), you move on a pathway toward the high end of independence and innovation and on toward the change-agile power of collaboration in an interdependent culture.

The higher the CQ,

- The less control you retain at the top.
- The more freedom you allow and responsibility you expect.
- The more you distribute authority and decision making.
- The more innovation, problem solving, and quality you get at the local level.
- The more uncertainty you can tolerate.
- The more conflict can emerge as a creative, viable force.
- The higher the level of individual and collective learning.
- The more ambivalence and paradox are accepted.
- The higher the level of feedback you want and get.
- The greater the levels of synergy and teaming.
- The more shared knowledge is engendered.
- The more intersystems thinking is the norm.
- The greater the level of leadership capacity and capability.
- The more you value and get organization-level capability and shared competence.
- The greater adaptability and agility of the organization.
- The greater the level of complexity and challenge the organization can face and take on with greater chances for success.

Examples of CQ's Effect

Let's say that you are facing the grizzly challenge of reengineering your corporation into a process-centered organization that requires collaboration throughout the value chain. This requires joining forces and resources in working partnerships not only within your employee base and culture, but also across the cultures of your supplier partners.

If you have a Dependent-Conformer culture in which the flow of work is coordinated (managed and directed) through a hierarchy controlled from the top, your chances of success in collaborating are exceedingly low because the tripod of leader-follower-goal makes process exceedingly slow. Reengineering requires distributed, local decision making and free access to information—qualities a Conformer culture does not have. This explains why failure rates in corporate reengineering programs, which often start in Dependent cultures, are in the 90 percent range.

Technology Inc. tackled reengineering, starting out as a Conformer culture. However, it mastered this challenge by moving the entire leadership culture to the cooperative Independent-Achiever level. At the same time, it was working toward some leadership practices at the Interdependent-Collaborator level.

In the next section, we apply the CQ framework to each of the three main stages of leadership logic.

Voice of Change

Every executive wants results—clear operational results. Here are a few examples from Technology Inc. Recall the story in which Bart called us and said that, as if a miracle, following the company's Headroom-generating work session, the group at the plant had made variable group compensation for the first time ever.

When we started working with Technology Inc., unforced turnover was in the double digits, but within a few quarters it had dropped so low it could be called zero. Recruitment costs have plummeted because almost all new employees come from internal referrals. Of the many metrics improvements from the shop floor, one stands out: product returns have dropped by 50 percent year over year over year over year—and nobody even used the word *quality*.

Change your leadership culture's beliefs and practices to the right level of CQ for your strategy (by creating Headroom and using action development), and your organization can enjoy similar sustainable outcomes.

Leadership Cultures and the CQ Framework

In the following sections, you will see similarities to our descriptions of the individual leader logics, but notice that we have shifted attention toward the three leadership culture types found at the organizational level.

Dependent-Conformer Logic: A Culture of Coordination

Within the senior leadership team and throughout a hierarchically coordinated structure, command and control is the organizational mind-set in this culture. Authority emanates from the top, and honoring the code of beliefs is preferable to adaptive learning, which can either extend or threaten the status quo. Knowledge, because it is power, is also held at the top. Members succeed insofar as they obey authority because belonging to the order and loyalty to the code are the primary tenets of membership. The unspoken ethic is, "Us first, me second." Recognition of good work and mastery takes place mainly at the level of technical expertise. Mistakes are treated as weakness, and feedback tends to be negative and is not sought after.

Wherever they are in the hierarchy, leaders in such a culture tend to range between authoritarian and paternalistic, expecting organizational success by virtue of compliance and conformance to their wishes. Thinking tends to be either-or (right or wrong), and expertise and technical mastery are honored. Achievement of goals is the way to ensure continued belonging in the culture. These cultures create members who avoid risk and are averse to change. Extreme forms of this culture are secretive and demand loyalty over many other values.

DAC Implications. Direction and alignment of the flow of work, two necessary outcomes of leadership, are achieved by coordination controlled by executive authority at the top and passing down through the ranks. This coordination restricts local decision making and regulates activities to the execution of tasks prescribed by management. Commitment, as loyalty, is assumed as a matter of membership.

Illustrations. Coordinated Dependent-Conformer cultures are found in all manner of postindustrial environments, including manufacturing, some public utilities, government institutions, policing and security, and many religious institutions. For these types of activity, these cultures can present distinct advantages. Consider regulating and ensuring safety in running trains or air traffic control. Centralized control from the top may provide the best alternative of safety. Reliability in unchanging rote tasks is one advantage. As long as the external environment remains relatively stable, the top-down coordinated culture can continue to produce predictable results.

A disadvantage (as Table 9.1 suggests) is that extreme forms of such cultures can co-opt members into complying and conforming to usual orders when adaptive learning and change are really what is needed. Consider unions, some of which have outlived their usefulness. We would probably be overstating the case if we said, "Show us a union shop and we'll show you a Dependent-Conformer culture," but not by much. The airline industry and public school systems are good examples. We love and value public schools, and yet unions often create barriers to constructive change when the knee-jerk answer to any significant change is a No bolstered by self-interest.

Independent-Achiever Logic: A Cooperative Culture

In an Independent-Achiever organization, authority and control are distributed well down through the ranks of individual managers. The general mind-set is about being successful in a changing world and adapting faster and better than the competition. "Me first and us second" is the unspoken ethic. Successful individuals master systems that produce results; they are focused first on "me" and then "my team" to achieve results, but can ultimately contribute to the success of the organization. Mastery of work and the recognition of successful outcomes tend to happen at the systems level for leveraging technical expertise. Mistakes may be treated as opportunities to learn within a team, and feedback is valued where it contributes to learning and the ability for individual advancement and success.

Throughout the Independent-Achiever organization, thinking tends to focus on solving problems, mainly by analyzing empirical data, and management by the numbers is likely the primary basis and driver for decisions. Achieving goals is the path to political power. Knowledge is a tool for competitive edge not only in the marketplace but within the organization itself. Individuals or teams share knowledge at the system level when it benefits them to do so. When change looks like an opportunity for advancement, individuals and teams are prepared to take risks. Extreme forms of this culture are highly competitive internally and place individual achievement above many other values. In such organizations, decisions and outcomes may become random; that is, decisions may not create strategic coherence for the organization, leading to such outcomes as disconnected product lines and divisions competing for share in the marketplace. (This, incidentally, describes the fate of Digital Equipment Corporation.)

DAC Implications. In Independent-Achiever environments, leaders can improve alignment through cooperation if executives at the top demonstrate cooperation themselves. Their demonstration leads lower-level individuals and teams to see cooperation as a path to achievement also at the local level. However, when executives are not cooperating, there is significant risk for multiple and competing directions and poor alignment of corporatewide resources. Commitment holds self-interest and the organization in balance through cooperation.

Illustrations. Cooperative Independent-Achiever cultures have distinct advantages. *Faster, better, cheaper* and *execution* are watchwords for these highly competitive industries. They provide beliefs and processes for competitive capability, and more advanced forms lead and create markets through product development. Microsoft and Google, for example, have exponentially extended globalization through PC and networks functionality and provide tools for the information age with wide impact. High-end financial services and many consulting companies are also examples. As external environments shift, they harbor initiative, foster innovation, and provide varying and flexible levels of cooperation as needed. Independent-Achiever cultures can be entrepreneurial and market focused. Their analytical problem solving can move beyond mere science to artistic expressions in leading-edge design.

Interdependent-Collaborator Logic: A Collaborative Culture

The "co" word *collaborate* is exactly what Interdependent-Collaborator logic and culture are about. Such cultures share authority and control throughout the organization in a way that maximizes the strategic competence of the whole. The culture's superordinate focus on learning is about collaborating in a changing world so that the construction of new social and operational orders can emerge through collective work. Individuals succeed by mastering integrating systems whose results fit and aid the overall strategy, producing results now and into the future. Satisfied customers, solid partnership, and organizational capability are all part of the ethic of the culture. Mastery and good work tend to be recognized at an integrated systems level where benefits can be seen to accrue across the whole value chain. Mistakes are embraced as opportunities for individual, team, and organizational learning; positive and negative feedback are valued as essential tools for collective success.

Collaborative cultures see leadership as collective work that benefits the whole in perpetually achieving the organization's outcomes. They locate leaders among people without management titles. Anyone willing and able to think and act in expanding DAC to build the capability of the entire enterprise can qualify. Because leadership is committed to collective, continuous, discovery-oriented learning, strategy and goals continuously emerge in an ongoing organic process.

Collaborative cultures foster dialectical thinking when dealing with complexity. They consider both-and solutions and actively seek out win-win answers. As evidence, they weigh both external hard data and internal soft data, and in equal measure. As they make decisions, they consider integrated organization systems and human systems. They often engage in dialogue to make sense of things. They achieve enterprise goals across the value chain by sharing social, political, and economic power. They share knowledge widely on a right-to-know basis and consider knowledge an organizational asset. These cultures breed informed risk taking. They regard taking risks as ongoing, emergent opportunities to learn, expanding vision and extending strategy. Extreme forms of these cultures may rely too much on consensus building. When information sharing and dialogue become confused with a ritual of consensus, these organizations can get bogged down.

DAC Implications. Collaborative cultures widen their collaboration across the enterprise and throughout the value chain by joining working partnerships. DAC becomes a working, organic whole system. They align work across parts of the organization by connected leaders and by distributing powers that develop collective learning. As their overall strategy unfolds, new knowledge informs its amendment, and they continuously develop systems, structures, and processes for production. Synergy is common, and the enterprise is greater than the sum of its parts.

Illustrations. Do such cultures exist? In both our primary and secondary research, it is difficult to find pure examples of Interdependent-Collaborator cultures, although we have found a few. An informal review conducted in 2001 showed that two-thirds of clients at the Center for Creative Leadership (CCL) aspired to become such a culture. Since then, CCL's case study research has revealed that a number of such aspiring Independent-Achiever organizations have made significant progress toward interdependence. In fact, two of the cases in this book have achieved this transformation: Technology Inc. and Memorial Hospital.

Leadership Culture Beliefs and Practices

In moving from independent to interdependent culture, just knowing which culture type and logic is right for your strategy is not enough. Transformation also requires defining some specific leadership practices as development targets. In Table 9.2, we have integrated DAC and ten leadership practice categories, and have associated their primary orientation as Inside-Out and Outside-In. Primary orientation means that both are inherent but one trumps the other in balance. For example, the distribution of authority and power is an Inside-Out shared belief, but when you have that decision-making power to affect others, it is definitely Outside-In; so all ten practices carry both implications in relative balance.

Following are examples of specific practices that advance leadership cultures into Interdependent-Collaborator capabilities. These examples are drawn from a multiyear, multiclient, ongoing CCL case study project that seeks to find and explain interdependent organizations and their leadership practices (McCauley and others, 2008). We present them here as actual examples of the new practices that are concurrent with new leadership logics. These examples illustrate the leadership practice categories in Table 9.2.

Table 9.2 Leadership Practices Categories That Generate DAC

Practices Categories	Primary Orientation
Direction and decisions	
Direction-setting decisions (mission, vision, strategy making)	Inside-Out
Generation and articulation of beliefs and values	
Governance—policies and compliance	
Alignment in operations	
Forming organizational structures	
Initiating work support systems in IT, HR, logistics, and other areas (enterprise systems)	Outside-In
Developing work processes for lateral integration of work flow and production	
Human systems and talent readiness	
Commitment through relationships	
Authority and power distribution, communication of ideas, and information flow	
Social formations: purposes and scope for teams or groups, partnerships, alliances, networks, communities, social responsibility, and others	Inside-Out
Culture, climate, and generation and maintenance of collective spirit	

Direction

Direction Setting. From the case of Technology Inc.: "During the annual planning process at Technology Inc., process engineers gather data from process team associates on their manpower and resource needs. This information is the basis for the plans created by the strategy process team (the senior team). Process engineers also bring plans to process team associates for discussion, and some modification of plans can result from this. At the annual September meeting, the process engineers, all representing their processes, present their operational plans, and a discussion follows in which plans are modified based on areas

Voice of Change

Joy, the finance manager at Memorial Hospital, discusses with her colleagues how a committee's operations have changed since the advent of the culture transformation work:

This committee has transformed! We trade team leadership, different people from different functions share chairman role, different people are in charge—the committee chair shifts. This used to be a pricing committee for product purchases, and it was run by logistics. Now it's about what is the best solution for the patient, not just efficiencies. Price is not the driver anymore, it's the patient now. The patient solution is the driver in how we make decisions. We use all our learning tools in this committee and rely on our relationships. This is one place where we really get a lot of headroom and multiple right answers and then combine them for the best answer. The reasons (criteria) for how we choose vendors have multiple factors for why—and price is only one of them and not the most important.

Our vendors are confused, they don't know how to approach us—how to sell to us now because they can't just compete on price anymore. Can you imagine how much change this is? We've all changed together. All the committees are like this.

of conflict and synergy. Further modifications come from discussion of plans with operational associates" (McCauley and others, 2008).

Beliefs and Values. From the study of a multistate service agency: "Since inception, [client] has been based on explicit values and a 'few simple rules' pertaining to 'the common good corporation.' These values create *both* individual autonomy and responsibility *and* interdependence in tasks and relationships. A single document called the Bill of Rights summarizes this system of beliefs and practices. The Bill of Rights is then used as the reference point for all matters of enculturation (for example, employee orientation, training) and discernment (for example, conflict resolution, complex decision making). Perhaps the simplest distillation of these values is (per the founder): *People are basically good and trustworthy. The path between here and there is not singular, but multiple. Welcome diversity. There is no single right way.* The intended (and often realized) result of these values is collaboration among multiple strong ('right') and sometimes conflicting perspectives and paths. This type of values-based collaboration is seen as the engine of creativity and emergent strategic directions for the corporation" (McCauley and others, 2008).

Alignment

Organizational Structures. From Technology Inc.: "A process-centered organization is organized around work processes rather than around functions and positions. There are no traditional vice presidents, managers, or supervisors. Rather there are 'process engineers,' whose responsibility is to collaborate with members of the process to improve its overall efficiency and effectiveness, and 'coaches' for individual and team development. The process-centered organization encourages a potentially high degree of interaction both within and across processes. As such interaction grows and continues to develop, and as it is increasingly directed toward an understanding of what work is being done and why, employees can begin to acquire a more comprehensive perspective on the organization overall" (McCauley and others, 2008).

Work Systems. From case work with Credlow, a national auto dealer: "Interdependent mechanisms for lateral integration in work systems allow for direct collaboration across organizational boundaries and for co-construction of new perspectives, knowledge, and identity across boundaries. In creating the specialized proprietary analytical software needed for their business, Credlow has begun using what the information technology (IT) field calls an agile IT development methodology. This version is called Scrum. Scrum uses collaborative, cross-functional, rapidly moving teams to iteratively and incrementally develop systems and products when requirements are complex and shifting. Scrum encourages interdependence by being radically open to continuous input, formal and informal testing, and revision from anywhere in the organization. Scrum surfaces and engages conflicting needs and perspectives about the software under development by problem solving through rapid iterations (daily and monthly) of prototypes. Scrum thus accommodates continuous transformation in the organization by deliberately revisiting priorities from one iteration to the next" (McCauley and others, 2008).

Developing Work Processes. From the case notes for Memorial Hospital: "Meetings became an integral part of work as the leadership beliefs and thought process shifted to engagement. All management meetings are now focused on action development. Opportunities to interact cross-functionally provide deep learning, and complex issues about cross-boundary processes get addressed and solved. Committees are a time and place to create Headroom and trigger action development. Leadership is understood as a verb (not a noun). Through working issues and doing active learning together (much more than the previous meeting practice of information sharing only) meetings are learning forums and serve to push our learning organization agenda forward" (McGuire, 2008).

Human Systems and Talent Readiness. From work with Technology Inc.: "Interdependent pay and benefits systems were designed to engage a dialectical tension in the organization by using multiple, conflicting criteria for rewarding employees, for example, individual rewards based on own, subsystem *and* total system performance. Peer reviews are integral to the process. People are compensated at the individual, team, and organization level. Annual performance reviews have a merit increase attached to reward individual performance of the skills and abilities to effectively work in the process-centered organization. A quarterly incentive compensation program based on team performance (products shipped) rewards people for being good team members. And the annual profit-sharing system rewards associates for the overall profitability of the company" (McCauley and others, 2008).

Commitment

Authority and Power. From the case study notes for Memorial Hospital: "The goal of distributed decision making has been surpassed and replaced with the practice of the distribution of ownership for patient-focused care throughout the hospital. The leadership culture committed to this practice is much bigger than the management ranks, and there is maturity of leadership from the middle. Patient-focused challenges are not prioritized— the leadership collective owns it all. There is not one patient issue silo more important than the others, and everyone takes ownership of all of them all the time" (McGuire, 2008).

Social Formations (Teams). From work with Technology Inc.: "The key purpose of this practice through teams is for direct collaboration across organizational boundaries, with minimum coordination orchestrated by higher management. The practice is used as a process for making decisions and solving problems. This collaborative work brings people with diverse perspectives together for mutual influence, co-construction of new perspectives, and self-authorized decision making. The practice of collaboration within and between process teams creates interactions that produce alignment and mutual learning. Within process teams, associates work together to solve problems and make decisions that affect work flow, product quality, product and process innovation, manpower needs, and personnel problems. For example, associates often reconfigure themselves, swapping team members among different process teams, to meet emergent man-ufacturing or delivery challenges" (McCauley and others, 2008).

Taking It to the Middle

When clients ask us whether effective change happens at the top or in the middle of the organization, without hesitation we say, "Yes, both." Concertedly seeding transformation at the top of the organization is essential—necessary but not sufficient. The real work to follow is what we call "taking it to the mid-dle," the heart of the culture. This is where Headroom really gets applied and tested. At the middle of any organization lies its heart. You'll find truth there.

By the middle, we mean primarily where the core of opera-tions is: where production of products and services is and where middle management sits, absorbing direction from the top and operational realities from below. Without engagement of change at the middle, transformation is dead on arrival. When the middle is engaged in Headroom and action development of new leadership beliefs and practices, then change happens in the organization. In important and essential ways, change at the top, such as in building the credibility that creates believability, is just practice for taking change to the middle.

Barry Oshry (1992) offers keen insights about how one's location in an organization shapes one's perspective on it. He writes that you need to have organizational readiness when you go to the middle because these "Middles," as Oshry calls them, are in a constant state of being torn between ongoing demands of the top and reaction to the unintended consequences of change from the bottom. But when you are ready and the top is actually engaging with the middle, then partnerships form and the tearing is mitigated because those in the middle are active players in the action development and change practices.

Taking it to the middle is the supreme test of how authenti-cally senior leadership has put its own self through the throes of transformation. When you take it to the middle, your Inside-Out mettle will be tested. Your time sense and control center will be on display. And your intentionality will get shoved around by people who want to know how serious you are about this new work.

Seeing is believing. Those in the middle want evidence that you've got a stake in the game, and they'll want to see that stake. People in the middle can smell a rat a mile away; they can also spot genuine intention in a heartbeat. If you ask them for more risk and vulnerability, they will want those things in and from you first—in fact, they will demand it.

When the top of the organization takes its own change to the middle and the middle believes it, the organization is on its way. Why does it work? Because to the people who have spent their organizational lives in that middle tearing zone, always being asked to do more and trying to please everyone, when senior people come to them, roll up their sleeves, and say they don't know everything, those actions invite the people in the middle into full-fledged membership in the leadership culture. When senior people start doing and being that change they want the organization to become, the response from the middle is to engage in partnership to make that change happen.

Let us be clear, again. We are not talking about morale-boosting company picnics and T-shirts; nor are we talking about the leadership rally with executive speeches, infotainment, and a golf tournament. Nor do we mean classroom learning. These activities have a place, but they cannot substitute for the real work of Headroom and culture change. Such activities do not help to produce Headroom, and Headroom is the "it" you are taking to the middle. Recall the three process steps to transformation we discussed in Chapter Three in relation to individual senior leaders and in Chapter Six as they relate to the culture. Working out from the middle entails those same steps because they are the steps to Headroom. And we would add this to our Headroom mantra: show up, own up, stand up, grow up—*then take it to the middle together.*

Headroom and Critical Mass

Beyond introducing Headroom to the middle, you will need to ensure and sustain it by example and ongoing practice. As repeated practice reinforces Headroom in an individual or team, so repeated practice leads to self-replicating Headroom in the middle. At all levels, Headroom can become integral to practice.

The dynamics of Headroom contain multiple essential perspectives that make it practical. By practicing and holding multiple perspectives simultaneously, you can inform and develop more realistic and feasible change strategies from multiple vantage points that create more practical leadership beliefs and practices that create and sustain change.

This phenomenon becomes viral, spreading from group to group, where it continues to grow. These self-replicating social clusters can gain energy from the perceived successes of other similar groups around them. Belief is key. When it catches on, it seems to do so by some spirit that moves through people who want to believe, and so do believe.

Ultimately the challenge is to establish momentum in the organization as a whole. When you release a naturally occurring force that favors the collective future good, that force will gain energy. Malcolm Gladwell popularized this general observation in his book *The Tipping Point* (2000), illustrating that phenomenon in public societies. Once a catalyst begins to take effect, a momentum can build that carries whole societies into a new reality. When Headroom has grown large enough to begin to sustain itself, we say it has reached a critical mass.

Effective social discourse and social agreements in the Headroom process provide evidence to organizational people that others among and above them are actually serious about what they are saying. When powerful people are seen to be engaged, taking risks publicly themselves, things start to change in operations. The skeptical find it harder to be skeptics. The cynical find it harder to be cynics. And the optimistic find it easier to engage, take on a risk, and give transformation a try.

Exercises

Questions for Reflection

- What is the predominant stage or type of leadership culture and leadership logic in your organization?

- To build the right level of talent to execute strategy, what stage of leadership culture do you have to have? What is required, not just desired?

- Do you have multiple subcultures across functions or business units, and are they appropriate to the work in those different environments?

Questions for Dialogue

Answer the following questions for your organization as it is at this time. Then take the questions to your senior leadership team, and ask each member to respond to the questions individually. After all have responded, together explore the implications for actions to develop a collectively bigger mind and a later-stage organization culture, which is required to sustain your organization's future.

Organization practices assume a learning mind-set that emphasizes . . .

1	2	3	4	5	6	7	8	9
adaptation to immediate problems			success in a changing world			generative learning in a new world order		

The thinking styles in this organization can be best described as . . .

1	2	3	4	5	6	7	8	9
either-or, black-or-white thinking, according to social convention			problem-solving thinking within a system to achieve goals			both-and thinking: integration of intuition and embracing paradox		

In this organization, information is shared primarily on a . . .

1	2	3	4	5	6	7	8	9
need-to-know basis			want-to-know basis			right-to-know basis		

In this organization, knowledge is . . .

1	2	3	4	5	6	7	8	9
closely held at the top			power for me and us			always evolving		

The environment of the organization is characterized by beliefs that . . .

1	2	3	4	5	6	7	8	9
leadership at the top will direct and protect us for our common good			self-reliance in my own and others' mastery will guarantee a good future			expansion of our shared awareness is ours to participate in together		

10

STRATEGIES, CULTURE, AND READINESS

The Pattern in Six Case Studies

> Still the question recurs, Can we do better? The
> dogmas of the quiet past are inadequate to the
> stormy present. The occasion is piled high with
> difficulty, and we must rise with the occasion. As our
> case is new, so we must think anew, and act anew.
>
> —*Abraham Lincoln*

Throughout this book, we have discussed six organizations, using their stories to illustrate the ideas, practices, challenges, and outcomes that arise when transforming leadership cultures. Three of these companies were successful in their transformation efforts: Technology Inc., Memorial Hospital, and Credlow. Three of the organizations failed to change: NuSystems, Professional Services Inc., and Global Electronics.

In this chapter, we profile these six organizations in terms of their business strategy, leadership strategy, leadership culture, and leadership readiness for change. We believe everyone can learn as much from failure as from success, and we share with you this variety of perspectives for one primary reason: understanding feasible change. Our hope is that from reading these case study summaries, you will see again, and perhaps more clearly, why three companies created a good chance to achieve sustainable change and three others did not.

Pay particular attention to the actions of leaders in these stories, in particular, Liam at NuSystems, Art at Professional Services Inc., and Dawson at Global Electronics. The profile of their strategies, leadership logics, and readiness in the face of their particular challenge reveals a great deal about the feasibility of addressing the change they were facing.

Keep in mind the difference between change (an adjustment or adaptation within the current level of culture) and transformation (a major shift in the culture from one leadership logic, or mind-set to another). As you read each profile, see where incremental change may have been the only practical course. Also look for instances where incremental change was impractical, considering the organization's strategy, its leadership logic, and the situation it was in.

As you read the profiles of the unsuccessful organizations, ask yourself:

- What would I have done in their place?
- How would I have advised them?
- What were their chances for transformation?
- What is missing from their profiles that is essential for transformation?
- What might have happened if they had aimed at some incremental change but not at total transformation?

As you read the profiles of the successes, ask:

- What are the strengths in their strategies, logics, and readiness that pushed them over the top to success?
- How did their profiles and actions square with their particular challenge?

We have argued at different places in this book that leadership strategy can be seen in an organization's choices (conscious or not) about its leadership culture, its beliefs and practices, and the kind of people systems it chooses to manage the development of leadership. Leadership strategy is also the strategic intent for future leadership culture and systems. After you finish reading this book, you should be able to build a coherent, reliable leadership strategy for changing or transforming the leadership culture in your organization.

Recall our saying early on, and often, that business goals and strategy come first and that leadership strategy and logic need to take whatever form best serves the business strategy. As you read each profile, think about the challenge each organization faced and examine the organization's strategies, logic, and readiness in relation to that particular challenge. By adopting that point of view, you will more easily recognize the degree to which, in each case, major change was really feasible. In Chapter Eleven, we continue this analysis by applying a process that we call feasibility mapping to each case. You will learn how to perform that same feasibility mapping on your own organization. Your feasibility analysis will tell you whether change (incremental adaptation) or transformation (movement from one leadership logic to the next) is the right choice.

Technology Inc.

Bart's challenge was to reshape this traditional, hierarchical manufacturing organization in order to keep it competitive into the future, continue sustaining a local economy, and make it a better place to work.

Business Strategy

Technology Inc. was a global market leader in multiple niches and intended to maintain that position and develop other product lines. The strategy team committed to leading a transformation from a typical top-down managed hierarchical manufacturing organization to a flat, lateral process-centered organization (PCO).

Leadership Strategy

For ten years the senior strategy team had invested consistently in developing individual leader skills and leadership team capabilities. Now it was time for them to seek a return on their investment. The leadership strategy for the PCO was simple and elegant: take time out for learning, and build toward a learning organization. This strategy was revolutionary in that it would prepare the way for leadership in collectives. It would focus on eighteen process teams in the central plant and many other teams in four plants across North America. There was a vision for more self and group determination to transform the leadership culture and create a more humane, better way to work together.

Leadership Culture

The fundamental culture challenge for Technology Inc. was to move from a hierarchy-based Dependent-Conformer kind of leadership culture to an Independent-Achiever leadership culture with a corresponding level of engagement. Furthermore, the strategy ultimately called for some level of Interdependent-Collaborator leadership beliefs and practices to sustain the horizontal, customer-focused PCO in the long run.

Leadership Readiness

These development initiatives were sponsored by Bart, the entrepreneurial, goal-oriented, results-driven owner. All of Bart's actions manifested his Performer-Freethinker into Collaborator leader logic range. Bart had consistently unfrozen himself, expanded his worldview, and, with the strategy team, personally modeled the new roles of leader and manager for the rest of the organization. When the decision was made to undertake such a dramatic transformation, Bart's actions had already positioned a cadre of the process engineers as leaders who had experienced some degree of personal readiness. Their readiness enabled them, as the change leadership team (CLT), to embrace the challenges and opportunities of culture transformation. The CLT was aligned in its effort toward transformation and had adopted Freethinker understanding and practices.

Ongoing developmental experiences enabled and motivated the team members to make themselves vulnerable to the uncertainties inherent in change work. Most were willing to face up to new challenges because they already had experienced positive impact and payoff from taking risks and staying the course of well-planned, incremental change. As employees had become part of a largely Dependent-Conformer workforce and culture moving toward more independence in thinking and decision making, those employees were becoming more willing to share decision-making responsibility and authority, with the assistance of the coaching team. However, along the way, one key member of the senior strategy team covertly determined to undermine these changes, and that fact had to be dealt with by Bart and his leadership team.

The leadership team was committed to the belief that the organization could increase profitability while taking the time to develop individuals and teams throughout the process and that the organization culture could become a learning culture. The informal but oft-stated, clear intention was to develop a culture of interdependence that linked and eventually reengineered internal processes and linked the organization more fundamentally with customers and external drivers in the economic and industrial environment. Equally important, the leadership team was aware that without such changes, Technology Inc. (still the largest source of jobs for a semirural community with limited educational opportunities) might be forced to downsize its workforce, damaging the local economy.

Our View

The leadership at Technology Inc. was strong, clear, and engaged in its intention to avoid such a step, and its resolve added impetus to the culture change initiative. Bart and his team demonstrated the advantages of sharing control; they also maintained good time sense and continually clarified their intentions behind any changes. To be sure, the journey may never be complete, but there is a sense that the organization had made fundamental, sustainable changes that yielded competitive advantage in its industry.

Professional Services Inc.

Initial challenges to Professional Services Inc. (PSI) included a loss of strategic focus following on the heels of numerous mergers and acquisitions and a longstanding sense of entitlement held by the core workforce.

Business Strategy

PSI's strategy was twofold: (1) integrate divisions for shared learning and gain efficiencies from shared systems and (2) differentiate and drive product lines in each of its markets. Its main focus would be flawless execution. Its management imperative to each executive was to return stakeholder value. The business strategy emphasized winning in each segment even if success in one was detrimental to success in others.

Leadership Strategy

Because execution was the primary focus, there was no substantial commitment to the development of the leadership culture. PSI had limited tolerance for development activity. Action development was not a priority. Specific leader development activities were limited to individual training for executives and specialized half-day events for the divisions.

Leadership Culture

An Independent-Achiever mind-set drove PSI senior managers; however, significant segments of stagnant Conformer subcultures remained resident across divisions. All activities were focused on achieving results. Minimal regard was paid to the kind of engagement required to integrate divisions and systems to benefit the whole enterprise.

Leadership Readiness

Some members of the senior CLT were at a higher level of readiness than the company's CEO, Art, but they were unable to leverage their readiness to affect the organization. These members with advanced leader logics spoke out for developing collaborative capability for the shared work of integrating divisions and systems, but received only lip service as a response. The senior team was not aligned toward the change effort required.

Although Art attended executive development programs that he described as profound personal change experiences, he was not ready to take on the personal and public risks of culture change. He would not tolerate becoming vulnerable to a board or to shareholders who had made it clear that the short-term bottom line was what mattered. Nor was he able to create the direction for his team to develop its readiness to transform the business and culture.

Despite their bringing in coaching and consulting services from multiple vendors for organization development and culture work, Art and his CLT focused almost exclusively on business strategy and systems, structures, and process of change management. Their drive for short-term results overwhelmed any commitment to a process of engaging and leveraging the personal and collective readiness of the team to bring about durable change.

In a mature and crowded segment of the professional services industry, PSI was able to increase its profits in the short term in some markets but was unable to create the culture of innovation it needed in order to develop market share and keep it competitive. Within a few years, separate business units were sold off, and the enterprise was reduced to one last operating division.

Our View

The business and leadership strategies at PSI were doomed by its leaders' lack of intentionality about advancing its leadership logic. Expecting employees simply to get results and make money reinforced the stagnating culture by reinforcing a resistance to change. In the absence of Art's meaningful commitment to apply his own personal transformation, his reaching outside to consultants without reaching inside for intentionality was a sign that transformation was not really feasible. Committed to tight fiscal control from the top and its short-term time sense, and focused on satisfying the demands of financial analysts, Art never became ready to alter and develop himself and his team, much less the organization.

Memorial Hospital

The challenge to Memorial Hospital was that its catchment area was economically depressed, demographics were shifting, and competition was rising around it in the regional health care industry. For example, several outside specialty health care centers threatened to siphon off customers.

Business Strategy

Memorial Hospital's strategy was to achieve competitive advantage through more customer-friendly operations. Facing increasing competition and regulation, the organization sought to become more dominant in its catchment area by emphasizing "an exquisite customer experience." Business operations such

as single-station services and improved emergency room facilities would be made possible by new physical planning and
reconstruction.

Leadership Strategy

The challenge called for more collaborative customer focus
with distributed decision making in the leadership culture and
throughout the organization. The CLT and all operating committees would be the vehicles of action development.

Leadership Culture

Memorial was a classic Conformer culture. Set in a conventional part of the country, the "don't make waves" local society
reinforced cautious, follow-the-rules conformance to standards.
Moving first to an Achiever culture with independent decision
making was essential in implementing the hospital's business
and leadership strategy and to building pockets of interdependent leadership beliefs and practices over time.

Leadership Readiness

The CLT continued to guide and encourage transformation
even though chief executive officer Glen struggled to remain
only partially engaged at the beginning of the journey. However,
Glen's ultimate willingness to develop his own leadership logic
to include Freethinker and aspects of Collaborator was a key
contribution to the transformation that was achieved. In fact,
the entire executive team rose to Freethinker logics as well.

One powerful member of the senior leadership team worked
covertly to undermine the transformation, however. And being
ready to deal with this individual was a fundamental challenge.
Ultimately the CLT was able to support Glen's decisive action to
sever ties to this disruptive team member, a senior vice president,

which led to astounding positive results in the leadership culture. This significant catalyst opened up the path for all management in the expanding leadership culture and boosted alignment in the transformation work.

Our View

At Memorial, change came about through personal examples set by the CLT and its balanced attention to both change leadership and change management. The team developed into Freethinker leadership logics and made a remarkable commitment to the hospital's transformation.

Change also came about because leadership could tolerate the length of time required to engage with teams, the organization, and the culture and to strengthen intentionality for deep engagement throughout the organization.

Global Electronics

The initial challenge at bustling Global Electronics was the odd fact that for six years, the same unchanged business strategy had called for a biannual doubling of revenues, but revenues had not gone up, and the strategy had been unexamined.

Business Strategy

For all intents and purposes, Global Electronics had no discernible business strategy, and growth remained flat year after year. It retained a corporate strategy officer, but his activities seemed peripheral. The company simply reacted to current conditions with annual downsizing and other cost-cutting measures. Emergency meetings were common. The company confused strategy with unrealistic and unfeasible stretch goals that it consistently failed to attain.

Leadership Strategy

Significant investments in a new corporate university appeared to imply some leadership strategy, yet the executive group was practically void of strategic intent. The university curriculum, primarily training programs, focused only on competencies meant to ensure a talent pipeline. The company's executives had a history of hiring consultants to do organizational and culture development work, but the efforts had had little effect.

Leadership Culture

Dawson, the CEO, himself a Moderator, presided over a Dependent-Conformer culture. Nested in hierarchy, leaders protected themselves from feedback, isolating themselves in a conflict-free field of diplomacy surrounded by operational chaos and annual layoffs. The core organizational culture was mostly made up of people with Specialist logic. The low ceiling of the leadership logic allowed no Headroom, and so there was no truth telling or facing up to the restrictions of the leadership culture. The situation demonstrated reciprocal interplay between a dependent and frustrated workforce and no clear intentionality in the leadership culture to encourage any meaningful engagement.

Leadership Readiness

After years of repeated, unchecked organizational behavior, Global Electronics had only eroding margins and a string of layoffs to show for its efforts. At the start of our work with the company, Dawson expressed strong commitment to the need for aligning leadership with the business strategy. He said this was the only way for the organization to survive and then thrive in a rapidly changing high-tech environment. But as we observed Dawson and his team, we noticed little readiness to challenge any of the major assumptions and beliefs that operated in the organization.

During our efforts to support Dawson in unfreezing his team and the organization, he was very open and personable. Yet in the presence of the team, he glossed over whatever significant challenges were presented. He avoided challenges that he could have used as an opening for engaging deeply with his team and instead pushed that task to us. Whenever team members challenged our framework and process, Dawson reassured them instead of standing up and creating some Headroom for change. It became clear that Dawson used consultants as pawns in his hide-and-seek game of avoiding serious change issues.

The senior team contained a few talented leaders ready to make changes, but when these few risk-taking team members confronted Dawson publicly about the absence of a real business strategy, he became ambivalent and shifted the conversation to operational issues and emergencies. Thus, in public, his Moderator leader logics undermined the change process that he had consistently endorsed in private. At the same time, he sheltered team members who did not want to do change work, assuring them that their wishes mattered.

Our View

Eventually we came to believe that Global Electronics was largely incapable of change and transformation because neither the team nor individuals on it were ready to lead change, and we disengaged. The major obstacles were the CEO's wavering intentions about the need and focus for change, his capitulation to the team around issues of control, and his constant activity without much awareness of the need to think beyond the immediate pressures of time.

A key insight from this case is that Dominators and Moderators in powerful positions will do anything in their power to block significant change. Their logic demands ultimate control and prevents positive conflict in public forums, where learning needs to occur for transformation to take effect. Guided by that leader logic, they disallow inquiry, intentionality, and engagement. The company doggedly pursues an unrealistic goal—doubling revenue every two years—while retreating from the necessary changes required to achieve that goal.

Credlow

The basic challenges for Credlow were dissatisfied customers, increased competition in used car sales, and unstable financial and credit markets.

Business Strategy

Credlow's business strategy was distinct in its market of bad-credit North American car buyers: it wanted to become first choice. To do that, it would deliberately break the old stereotypes about used car dealers preying on customers, usury, ruthless repossession departments, bait-and-switch, and strong-arm tactics for selling whatever cars were on the lot. To sell and finance used cars in this difficult market, a strategy that embraced community support services in underserved neighborhoods required both the right business model and the right culture.

Leadership Strategy

Credlow's top executives spanned a diverse array of leader logics that were dedicated to a systemwide Achiever culture. They were remarkably adept at discerning the need for various levels of leadership logic in various roles, levels, and divisions across the enterprise. They chose a tiered strategy to develop all individual managers toward an Achiever leader logic. Various teams would reinforce that ethic and push for excellence and performance. The strategy also called for raising the entire senior leadership culture to Freethinker leadership logics where feasible. One distinct advantage was that Roger, the CEO, demonstrated leader logic that spanned the range from Achiever to Transformer.

Other elements of the leadership strategy included emphasizing and rewarding cross-functional problem solving, promoting action and frequent informal communication, eliminating complacency, and fostering constructive debate to build an environment that would move the senior leadership culture toward a self-generating organic enterprise capable of facing and executing the challenging business strategy.

Leadership Culture

Credlow started out as a mixed Conformer and Achiever culture. The senior team was clearly committed to developing a leadership culture that stood out from the rest of the industry. Credlow's leadership wanted to stand out by enacting values based on service relationships in an underserved market. They provided security and safety to customers in terms of how well the used cars would perform and be serviced and in terms of the financial transactions offered under the Credlow banner.

Leadership Readiness

CEO Roger was committed to leading a transformation. To that end, he and his senior leadership team went through leadership culture development work together. The collective learning was that Credlow could build interdependence only on a foundation of independence. The senior leaders committed to deliberately pursuing both independence (up from dependence) and interdependence.

The senior leadership team members felt exhilarated by their experiences as Freethinkers. During our work with Credlow, we have seen the emergence among them of a number of Interdependent leadership practices. Role definitions of managers are purposefully left open-ended, and managers work across functional and territorial boundaries to integrate their work as a whole. Decisions are guided by lots of informal and formal conversations, including multiple perspectives from both specialists and nonspecialists. The hierarchy shares power with the network of dealerships. Experimentation is normal, and failure is an expected part of the change process. Individual and organizational development are seen as part of the work to fulfill the business strategy.

Our View

From the start, Roger's intentionality regarding culture transformation and his continuous engagement with leaders, the workforce, and clients have been crucial in embedding change at Credlow. His actions are also a constant reminder to his team and the larger workforce that business strategy and leadership strategy are linked and that both must be reflected in problem solving, decision making, and execution.

NuSystems Inc.

This public service specialist institution had enjoyed many years without much competition, but now, in the face of such competition, the organization was dwindling.

Business Strategy

NuSystems' strategy was a mosh of competing priorities. Unable to choose and prioritize a few areas of central focus (the essence of strategy), it continued to burden itself with reactive operations, unguided by clear goals or strategic priorities. To the extent there was a strategy, it was simply a matter of different units within NuSystems attempting to generate products, services, and cost savings in order to increase their influence and degrees of freedom in the organization. This behavior placed the organization at a Conformer level; more specifically, the Specialist leader logic was prominent.

Leadership Strategy

Having no coherent business strategy, NuSystems had never discussed a leadership strategy or invested significantly in leadership development systems or events. That it had no leadership succession pipeline was not a matter of concern.

Yet an implicit and informal leadership development strategy was in play. Having one's expert talents and achievements showcased and touted was the pathway to management. Endemic to this Specialist culture was the informal practice of promoting good individual performers to management. That was the only succession system operating.

Leadership Culture

As experts in their craft, Specialists form a leadership logic and culture that naturally tends to be in transition between Conformer and Achiever. But NuSystems, made up almost entirely of Specialists, was embedded in a Dependent-Conformer core culture. It was also stuck there because it was unable to focus on the broader competitive situation and the innovations that would allow it to move naturally toward an Achiever culture.

Leadership Readiness

NuSystems' CEO, Liam, was devoted to his company's preeminence in the service industry, but the workforce was divided over both the mission of the organization and the way it was being managed and led. Hard work was common, but strong professional management was not the organization's strong suit, and this was true for Liam and most of his executive team. Still, when Liam engaged us, he pledged to support the culture work and the work of his team first.

As the work unfolded at NuSystems, we began to see that Liam wasn't really ready to be an instrument of culture change. For example, he insisted that all ideas pass through him before they were explored with the executive team. The effect of this need for control was a narrowing of issues that could be explored within the executive team or in the general leadership culture. Moreover, the executive team's significant issues and its pursuant questions were often undiscussable and were taken off the table. It became clear that NuSystems would not allow the conflict necessary for learning.

As a consequence, we recommended the creation of a CLT that could explore further into the company's human and operational systems. As we continued to work for discovery using information obtained through surveys, focus groups, and other internal sources, Liam increasingly insisted that all the information generated in the culture work be distilled for his editing and release. In advance of any face-to-face meetings with his team or other change leaders in the organization, he wanted control of the organizational messages. Liam wanted no surprises.

Because of the commitment of some on the change leadership team, we continued to work with NuSystems over several quarters. However, ultimately it was clear that Liam wanted primarily to manage the board's perceptions of him, the executive team, and the organization, not to change the leadership culture. Managing appearances and avoiding conflict were personal drivers that he was unable to control. Several of his key supporters also wanted activity but not real change. They wanted only to mollify constituents with an appearance of good-faith effort.

Our View

The NuSystems story illustrates the power of the leader in shaping what change is acceptable. It shows how important it is that leaders be personally ready and committed if real organization change is to occur. The end game for NuSystems was a continued appearance of a culture change effort until Liam moved on and passed the challenges facing NuSystems to his successors. This story is also an illustration of the negative influence of tightly held central controls, exaggerated time pressures, ill-defined intentions, lack of engagement, and the contradictions between Performer and Freethinker aspirations and ingrained Moderator leader logics.

The Pattern

After reviewing these cases, is it clear to you which leadership logics prevent change almost no matter what other conditions exist? Do you see also the power of leadership readiness?

When they call us, some clients are raring to go with immediate work in the culture. We advise them that first they should ready the team. After that, it may be feasible to launch further work in the middle. A thorough process of discovery is the most important investment that any company can make in doing serious change work. A nickel's worth of discovery and feasibility analysis up-front can save a fortune and eons of wasted time spent on unsuccessful change efforts.

Exercises

Questions
Reflect on and record your insights from each of this chapter's six stories:

- What insights do they give you into your own readiness to lead others in the change process?

- Can you recall a personal change or transformation experience that provided you with lessons and insights that you use whenever confronted with the dynamics of change in others at the individual, team, and organization levels? Can you name the lessons and tell a story about how you have used these lessons intentionally and the impact you have observed?

- Are you clear about what type of leadership culture and logic your organization needs in order to achieve direction, alignment, and commitment now and into the future?

- What do you still need to clarify?

- What will you do to make yourself ready?

Profile Your Organization

Write a profile of your organization's business strategy, leadership strategy, leadership culture, and leadership readiness. Note where the profile seems clearest and where it reflects confusion or gaps.

11

FEASIBILITY MAPS AND CHANGEABILITY

So, if you find nothing in the corridors open the doors, if you find nothing behind these doors there are more floors, and if you find nothing up there, don't worry, just leap another flight of stairs. As long as you don't stop climbing, the stairs won't end, under your climbing feet they will go on growing upwards.

—*Franz Kafka*

Whew! Oh my! All right! Can it be? From our experience, these are likely to be words and questions that are circling in your mind and the emotions palpitating your heart. We are with you. As authors, we have shared similar reactions within ourselves and observed them in our clients. In the case of the six organizations and their leadership profiled in this book, the feelings observed and reported have ranged from confusion, to anxiety, to elation, and finally to validation.

Deep change may well be feasible in you and your organization. It was for Bart at Technology Inc., for Glen at Memorial Hospital, and for Roger at Credlow. If things had been a little different, it might also have turned out more feasible at NuSystems, Global Electronics, and Professional Services Inc. What matters now is figuring out what change you want to bring about and how feasible that is in terms of your leadership logic, leader logics, and culture.

Both of us are avid fly-fishing anglers. As part of our journey, we have learned the importance of being prepared before we set out. We need to have some forecast of the weather, the water conditions, the current insect hatch, as well as the lessons of prior experience (when we lost flies and did not have replacements, for example, or did not have the right flies and lost out on the potential for a big catch). These experiences are analogous to gauging readiness and feasibility to handle the emergent and the changeable as part of our responsibility in guiding leadership culture transformation. From our engagements with Technology Inc., Memorial Hospital, and Credlow, we look for the lessons of experience as well as project forward from those experiences to assessing readiness and feasibility. Moreover, through our own reflections on our work with NuSystems, Global Electronics, and Professional Services Inc., we have come to understand better what could have been a more insightful preparation for readiness and feasibility.

Mapping Feasibility of Success: A Tool

It took us a while ourselves to see that leaders and organizations need to take steps early on to map the feasibility of culture change or transformation. Once we saw that need, we began to apply our research and practice to creating a helpful tool.

Figures 11.1, 11.2, and 11.3 present numerical scales and graphic frameworks (we call them maps) on which to chart feasibility results for an organization. As you can see, Figure 11.1 concerns individual senior leaders, 11.2 concerns the senior team, and 11.3 looks at the broader leadership culture. Notice also that the scales differ from map to map, as summarized in Table 11.1. Each exercise (Exercises 11.1, 11.2, and 11.3) derives from the concepts and research contained in previous chapters. Completing all three exercises should deepen your appreciation of the interconnectedness of all the concepts we have discussed.

We recommend you first complete the exercises yourself; then ask other individuals on your team to do so, both individually and as a group. By completing the scales and graphs, you can

Table 11.1 Feasibility Map Scales

Individual	Senior Team	Leadership Culture
Control source	Team work style	Scope of awareness
Time sense	Trust	Learning orientation
Intentionality	Learning environment	Strategic scope
Leader logic	Strategic action logic	Senior team change orientation
Values	Information	Development
Change guide	Partnership	Belief system

compile data that will help you judge your and your organization's level of feasibility for transforming its leadership culture. The results will be useful for your own thinking and for discussion among your senior team.

Following the exercises, we discuss how each of the six case organizations would likely have scored on each of the three feasibility maps had we been mapping them when we began our work with each.

Exercise 11.1   Individual Leader Feasibility Exercise

Circle the number that best represents your position on each continuum.

Control source. When making decisions I am guided primarily by:

1	2	3	4	5	6	7	8	9
goals and objectives for my role						my internal compass oriented to linking present with future		

Time sense. In carrying out my responsibilities, I:

1	2	3	4	5	6	7	8	9
carefully plan each day with lists of specific tasks to be done						leave open space each day to engage with people or the unexpected		

Intentionality. In setting direction for developing the organization, I focus on and emphasize:

1	2	3	4	5	6	7	8	9
objectives for the year and targets for each quarter						objectives that will stretch my leadership logic and those of the people in the organization		

Leader logic. In leading the organization, I actively:

1	2	3	4	5	6	7	8	9
take control while exploiting opportunities						reach out to others to partner with me in going beyond the expected		

Values. It is important to me that managers and employees:

1	2	3	4	5	6	7	8	9
are loyal and consistently do what top leadership expects						actively pursue creativity in work and relationships and constantly look for ways to serve the greater good		

Change guide. When confronted with the need for change, I:

1	2	3	4	5	6	7	8	9
focus on methods that have proven to work in the past in this or other organizations						engage with diverse people to generate as many possibilities for successfully guiding change as possible and explore the choices that are on the leading edge		

Figure 11.1 illustrates how responses to the prompts in Exercise 11.1 can be mapped.

Figure 11.1 Individual Feasibility Map

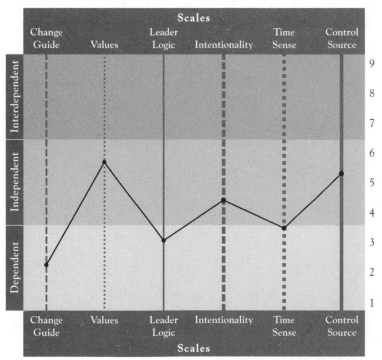

Individual Map

Exercise 11.2 Senior Leadership Team Feasibility Exercise

Circle the number that best represents your position on each continuum.

Team work style. The work of the senior team is characterized by:

1	2	3	4	5	6	7	8	9
a strong leader who makes most operational decisions and expects compliance from team members						regular team and frequent subgroup meetings with the main focus on big issues		

Trust. The team is:

1	2	3	4	5	6	7	8	9
closed and secretive and operates with many hidden agendas						open, transparent, and trusting of team members and others in the organization		

Learning environment. The team supports and reinforces a work environment where:

1	2	3	4	5	6	7	8	9
being right is highly valued and mistakes are frowned on						learning happens together in public, and mistakes are treated as learning opportunities		

Strategic action logic. This is a senior team that is:

1	2	3	4	5	6	7	8	9
insular, reactive, and simplistic in its perspective about business strategy and the external world						proactive, dynamic, and global in its perspective about business strategy and the external world		

Information. The senior team:

1	2	3	4	5	6	7	8	9
keeps most information to itself and shares only what it must						is very open and transparent in sharing information		

Partnership. Members of the senior team are:

1	2	3	4	5	6	7	8	9
self-centered and emphasize the importance of their authority to the success of the organization						partners in addressing current and future success for the organization, not for their individual benefit		

Figure 11.2 illustrates how responses to the exercise prompts in Exercise 11.2 can be mapped.

Figure 11.2 Senior Team Feasibility Map

Senior Team Map

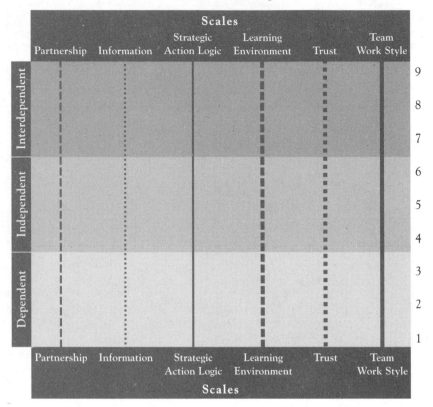

Exercise 11.3 Leadership Culture Feasibility Exercise

Circle the number that best represents your position on each continuum.

Scope of awareness. Leadership in this organization focuses on:

1	2	3	4	5	6	7	8	9
the task—getting the job done now						business strategy, leadership, and execution		

Learning orientation. The organization emphasizes learning that is:

1	2	3	4	5	6	7	8	9
focused on technical knowledge and skills to increase performance and productivity today						for the collective, transcending the here-and-now, with potential for moving people and the organization toward the next leadership logic		

Strategic scope. Strategic work in this organization is:

1	2	3	4	5	6	7	8	9
incremental and driven by reflections on past successes and image in the marketplace						generative and driven by an expansive view of the future and its creation		

Senior team change orientation. The top leadership team is:

1	2	3	4	5	6	7	8	9
opportunistic, directive, and controlling						strategic, imaginative, and collaborative		

Development. This organization is characterized by:

1	2	3	4	5	6	7	8	9
a short-term focus on improving talent, systems, and processes						a comprehensive approach to developing human systems and operational systems to sustain outputs and changeability		

Belief system. The prevailing assumptions and attitudes are:

1	2	3	4	5	6	7	8	9
conservative, "either-or" in solving problems and making decisions—a black-and-white mind-set						creative and transformative in terms of "both-and" problem solving; people use paradox to generate action and invite open expression of intuition and emotions		

Figure 11.3 illustrates how responses to the exercise prompts in Exercise 11.3 can be mapped.

Feasibility in the Cases

To illustrate the application of the feasibility mapping exercises to leadership culture transformation, we have gone back to our six cases and done a retrospective mapping. These stories and illustrations can help you guide a similar discovery and dialogue process for your executive team, for a CLT (if one exists in your

Figure 11.3 Leadership Culture Feasibility Map

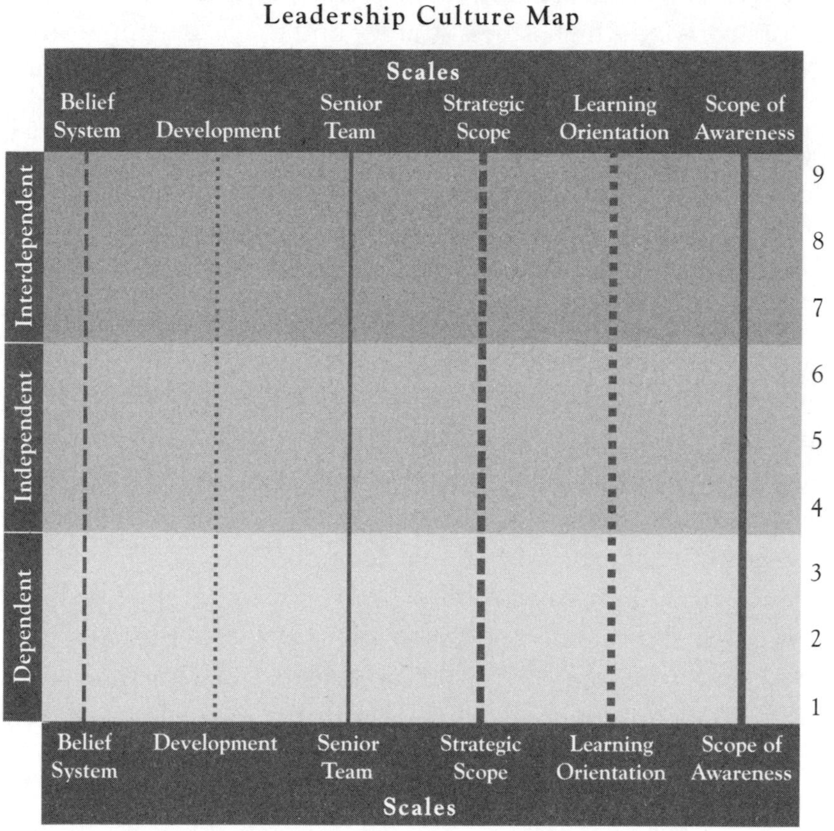

Leadership Culture Map

	Scales					
	Belief System	Development	Senior Team	Strategic Scope	Learning Orientation	Scope of Awareness

(vertical axis labels, top to bottom: Interdependent, Independent, Dependent; right-side numeric scale 9, 8, 7, 6, 5, 4, 3, 2, 1)

	Belief System	Development	Senior Team	Strategic Scope	Learning Orientation	Scope of Awareness
			Scales			

organization), and for a leadership culture discovery process. Following this or a similar process, you will be able to navigate from your leadership collective's current stage to a desired future stage.

Technology Inc.

When we first connected with Bart at Technology Inc., it quickly became apparent that Bart was a smart entrepreneur with a genuine desire to develop the company toward a more Interdependent-Collaborative leadership culture. As we reported in Chapter Ten, the business strategy and the leadership strategy were in sync. Still, was it feasible to move this well-established, Conformer leadership culture to an Achiever culture with some pockets of Collaborative leadership? Could Bart's intentionality and engagement have an impact on the feasibility and readiness to lead change among the rest of the senior leaders?

Individual Level. Let us look retrospectively at Bart. If we had mapped him on individual leader feasibility on the control source scale, he would have scored at a Conformer level; his time sense would have placed him on the transitional cusp between Achiever and Collaborator; his intentionality would have been transitional between Conformer and Achiever. He operated with Freethinker leader logic, but his values were still defined by a Conformer culture. On the change guide scale, he was down the middle and pragmatic. Of these, the four measures that were most favorable for success were his time sense, his evolving intentionality, his Freethinker leader logic, and his change guide pragmatism. These four enabled him to engage fully with his senior team and the workforce and to relinquish enough control to support the Headroom necessary to develop the leadership culture in line with the leadership strategy.

Senior Team Level. Mapping senior team feasibility at Technology Inc. would have revealed three qualities that crucially supported Bart at his individual level of feasibility. The three also reinforced forward development in the leadership culture.

First, the senior group's team work style lined up with Bart's control source at the Conformer level, with the exception of one key member who had been with Bart since the company began. She was higher—more oriented to broader engagements and discussion of the bigger picture. She was an important internal supporter of Bart's individual development to more awareness of and comfort with his control source. She also drew out his intentionality, helping him toward deeper introspection and toward shifting it toward a more transformative perspective.

Second, the team score would be very high on trust, at a level strongly associated with a Collaborative leadership culture. This helps explain the deeper level of engagement within the team. It expanded their concept of a *learning environment* (and raised them on that scale) from technical skills to softer skills focusing on communications and interpersonal relationships, both of which are requisite for engagement and Headroom to move a leadership culture toward a bigger stage.

Third, on the strategic action logic scale, the team had a mixture of some individuals more comfortable with Conformer logic and some at a more global level. The team's overall middle-of-the-road pragmatic scores suggest it was feasible for it to guide change in support of the business strategy and the leadership strategy. Reflecting on what would have been revealed by the fifth scale, information, we would be less encouraged: a Conformer view of sharing information. In fact, we observed vigorous disagreement about how much to share and with whom to share outside the senior team. But this negative factor was counterbalanced by a clearly collaborative partnership score.

Leadership Culture Level. In retrospect, Technology Inc.'s leadership culture was the most constraining of the three feasibility assessments. Strategic scope would reveal that the company was on the cusp between Achiever and Collaborator, and the senior team change orientation reached the level of early-state Achiever, but the other four scales would all be Conformer. Among these four, the opening gambit had to take on the belief system. To move the leadership culture to support the business strategy and the leadership strategy, the dominant beliefs had to move beyond the Joe Sixpack perspective of "I do my eight and hit the gate."

Now What for Technology Inc.? If we had done the feasibility map for Technology Inc. prior to our working with the company, the maps would have revealed a better than zero-sum chance for sustainable change. A few key scale results would lead to an overall conclusion of feasibility. At the individual level, Bart's time sense, his leader logic, his change guide pragmatism, and his evolving intentionality were all constructive. For the senior team, the levels of trust, partnership, and evolving learning environment were key. In the leadership culture, the strategic scope level would help significantly in building and sustaining sufficient Headroom draft.

Professional Services Inc.

The transformation opportunity for PSI initially was cast as moving from Conformer over time to Collaborator in order to dispel the image of the legacy company from which PSI was renamed and was to be reinvented. PSI's business strategy was to integrate divisions and systems while emphasizing market-driven approaches for each strategic business unit. Yet the leadership strategy and the surrounding leadership culture were strongly oriented to the short term (a common pattern in Conformer cultures) and maximizing the gain of each business unit (a common pattern in Achiever cultures).

Individual Level. Initially we found the CEO highly committed to his own development and the development of the organization. Had we mapped his individual leader feasibility, it would have revealed both challenges and opportunities. Adam's control source profile would be in the Achiever range. As an Achiever, he was struggling to integrate his own internal compass with the Outside-In demands of the shareholders. His time sense, intentionality, and change guide scores would all be typical of a conformer. At the same time, his leader logic and values would scale out as those of an Achiever-Specialist-Performer.

Adam was clearly action oriented, exploring the possibility of bridging from a historically Conformer culture to a high-performer culture with collaborative characteristics.

Senior Team Level. PSI's senior team members held diverse perspectives on leadership culture, from Conformer to Achiever to Freethinker/Collaborator. The team's most striking result on the map would have been strategic action logic. Individually and collectively, the team emphasized being proactive, dynamic, and global in perspective around the business strategy. Clearly, from a development perspective, this was something that should be constructively leveraged. The dilemmas for this team in terms of feasibility involved trust and partnership. Although resources were constrained within the organization as a whole, each business unit head was expected to maximize that unit's contribution to the bottom line. Meanwhile, units were free to compete with each other for resources. This produced competition, withholding of information, and a culture made of people with the leader logic of dominating Achievers who emphasized the needs of their group over the needs of the company as a whole. The team work style and the learning environment were characteristic of an Achiever development stage. Members of the team took their lead from Adam and rarely pushed back unless his decision challenged the goals of their own individual business unit. The learning environment at our point of entry was clearly focused on knowledge and skills to perform better and produce more in response to Outside-In demands of the market.

Leadership Culture Level. Five of the leadership culture scales were in the Achiever zone; the sixth, scope of awareness, was borderline Conformer. Awareness was high about past, present, and future image, as defined almost solely by whether someone was delivering results with flawless execution. The leadership culture's learning orientation and development perspective emphasized a Conformer approach for the workforce but a more Freethinker/Collaborator approach for senior leaders and directors. From a feasibility perspective, this split emphasis reduced the feasibility of change in that it obstructed the development of Headroom draft; and without that draft, the leadership culture was unlikely to collaborate more.

While the senior team was strategic and imaginative, this was counterbalanced by the culture's Conformer scope of awareness.

Now What for Professional Services Inc.? In retrospect, feasibility mapping for PSI suggests that an assertive senior team with bigger leadership logic on several dimensions than the CEO could have become a force for transformation. To make this happen, work could have been done to address issues of trust and partnership. By developing more trust in each other and becoming partners, not competitors, the team might have leveraged its strategic action logic to generate the engagement and Headroom across the organization to support developing to a more fully formed Achiever leadership culture and the beginning steps toward a more collaborative leadership. Unfortunately PSI didn't go this route.

Feasibility at Memorial Hospital

The business strategy presented to us at Memorial Hospital emphasized achievement, and the leadership strategy was worded in the language of collaboration. At the same time, the culture at Memorial Hospital was clearly Conformer. In such a context, feasibility mapping would have been an important antecedent to determining the best direction for change.

Individual Level. Glen, the hospital's chief executive, had an individual feasibility map that registers Freethinker/Collaborator on the dimensions of time sense, intentionality, and values.

He sought to leverage these dimensions by playing the role of coach/facilitator in supporting the evolving leadership logic of various members of his senior team. His control source and leader logic scores illustrate his internal tensions around dealing with conflict and the oppositional voice of one of the senior vice presidents. So while Glen was very much guided by his internal compass, he often defaulted to goals and objectives for his role when confronted by this particular adversary. This tension manifested itself in a leader logic of controlling conflict while seeking to move the hospital culture initially to an Achiever stage (Glen's ultimate goal was to reach the collaboration stage). We believe these strains in his individual feasibility contributed directly to his pragmatic achiever/adapter change guide orientation.

Among all Glen's dimensions, what stood out most was values: he strongly believed and said that all employees could make a difference and everyone should try.

Senior Team Level. Assessing feasibility for the senior team is complicated by the presence of an outspoken, negative senior vice president who opposed any idea of change. His dominating personality and skill at leveraging Outside-In forces to support his position detracted from the overall feasibility profile for this team. Consequently the feasibility of the team's fully engaging in the early stages of the change process was limited by lack of trust, which in turn generated obstacles to truly meaningful partnerships within the team and between the team and the broader hospital community. The most promising signs of team feasibility were the team's profiles in learning environment, information, and strategic action logic. Its positive qualities in these areas were visible in the hospital environment and in dealings between the team and the broader hospital community. The team drew inner strength from these dimensions in the face of the constant conflict and tension generated by the opposing senior vice president.

Leadership Culture Level. Mapping the leadership culture would have shown an overall pattern of Achiever leadership. The leadership was using collaborative processes to engage the workforce and to move the Dependent-Conformer organization culture toward more independent achievement.

Scope of awareness, senior team change orientation, and development scales are all strongly Achiever. Learning orientation and strategic scope are on the cusp between Conformer and Achiever, which is not surprising given the nature of health care and the history of Memorial Hospital in particular. From a feasibility perspective, critical leverage could be found in the leadership culture's belief system. Despite the one outspoken naysayer, the belief system was early-state Collaborator, and it could generate creative, collaborative mechanisms for solving problems and serving the greater good. Although Conformer work environments don't generally foster open expression and constructive use of intuition and emotions, the most senior executives were fostering it at Memorial by their actions as role models.

Now What for Memorial? The overall feasibility map shows many indicators that Memorial can raise its odds for successful transformation, create draft for and reinforce Headroom, and generate deeper exploration and commitment to engagement. In turn we could reasonably expect an intentional, values-based evolution of both individual and collective leadership logics. At Memorial we could foresee a late-stage Achiever culture developing toward a transitional Achiever/Collaborator state.

Feasibility at Global Electronics

That Global Electronics had no serviceable business strategy limits the meaningfulness of mapping transformation feasibility. The leadership strategy was defaulting to whatever was designed and delivered by its corporate university. Moreover, the organization culture was strongly Conformer and struggling with defining an identity for a company that was both Asian and American.

Individual Level. Dawson, the CEO, was a Moderator, a conflict-averse pleaser aided and abetted by a co-CEO who was oriented toward results rather than change. In creating Dawson's individual feasibility map, we discovered that his intentionality and espoused values contrasted sharply with his profiles for control source, time sense, leader logic, and change guide. In terms of intentionality, he was an articulate voice for the importance of developing himself, the team, and the organization toward a bigger mind and an Achiever leadership culture with purposeful pockets of collaboration. Moreover, his value position was what we would associate with a Freethinker: it focused on creativity and intuition in work that served a broader purpose than technical quality alone.

However, Dawson's control source, time sense, leader logic, and change guide would have been more telling indicators of what was likely to happen. Related to control source, he often talked about being guided by his internal compass in discussions with us, but when he was with the team, he talked instead about the goals and objectives for his role. In turn, his team focused on goals and objectives for their respective roles, not on the bigger picture of the organization and its future. With regard to time sense, Dawson rarely left his office, expecting those who needed his involvement to come to him. He expressed pride in having lots of time to read the latest academic and trade books on strategy, leadership, and change. His leader logic mirrored his penchant for avoiding conflict while looking good to his team, his co-CEO, and the parent company and appearing to be willing to exploit emergent opportunities for the business. From a change guide perspective, he focused totally on exploring and then implementing what had proven to work in other organizations, regardless of whether it matched Global Electronic's strategy and culture.

Senior Team Level. Dawson's senior leadership team operated most comfortably with a Conformer style, although two outliers on the team sought to lead it toward Achiever practices using a collaborative process. In keeping with Conformer team work style norms, the team supported regular team meetings and frequent subgroup meetings to explore direction, alignment, and commitment. By all other measures on the map, the senior team was clearly Conformer. Trust level was low, and many hidden agendas operated among certain team members. Other team members chose to go it alone. For Global Electronics to develop in the direction espoused by Dawson, feasibility hinged critically on the team's learning to engage intentionally and meaningfully with each other and the broader workforce on change issues. But the learning environment supported by the team focused on formal programs, especially those being created by the corporate university. At meetings of the senior team, we could see that its strategic action logic was insular, reactive, and simplistic when it handled business strategy.

Remember that the company's revenue goal had been the same for six consecutive years, and during that time, no one had ever openly explored changes that might produce a different outcome. This avoidance was reflected as well in the team's approach to information. Discussions at the business unit and the senior team levels were tightly controlled, and information was shared only on a need-to-know basis. It was not surprising that in terms of partnership, the members of the team were largely self-centered, self-aggrandizing, and accustomed to playing blame games about performance, productivity, and strategic business outcomes.

Leadership Culture Level. Mapping the leadership culture's feasibility turned out much the same in tenor and impact as the mapping for Dawson and the senior team. Scope of awareness and learning orientation leaned modestly toward an Achiever culture. Feasibility in this regard would accrue more from a general desire to remain competitive in the industry than it would from any intentional belief system or strategic scope. Shifts in business strategy had been largely incremental, aimed at appearing proactive. Consistent with a Conformer culture, the belief system was conservative, with a cut-and-dried, black-and-white mind-set about defining and solving problems. Leadership cannot intentionally engage in climbing the stairs toward a bigger mind unless that process is supported by leadership's development philosophy. But Global Electronic's development view was all short term and based on the idea that talent was best developed by its own training programs in its corporate university. Changes to systems and processes related to productivity and effectiveness were seen largely as matters of fine-tuning what was already in operation. Our suggestions to explore a long-term strategic approach to the development of individuals, teams, work groups, and the leadership culture were treated as if we were speaking a foreign language.

Now What for Global Electronics? The Global Electronics feasibility maps demonstrate the importance and value of mapping feasibility before embarking on efforts to change, and the adage that hindsight is 20–20 certainly holds true for our engagement with the company. Granted, these feasibility mappings (like the other mappings in this chapter that focus on the six organizations whose stories we have told) are all post hoc, retrospective. But had we been ready with our feasibility mapping process at the time we were working with Global Electronics, we might have been able to see different opportunities there and to open some different doors. We might have been able to co-create a different path toward the Headroom that the company clearly needed.

Feasibility at Credlow

Credlow's business strategy was to break the old stereotypes about used car dealers and so become the company of choice for car buyers with bad credit. The leadership strategy was continuing to evolve, but at the time of our initial engagement, it was primarily an Achiever strategy with variation in the leader logics of senior team members, including Moderator, Specialist, Performer, Freethinker, and Collaborator. The CEO, Roger, was a Freethinker/Transformer in his leader logic. His strategic intent was to leverage the best qualities of Specialists, Performers, and Freethinkers among the management ranks to climb the staircase he was putting in place. In that way, Credlow could develop toward a leadership culture with sustainable change practices to ultimately become a transformative leadership culture and a model of serving not just its customer base but also the broader community.

Individual Level. Because of our previous remarks about our work with Credlow, you won't be surprised that our retrospective feasibility map verifies our initial view of Roger as a transformer, sage, guide, and creator. His scores are between 7 and 9 on all six scales. His leader logic and change guide scores match exactly. In modeling a consistent reaching out to partner with others, he surpasses typical behavior in used car companies. Moreover, he continuously engages with all comers—Moderator, Specialist, Performer, or Freethinker—to generate ideas and increase changeability, always intent on developing his team and Credlow's leadership culture to the bigger minds of a high-performing Collaborator culture.

Notwithstanding the significant business challenges in our early involvement with Roger and Credlow, he was still able to maintain his intentionality to stretch himself and others at Credlow while at the same time meeting aggressive financial and operational targets. For Roger, control source and time sense are about Inside-Out practices. They reinforce his own values and the value base among the senior leaders that can advance the leadership culture toward transformational practices and outcomes. For Roger, feasibility derives from and depends on his applying methods consistent with his own profile to move the feasibility and leadership logic of the entire enterprise.

Senior Team Level. As a whole, the senior team at Credlow showed Achiever level on its feasibility map. Although some on the team would defer to Roger and expect him to make decisions for them to execute, Roger's own style had created a team work style that is more typical of Performers than of Conformers. The team maintains a balance between doing what is best for "me and my function" and doing what is best for Credlow. This balance gives them the means to intentionally engage the large workforce in sustaining Headroom. In turn, Headroom allows them to climb collectively toward a next-stage leadership culture.

Trust, information, and partnership all score midway between Conformer and Collaborator. These are also encouraging results. The team's current practices along these three dimensions are constructive and instructive for a larger workforce that had displayed residual elements of a Conformer culture at the beginning of the journey. The learning environment is still more typical of an early-stage Achiever culture than of a late-stage Achiever culture. It can develop further within the team and the evolving leadership culture. The senior team's strategic action logic rests on Achiever mind-set soil but is openly pursuing a larger, more expansive understanding of the place of Credlow in the used car industry and as a good steward for the communities in which it operates.

Leadership Culture Level. Consonant with our earlier comments about Credlow's leadership culture, its feasibility map scores range from early-stage Achiever to early-stage Collaborator. Its high scope of awareness shows a leadership culture in an early Collaborator stage of development. From Roger to the senior team to functional and local dealer meetings, the conversations embrace strategy implementation, business development, and developing leadership logics and the leadership culture. This scope of conversation can help the climb continue by reiterating the benefits of organizational change. Strategic scope lags awareness because some leaders and some parts of the organization are still recovering from their experience fighting for survival after a downturn in the image and the profitability of the business. But some Performers and Freethinkers among the leadership are increasingly open to exploring what can be accomplished if they take an expansive view of the future they can achieve by leveraging values and belief systems. The belief system is largely consistent with what one would expect in a leadership culture that includes a substantial number of Freethinkers.

Credlow's senior team is not homogeneous in its mind-set and practices. The Specialists and Performers on the team still behave from time to time in directive, controlling, and self-centered ways. Meanwhile, the Performers and Freethinkers are more attuned to collaborating strategically and asking "What if?" to imagine and visualize a future developmental stage.

At the beginning of Credlow's transformation, development was largely about knowledge and skill building. Now, due to other elements at work in the leadership culture, there is movement toward a bigger mind in exploring the importance of self-awareness, spirit, values, and intentionality. That movement suggests the feasibility of developing human capital, operational systems, and an Inside-Out mentality to complement the Outside-In.

Now What for Credlow? Overall, there are many indicators that Credlow could develop a bigger mind regarding change. In the light of Roger's transformation leadership logic, the diversity of leadership logics within the senior team, and the overarching umbrella of intentionality, values, and belief systems, it seems highly probable that Credlow will surpass its current state. It is tempting to call Credlow our poster child case for leadership culture transformation.

Feasibility at NuSystems

In our earlier accounts of prospects for change at NuSystems, we noted disconnects between business strategy, leadership strategy, and leadership logic. You may recall that the "business strategy" simply directed business units to generate revenue in order to increase influence and degrees of freedom, presumed to be a potential pathway from a Conformer to Achiever leadership culture. We noted that that path was made difficult by a mind-set that "great men" were the same thing as "great managers" and a lack of any observable leadership strategy. Furthermore, we said that NuSystems was made up almost entirely of Specialists embedded in a Conformer organizational culture. This backdrop makes feasibility mapping all the more important.

Individual Level. As CEO, Liam's primary leader logic was that of a Moderator, a conflict-averse adapter with a generous paternalistic attitude toward his senior team and the workforce. His individual map is revealing.

On control source, he is assessed as an executive guided by an internal compass that pointed to the future while building on the present. His language was almost always couched in expressions of values and a better future without compromising the present. At the same time, he made continual references to being governed by the goals and objectives of his role. Such statements place him in the midrange on this scale.

If we had not looked at other scales, it would have been easy to conclude that Liam was poised to lead a successful change process. The other scales, however, paint a different picture of his individual feasibility for change. Liam's time sense was all about the here and now and the completion of tasks as structured and without debate. He focused constantly on the current year's financials—and this in a knowledge industry company where the typical scorecard would emphasize knowledge creation and dissemination. This behavior belied his publicly expressed intentionality to stretch his own leadership logic and that of his team and other key managers throughout the organization. The picture that emerges is of a CEO who espouses a leader logic of Freethinker/Transformer but acts with one of Conformer/Achiever.

Liam's ability to lead in stage development was severely compromised by his demands for loyalty and his conflict avoidance. In terms of feasibility, what frustrated his team and the organization were his frequent and persuasive communications about pursuing one's passion in service of the greater good (values) even while he himself avoided conflict, risk, and vulnerability. These are exactly the barriers that change guides need to overcome in a Conformer culture. Clearly Liam was not prepared to tackle issues of alignment and commit to a bigger mind, Headroom, or an Inside-Out leadership culture.

Senior Team Level. NuSystems' senior team was so diverse that it was difficult to sum up results of the team feasibility scales. Some members were strong Dominators, and some Moderators; others were strong Performers; still others were Performers/Freethinkers but unable to express that logic when confronting others on the team; and one was a noncommittal Freethinker. Still, as a whole on the map, what we see is a senior team much more advanced in its leadership logic than Liam was. And we also see a team paralyzed by its inability to acknowledge the present. It was unable to shape itself into an instrument for developing and sustaining change.

The team work style reflected regular team and small-group meetings, but more focus on operations than on big strategic issues. This reinforced short-term achievement rather than progress on larger strategic issues. Trust within the team was on the cusp between Conformer and Achiever, stuck there largely by hidden agendas maintained by Liam and one of the more dominant members of the team. The learning environment supported by the team was primarily about elevating "my" performance in helping "my group" meet its financial targets. The team resisted the concept of collective learning and learning in public, both important aspects of feasibility in moving a leadership culture from Conformer/Achiever to Achiever/Collaborator. The strategic action logic and rhetoric were consistent with a proactive, dynamic, global perspective about the business and the world, but observed behaviors were frequently insular, reactive, and narrowly functional.

Often absent was information that could drive higher leadership logic or culture, especially with regard to engagement and Headroom. Partnership within the senior team was assessed as one-off deals between two or three members of the team. Overall scale scores did not suggest partnering for future success of NuSystems as an enterprise; partnering simply advanced more narrow self-interests of functional groups.

Leadership Culture Level. Leadership culture at NuSystems was also an amalgam of Conformer and early- and late-stage Achiever—relatively devoid of early-stage Collaborator thinking or feeling. The company's scope of awareness and strategic scope were like those of late-stage Achiever cultures. The conversations were often about vision, strategy, and commitment, and less often about alignment for the sake of execution.

There was substantial high-profile activity promoting an expansive view of the future for NuSystems and the shared responsibility to make the future into a reality. But such activity was undercut when leaders defaulted to incremental approaches that honored and protected the past, even when past practice differed from the organization's espoused future practices.

NuSystems' learning orientation was typical of an Achiever leadership culture, emphasizing performance and productivity that drives unit-specific revenue generation but largely disregards the collective and the development of a bigger mind to support change. Learning orientation tended to run counter to the values and belief system that leaders were espousing in their pursuit of a more Collaborative/Transformative leadership culture. As we said, senior team members were largely preoccupied with advancing the well-being of their individual functions and drawing attention to themselves as exemplary managers. To the extent that there was a development frame at NuSystems, it most frequently focused on acculturating new members and helping longer-term members whose leader logics differed from those of Liam and one of his most outspoken and powerful vice presidents. In other words, development amounted to helping people fit in with the leadership cultural view of Liam and his most powerful ally.

Now What for NuSystems? Given this feasibility result for NuSystems, it is apparent that potential existed for developing the leadership strategy and supporting leadership culture to a bigger mind.

But the potential was likely contingent on Liam's engaging himself in his own intentional development. Only then could he and his team start the journey toward practicing and modeling collective learning that could help develop not only the team but the broader leadership culture. Only through these actions could one expect a mobilization of the collective to climb the stairs to a Collaborative/Transforming leadership logic widely shared and widely practiced.

Now What?

As you take on the task of feasibility analysis for change in your leadership culture, we offer what for us are some nuggets of knowledge that we have come to appreciate from this work. In the Introduction to this book, we pointed to three statements about this work that we felt you would not find in other treatments of change.

First, in this new world order, your work as a leader is about developing culture and talent, not about assigning it to someone else, and all culture development and change starts with you. Second, the key to successful transformation is doing the work in the senior leadership culture first before taking the change to the middle of the organization. Third, transformation is serious work for serious people; it is about getting bigger minds to deal with bigger and more complex issues that will continue to confront you, your leadership, and your organization. It is in this context of these three ideas that we share with you our reflections:

- *Developing a leadership culture starts with you and all of your colleagues in senior leadership.* You can no longer just delegate, defer, or demand development from others. The changing role of senior leaders in the changing new world order absolutely requires your commitment to your own Inside-Out development—a direct engagement within yourself. You must develop your internal self in action development with external challenges so that you can prepare for your critical role as a change guide for others. Don't ask anyone to do what you are not willing to do.

- *Advancing your leadership culture means executing your strategy while developing your leadership talent.* By choosing the right level of leadership culture that your organization absolutely requires for its future, your leadership talent as a collective can advance to new levels of organizational capability that secures success. This is a feasible alternative to advancing talent by developing individual competencies one leader at a time as they come through the pipeline. Instead, imagine if you could amass a flood of talent capable of implementing every new strategy for the next ten years.

- *Inside-Out development of leadership beliefs must come into balance with Outside-In changes in the organization's systems, structure, and processes.* Business strategy drives the challenge; leadership strategy meets and greets it. The organization is the playground where demand meets supply. Why not finally get the human system in alignment with the operational systems? That is the balance in the equation that really makes everything work.

• *Get a bigger mind.* Serious change demands serious people. Are you up for it? An expanding, learning-capable leadership mind-set can successfully face increasingly bigger challenges. Collective learning is the key to the elusive, popular vision of the learning organization. Collective, bigger leadership minds can address not only this year's business issues and goals but also the shifting strategic challenges that face the leadership culture in the future.

• *The three foundations of personal readiness—time sense, control source, and intentionality—are the keys to advancing your personal readiness for transformation.* When leaders demonstrate through their decisions and actions a willingness to counter traditional assumptions, they create the conditions for others to learn and advance, and they expand the arena of collaborative exploration, learning, and development. These people will together pursue multiple right answers and advance collaborative relationships, thereby addressing more complex emergent issues and build readiness together for leadership in the emerging new world order.

• *Achieving a vibrant leadership culture capable of executing your strategy while developing your leadership talent is the hat trick, the sweet spot, the big enchilada.* This creates the capability for self-perpetuating leadership collectives to continuously re-create the organization into endless new structural creations capable of satisfying the demands of emergent complex challenges.

• *Headroom is the primary development process engine for your leadership culture.* Engaging fully in the Headroom process includes time and space for Inside-Out discovery, action development for new leadership beliefs and practices, and advancement of leadership logics and culture. Headroom can and will generate a new level of organizational capability and talent.

As you progress to an Interdependent-Collaborative stage of culture and talent, no competitor void of that capability will challenge your organization's ability to survive and thrive.

• *The change leadership team (CLT) is the executive practice zone for emergence, generation, and launch of the new leadership beliefs and practices that are the seeds of change that you need.* Over time, it becomes the generator and the carrier of the next-order leadership culture. Ultimately the CLT is driver of and tender to transformation in the business, the organization, and the leadership culture.

• *Focus on the core.* Developing your leadership culture is developing your leadership talent to the next level of capability. Advance the collective beliefs of the culture to the next level of leadership logic, and you advance the practices of leadership to the next level of capability. When the next level of leadership culture is aligned with your strategy, your performance will be stellar. By focusing on the few core capabilities the organization needs, you can move the whole and expanding leadership culture forward as a unified force for change.

• *The development law of 3 × 3.* There are three steps of development in each of the three stages of development. This is true for individuals and organizations. The three-step language goes something like this: (1) find awareness, (2) try to apply new stuff, and (3) consolidate learning into the new logic frame. The steps take courage, belief, and a new idea that is better and bigger. You have to ride inspiration and gut it out at the same time. You can't skip steps. Development is earned. If it were easy, everyone would be doing it. How serious are you?

• *The culture development cycle represents the collective learning that results in the next advancement of leadership logic and culture.* Each dimension is an ongoing, self-contained entity. Your organization can and will go through the phases multiple times and yet be contained within the dimensions as they advance in capability and sophistication.

It is up to you and your team now to map and otherwise analyze your feasibility for change. The case examples should help you begin, as will the mapping tools and process we have described. Such a process will enable you to continue your pursuit of a bigger mind and whatever higher leadership logic your organization needs to reach.

Appendix A

A VERY BRIEF HISTORY OF DEVELOPMENTAL THEORY AND LEADERSHIP RESEARCH

The field of developmental psychology and theory began with studies of the development of children by Jean Piaget (for example, 1967) and expanded into a lifelong development theory elaborated by Erik Erikson (1980). Bob Kegan's ground-breaking book, *The Evolving Self* (1982), was also a key contribution to this field. Lawrence Kohlberg studied moral development (1981). Jane Loevinger pioneered a sentence-completion test that measures the stages of psychological development (for example, 1998), and Susann Cook-Greuter continued this work, discovering even higher, more advanced stages of development (1999). James Fowler's work examined the developmental stages of faith (1981).

Other researchers carried the human development inquiry explicitly into areas of organizations, with implications for leadership. Bill Torbert, for example, correlated individual action logics with organizational stages of development in his 1987 book, *Managing the Corporate Dream*. Clare Graves developed the concept of memes to describe units of cultural information that govern behaviors, and Don Beck and Christopher Cowan brought his work forward in their book *Spiral Dynamics* (1996), which correlated memes to stages of development in individuals and organizations.

Table A.1 Leadership Logics and Individual Stage Comparisons

Leadership Logics: CCL	Action Logics: Rooke and Torbert (2005)	Memes: Beck and Cowan (1996)	Stages: Kegan (1982)	Values: Hall (2006)	Stages: Erikson (1980)
Interdependent-Collaborator	Ironist Alchemist Strategist	Turquoise Yellow	5	Interdependent	Integrity versus Despair
Independent-Achiever	Individualist Achiever	Green Orange	4	Self-Initiating	Generativity versus Isolation
	Expert			Belonging	Intimacy versus Isolation
Dependent-Conformer	Diplomat	Blue	3		
	Opportunist	Red		Surviving	Identity versus Role Confusion

Another specialist in the field is Brian P. Hall, whose book *Values Shift* (2006) identifies 125 worldwide values and plots them on a developmental schema across four phases, each with individually and socially correlated values. Finally, our colleagues Chuck Palus and Bill Drath's *Evolving Leaders* (1995) broke early ground in the application of developmental theory to the field of leadership.

Other strands of research are woven into this picture. Abraham Maslow's work on self-actualization and the hierarchy of needs represents similar thought, as does James Collins's work denoting five levels of leaders. Although not strictly associated with development theorists, authors such as these have brought a commonsense view of development as natural, ongoing life stages.

At present, the core of the development stage theory field is constructive-development theory, called *constructive* to acknowledge that we actively construct ways of making sense of our world. For a thorough treatment, see McCauley and others (2008).

In Table A.1 we compare numerous key perspectives. We do not suggest a strict constructive-development point of view (according to Piaget, Kegan, or Torbert, for example), but rather include multiple perspectives on adult development. Experts in this general area might take issue with any attempt to compare Erikson or Hall with Kegan and Torbert. Mindful of that critique, we attempt in this table only to roughly correlate across multiple perspectives in order to illustrate general similarities. For a rigorous treatment of the subject in comparative tables, see Wilber's *Integral Psychology* (2000).

Appendix B

ROOTS OF THE HEADROOM CONCEPT AND RELATED METHODS AND TOOLS

The practice of Headroom has grown out of the influence of several strong players across multiple knowledge fields. We have integrated many of their concepts into knowledge clusters and hybrids on which we stand. It is from this network of knowledge that our work is evolving, and so we wish to acknowledge the general use of their theories within our practice.

In addition to the stages theorists selected for recognition in Appendix A, we add the work of these pioneers:

- Learning theories of Chris Argyris, Donald Schön, Peter Senge, and David Kolb
- Change approaches represented by Michael Beer and Nitin Nohria
- Organizational development work of Lee Bolman and Terrence Deal, and Kim Cameron and Robert Quinn
- Business and organizational strategy of Henry Mintzberg, Michael Porter, and Dave Ulrich

Following is a sampling of tools that support our work in creating Headroom in the leadership culture. These select tools feature developmental action inquiry and interdependent organizing, a subset of our organizational leadership development tools, featured in our joint work with Bill Torbert (McGuire, Palus, and Torbert, 2007):

Method or Tool	Description	Source or Reference
Difficult Conversations (two-column exercise)	Examining the assumptions, frames, and feelings left unspoken in a conflictual conversation	Argyris, Putnam, and Smith (1985); Senge and others (1994)
Learning Pathways Grid	Systematic analysis of a difficult conversation in terms of actual versus desired frames, actions, and outcomes	Taylor, Rudolph, and Foldy (2006)
LDP (Leader Development Profile) instrument with coaching groups	Assessment of individual action logics, supported by trained coaches and peer dialogues	Rooke and Torbert (2005); Cook-Greuter (1999, 2004)
Mapping organizational action-logic history	Understanding LDR (Leadership Development Resources) by tracing its history of development in action logics	Torbert and Associates (2004)
Culture Mapping Tool	Group exercise in which the "Culture Crew" at LDR mapped, and reflected on, their appraisal of the organization's actual and desired culture, according to two dimensions and four types	Cameron and Quinn (1999); Slobodnik and Slobodnik (1998)
Business Process Analysis and Mapping	Analysis of value-creating activities for specific products and services and aligning them into a "value stream" while eliminating activities that don't add value	Womack and Jones (2003)

(Continued)

Method or Tool	Description	Source or Reference
Culture Evaluation Tool	Survey instrument developed at LDR for assessing the relative strength of current organizational action logics; used as an internal assessment at LDR, with coaching	Ongoing research at LDR
Team Workstyle Continuum	Tool that helps a team self-assess current and future required functioning on a continuum from earlier to later action logics; used in the LDR culture-change discovery process	Tool created by LDR
Four Parts of Speech	Encourages framing, illustrating, advocating, and inquiring for effective communication in support of collaborative inquiry	Torbert and Associates (2004)
Group Dialogue	Conversation models that support the construction of shared meaning through exploring diversity in assumptions and perspectives	Isaacs (1999); Palus and Drath (2001); McGuire and Palus (2003)
Visual Explorer	A tool that uses visual imagery and the resultant metaphors to mediate group dialogue	Palus and Horth (2007)
First- and second-person journaling	Research staff keep personal as well as group journals of observations and experiences related to projects	LeCompte and Schensul (1999)

Body Sculpting of Roles and Relationships	Group workshop exercise in which people from diverse roles in LDR collectively, physically modeled their actual and desired interdependencies with each other, using physical postures in relation to one another as a metaphoric device to support group reflection	Moreno (1977)
Culture Walk-About Tool	LDR-designed ethnographic tool to capture subjective and objective observations in first-, second-, and third-person modes	LeCompte and Schensul (1999)
Open Space Technology	A tool for establishing effective affinity groups amid diverse interests; used in a variety of ways at LDR, including forming discussion groups at workshops and seeding idea communities	Owen (1997)
Idea Communities	Interest- and passion-driven greenhouses of future Research and Development efforts, leading in some cases to fully established communities of practice	Lave and Wenger (1991)

Source: Adapted from J. McGuire, C. Palus, and W. Torbert. "Toward Interdependent Organizing and Researching." In A. B. Rami Shani and others (eds.), *The Handbook of Collaborative Management Research.* Thousand Oaks, Calif.: Sage, 2007. Used with permission.

Appendix C

HELPFUL SOURCES OF STUDIES ON INTELLIGENCE AND BRAIN RESEARCH

A plethora of work in the past decade has addressed connections between forms of intelligence, how we learn, emotions, and the functioning of our brains. These cross-disciplinary fields are still poorly understood by nonspecialists, and yet some authors are attempting to make new data available in more accessible forms. One specialty area is the field of neuroscience, which seeks to understand the biological basis of consciousness and the mental processes by which we perceive, act, decide, learn, and remember. We have listed a few select readings that we have found to be useful in exploring human perception and decision making.

Cooper, R. K., and Sawaf, A. *Executive EQ: Emotional Intelligence in Leadership and Organizations*. New York: Berkley, 1997.

Damasio, A. *The Feeling of What Happens*. Orlando, Fla.: Harcourt, 1999.

Doidge, N. *The Brain That Changes Itself*. New York: Viking Penguin, 2007.

Gardner, H. *Intelligence Reframed: Multiple Intelligences for the Twenty-First Century*. New York: Basic Books, 1999.

Goleman, D. *Working with Emotional Intelligence*. New York: Bantam Books, 1998.

Goleman, D., and Boyatzis, R. "Social Intelligence and the Biology of Leadership." *Harvard Business Review*, Sept. 2008, pp. 74–81.

Gore, A. *The Assault on Reason*. New York: Penguin, 2007.

Hawkins, D. *Power Versus Force*. Carlsbad, Calif.: Hay House, 1995.

Kandel, E. R. *In Search of Memory: The Emergence of a New Science of Mind*. New York: 2007.

Rock, D., and Schwartz, J. "The Neuroscience of Leadership." *strategy+business*, Summer 2006, pp. 1–10.

Scientific American Mind Magazine. Retrieved from http://www.sciam.com/sciammind/.

Wexler, B. *Brain and Culture.* Cambridge, Mass.: MIT Press, 2006.

Glossary

Action development: The process of helping clients to implement key organizational strategies while simultaneously transforming their leadership culture.

Bigger minds: New, advancing, more complex mind-sets that can anticipate and prepare organizations that secure new capabilities to address successive future challenges.

Change: Incremental adaptation.

Change Guide: Senior leaders who model new ways of being and doing, find pathways through unexplored territory, have the trust and respect of others, and take people at varying levels of capability and work with them to accomplish success.

Change leadership: Leading change primarily through adaptive and generative human systems in the leadership culture and its beliefs and practices.

Change leadership team: A special representative team assembled to be responsible for stewardship of transformation. The team comprises key executive team members, influential leaders across and down a few layers into the organization, a company folk-hero maven or two, select members of the board, and representatives from the supply chain or client and constituent groups.

Change management: Managing change primarily through technical solutions and operational systems, structures, and processes.

Collaborator: An excellent strategist with extraordinary strategic influencing skills; a powerful change agent.

Collective learning: Learning done by groups throughout the Headroom process. Collective learning becomes organizational learning in that the knowledge is helped by the collective.

Control source: A personal belief system about choices available in taking actions for change.

Core capability: The few key qualities and things an organization needs to have and be able to do in order to implement the business strategy and be successful in navigating the new organizational direction.

Culture: The tools and beliefs of collectives that expand behavior, extend learning, and channel choice.

Culture development cycle (CDC): An organizational learning and development framework that interrelates six dimensions of leadership work as phases, or steps, in an organizational transformation process. An organization that evolves through all six phases of this collective, organizational learning cycle can advance in its culture stage. Within the cycle framework, there are continuous, simultaneous interactions among the six dimensions. The CDC represents the dynamic phenomenon of collective learning and culture advancement to bigger minds.

Dependent-Conformer leadership culture: Authority and control are held at the top; success depends on obedience to authority and honoring the code; mistakes are treated as weakness; and feedback is not valued.

Dominator: An authoritarian opportunist who requires control over others.

Double-loop learning: Going beyond detecting and correcting a system error (single-loop learning) to also question the values, variables, and root sources of the system error. A term coined by Chris Argyris (1995).

Engagement: The authentic, multilateral Inside-Out process that generates connectedness in the leadership culture. Levels of engagement vary with levels of leaders logics and determine the depth of engagements and how people interact with each other.

Feasibility mapping: The analysis of data and the synthesis of information that plots a realistic, feasible plan for change or transformation in an organization.

Freethinker: An individualist who has mastered the idea that reality is constructed and is what he or she makes it from his or her own perspective.

Guide: People who are at the Freethinker leader logic or beyond who simultaneously are aware of their own development, take responsibility for the development of others, find pathways through unexplored territory, and have the trust and respect of others.

Headroom: Supporting growing, bigger minds in yourself and others in order to face and unravel big organizational challenges, puzzles, and the leadership culture systematically and to intentionally develop toward an interdependent collective leadership logic. The space and time created to allow systemic development of the leadership culture.

Independent-Achiever leadership culture: Authority and control are distributed through the ranks; success means mastery of systems that produce results; mistakes are opportunities to learn; and feedback is valued as a means to enhance advancement.

Inside-Out: The subjective, internal perspective that uses emotion, intuition, imagination, beliefs, and spirit for deep experience and expression and is the realm of an essential self. Inside-Out is interpretive and includes a sense-making process in culture that involves dialogue with others.

Intentionality: Actively using the zone of intentional change by bringing the unconscious into conscious expression of values, beliefs, assumptions, and aspirations, which are then translated into strategic actions for change.

Interdependent-Collaborator leadership culture: Authority and control are shared based on strategic competence for the whole organization; success means collaboration across all systems for shared results; mistakes are embraced as opportunities for organizational learning; and feedback is valued as essential for collective success.

Leadership: What is done through leadership collectives to realize the outcomes of setting direction, achieving alignment, and getting commitment in increasingly peerlike, collaborative relationships.

Leadership culture: The web of beliefs and practices that realize collective organizational outcomes of direction, alignment, and commitment.

Leadership logics: Distinctive, consistent mind-sets that tend to pervade the culture of leadership in every organization. Each stage of logic contains a set of beliefs and interpretations that underlie choices.

Leadership strategy: An organization's implicit and explicit choices about the leadership culture, its beliefs and practices, and the people systems needed to ensure success—a strategic intent that includes the whole organization.

Middle: Where the core of operations is: where production of products and services is and where middle management sits, absorbing direction from the top and operational realities from below.

Moderator: A diplomatic, conflict-avoidant pleaser who requires control over self.

Operating space: Where and how people in organizations do their work every day.

Outside-In: The objective, external perspective that uses reason, logic, senses, and empirical tools for mastery of the perceived material world and is the realm of the functional self. Outside-In is an analytical, measurable, scientific process that involves self-directed action.

Performer: An independent, self-possessed person who has created his or her own internally generated values and standards.

Specialist: A technical expert who requires mastery and control over things and his or her craft.

Stage: An ongoing situation—durable, consistent state of experience; follows a sustained new state of an advanced leader logic.

State: A fleeting situational experience of a later leader logic or stage; precedes a stage.

Time sense: A personal belief and orientation about time experienced as a constraint to be managed versus time experienced as a resource to be leveraged.

Transformation: Movement from one leadership logic to the next.

Transformation principle: Sustain and practice a new state, and you will make it to the next stage; maintain the new bigger idea long enough, and you will advance to the next leadership logic.

Transformer: Someone who can transform organizations through an unusual capability to simultaneously deal with multiple situations at many different levels.

Zone of intentional change: The zone where expanding, conscious attention to Inside-Out and Outside-In forces simultaneously creates greater awareness of the span of potential decisions.

References

Argyris, C. "Teaching Smart People to Learn." *Harvard Business Review*, May-June 1991, 99–109.

Argyris, C. *On Organizational Learning.* Cambridge: Blackwell, 1995.

Beck, D. E., and Cowan, C. C. *Spiral Dynamics: Mastering Values, Leadership, and Change: Exploring the New Science of Memetics.* Cambridge: Blackwell, 1996.

Beer, M. "How to Develop an Organization Capable of Sustained High Performance: Embrace the Drive for Results-Capability Development Paradox." *Organizational Dynamics*, 2001, 29(4), 233–247.

Beer, M., and Nohria, N. *Breaking the Code of Change.* Boston: Harvard Business School Press, 2000.

Bennis, W. G. "The Challenges of Leadership in the Modern World: An Introduction to the Special Issue." *American Psychologist*, 2007, 62(1), 2–5.

Bohannan, P. *How Culture Works.* New York: Free Press, 1995.

Bolman, L., and Deal, T. *Reframing Organizations: Artistry, Choice, and Leadership.* (4th ed.). San Francisco: Jossey-Bass, 2008.

Boyatzis, R., and McKee, A. *Resonant Leadership.* Boston: Harvard Business School Press, 2005.

Bradford, D. L., and Burke, W. *Reinventing Organizational Development.* San Francisco: Jossey-Bass/Pfeiffer, 2005.

Brand, S. *The Clock of the Long Now.* New York: Basic Books, 1999.

Cameron, K. S., and Quinn, R. E. *Diagnosing and Changing Organizational Culture.* Reading, Mass.: Addison-Wesley, 1999.

"Chrysler Chief Tries to Rally Troops." *Atlanta Constitution*, Mar. 23, 2007, p. G2.

Collins, J. C., and Porras, J. I. *Built to Last: Successful Habits of Visionary Companies.* New York: HarperCollins, 1997.

Cook-Greuter, S. "Post-Autonomous Ego Development." Unpublished doctoral dissertation, Harvard University, 1999.

Damasio, A. *Looking for Spinoza: Joy, Sorrow and the Feeling Brain.* Orlando, Fla.: Harcourt, 2003.

DeMartino, B. "Frames, Biases and Rational Decision-Making in the Human Brain." *Science*, 2006, *313*(4), 684–687.

Di Pego, G. (Writer), and Turteltaub, J. (Director). *Phenomenon*. Touchstone Pictures, 1996. Motion picture.

Drath, W. D., and others. "Direction, Alignment, Commitment: Toward a More Integrative Ontology of Leadership." *Leadership Quarterly*, 2008, *19*(6), 635–653.

Erickson, E. *Identity and the Life Cycle*. New York: Norton, 1980.

Fowler, J. *Stages of Faith*. New York: HarperCollins, 1981.

Gardner, H. *Changing Minds*. Boston: Harvard Business School Press, 2004.

George, B. *Authentic Leadership: Rediscovering the Secrets to Creating Lasting Value*. San Francisco: Jossey-Bass, 2003.

Gerstner, L. V. *Who Says Elephants Can't Dance?* New York: HarperCollins, 2002.

Gladwell, M. *The Tipping Point*. New York: Little, Brown, 2000.

Goldsmith, M. *What Got You Here Won't Get You There*. New York: Hyperion, 2007.

Goodwin, D. K. *Team of Rivals: The Political Genius of Abraham Lincoln*. New York: Simon & Schuster, 2006.

Gratton, L. *Hot Spots*. San Francisco: Berrett-Koehler, 2007.

Gunning, T. "Evolve or Dissolve—Creating Meaningful Businesses." Unilever, 2006.

Hall, B. P. *Values Shift: A Guide to Personal and Organizational Transformation*. Eugene, Ore.: Wipf and Stock Publishers, 2006.

Hawkins, D. *Power vs. Force: The Hidden Determinants of Human Behavior*. Carlsbad, Calif.: Hay House, 1995.

Hughes, R. L., and Beatty, K. C. *Becoming a Strategic Leader: Your Role in Your Organization's Enduring Success*. San Francisco: Jossey-Bass, 2005.

Joubert, J. *The Notebooks of Joseph Joubert*. (P. Auster, trans. and ed.) San Francisco: North Point Press, 1983.

Jung, C. G. *The Undiscovered Self*. London: Penguin, 1957.

Kafka, F. *The Diaries 1910–1923*. (M. Brod, ed.) New York: Schocken, 1949.

Kegan, R. *The Evolving Self: Problem and Process in Human Development*. Cambridge, Mass.: Harvard University Press, 1982.

Kegan, R., and Lahey, L. L. *How the Way We Talk Can Change the Way We Work*. San Francisco: Jossey-Bass, 2001.

Kohlberg, L. *Essays on Moral Development*. New York: HarperCollins, 1981.

Kotter, J. P. *Leading Change*. Boston: Harvard Business School Press, 1996.

Kotter, J. P. "What Effective General Managers Really Do." *Harvard Business Review*, Mar. 1999, pp. 145–159.

Landler, M. "Daimler's Chief Confirms Talks for Sale of Chrysler." *New York Times*, Apr. 5, 2007, p. C1.

Lawrence, J., and Lee, R. E. *Inherit the Wind*. New York: Ballantine, 2007.

Lipman-Blumen, J., and Leavitt, H. J. *Hot Groups*. New York: Oxford University Press, 1999.

Loevinger, J., ed. *Technical Foundations for Measuring Ego Development: Washington University Sentence Completion Test*. Philadelphia: Lawrence Erlbaum Associates, Inc., 1998.

Maclean, N. *A River Runs Through It*. (25th Anniv. Ed.) Chicago: University of Chicago Press, 2001.

McCarthy, B. *About Learning*. Wauconda, Ill.: About Learning, 2000.

McCauley, C. D., and others. *Interdependent Leadership in Organizations: Evidence from Six Case Studies*. Greensboro, N.C.: Center for Creative Leadership, 2008.

McGuire, J. B. [Case study notes.] Unpublished research material, 2008.

McGuire, J. B., and Palus, C. J. "Conversation Piece: Using Dialogue as a Tool for Better Leadership." *Leadership in Action*, 2003, *23*(1), 8–11.

McGuire, J., Palus, C., and Torbert, W. "Toward Interdependent Organizing and Researching." In A. B. Rami Shani and others (eds.), *The Handbook of Collaborative Management Research*. Thousand Oaks, Calif.: Sage, 2007.

McGuire, J. B., Rhodes, G. B., and Palus, C. J. "Inside-Out: Transforming Your Leadership Culture." *Leadership in Action*, 2008, *27*(6), 3–7.

O'Reilly, C. A., III, and Pfeffer, J. *Hidden Value*. Boston: Harvard Business School Press, 2000.

Oshry, B. *The Possibilities of Organization*. Boston: Power and Systems, 1992.

Palus, C. J., and Drath, W. H. *Evolving Leaders: A Model for Promoting Leadership Development in Programs*. Greensboro, N.C.: Center for Creative Leadership, 1995.

Palus, C. J., and Drath, W. H. "Putting Something in the Middle: An Approach to Dialogue. *Reflections*, 2001, *3*(2), 28–39.

Palus, C. J., and Horth, D. M. *Visual Explorer: Picturing Approaches to Complex Challenges*. Greensboro, N.C.: Center for Creative Leadership, 2001.

Palus, C., and Horth, D. *The Leader's Edge: Six Creative Competencies for Navigating Complex Challenges*. San Francisco: Jossey-Bass, 2002.

Patterson, K., Grenny, J., McMillan, R., and Switzler, A. *Crucial Conversations*. New York: McGraw-Hill, 2002.

Peck, M. S. (Speaker). "Further Along the Road Less Traveled." *Blame and Forgiveness*. New York: Simon & Schuster Audio, 1992. Cassette recording.

Phillips, D. T. *Lincoln on Leadership*. New York: Warner Books, 1992.

Piaget, J. *Six Psychological Studies*. New York: Random House, 1967.

Quinn, R. E. *Deep Change*. San Francisco: Jossey-Bass, 1996.

Rooke, D., and Torbert, W. "Seven Transformations of Leadership." *Harvard Business Review*, Apr. 2005, pp. 1–12.

Savitz, A. W., with Weber, K. *The Triple Bottom Line*. San Francisco: Jossey-Bass, 2006.

Sawyer, K. *Group Genius: The Creative Power of Collaboration*. New York: Basic Books, 2007.

Schein, E. *Organizational Culture and Leadership*. San Francisco: Jossey-Bass, 1992.

Selznick, P. *Leadership in Administration: A Sociological Perspective*. New York: HarperCollins, 1957.

Torbert, B., and Associates. *Action Inquiry: The Secret of Timely and Transforming Leadership*. San Francisco: Berrett-Koehler, 2004.

Torbert, W. R. *Managing the Corporate Dream: Restructuring for Long-Term Success*. Homewood, Ill.: Dow Jones-Irwin, 1987.

Wilber, K. *A Brief History of Everything*. Boston: Shambhala, 1996.

Wilber, K. *Integral Psychology*. Boston: Shambhala, 2000.

Index

169; senior team feasibility exercise assessing, 261*e*
Collective-consciousness culture, 216*t*
Collective learning. *See* Learning
Collins, J. C., 118
Command and control culture, 5
Commitment practice, 226*t*, 229–230
Conformist culture: culture development cycle (CDC) role of, 183*fig*–184; Dependent-Conformer logic and, 38–39; Dependent-Conformer logic and engagement in, 86–87; organization CQ and, 214, 216*t*, 218, 219–220. *See also* Dependent-Conformer logic
Connectedness, 84–85
Conscious awareness: leadership culture feasibility exercise on, 262*e*–263*e*; operating space increased through, 47*fig*, 48; zone of intentional change expanding, 46–48. *See also* Big Mind
Continental Congress (1776), 140
Controller educational role, 104–106
Control source: as balance wheel of personal readiness component, 107*fig*, 115–117; examples of, 117–120; individual feasibility map on, 259*fig*; individual feasibility map scale/exercise on, 257*t*; as personal readiness key, 284
CQ. *See* Organizational CQ (coordinate, cooperate, collaborate)
Credlow: alignment practice at, 227–228; control source at, 119–120; emotional decision making at, 192; time sense at, 124–125; Transformer leader and engagement at, 99–100

Credlow case study: business strategy, 247; feasibility analysis on, 275–278; leadership readiness, 248–249; leadership strategy and culture, 247–248
Culture and Systems Readiness Audit (exercise), 50–51
Culture development cycle (CDC): assessing feasibility of successful, 193; collective learning represented by, 285; description of, 182–184; exercises on, 208–209; four learning questions and leadership logics of, 183*fig*–184, 203–207; as learning cycle for leadership culture, 183*fig*–184; ongoing cycles and shifts in, 207–208; six phases of, 184–203. *See also* Leadership culture transformation
Culture development cycle (CDC) phases: 1: Inside-Out, role-shifting experience phase, 185–190; 2: readiness for risk and vulnerability phase, 190–192; 3: Headroom and widening engagement phase, 193–195; 4: innovation phase, 195–197; 5: structure, systems, and business processes phase, 197–199; 6: leadership transformation phase, 200–203
"Culture eats strategy for breakfast" (cartoon), 39, 40*fig*
Culture. *See* Leadership culture; Organizational culture
Culture work: as beginning with the individual, 20–21; intimate and revealing nature of, 21

D
DAC (direction, alignment, commitment): adaptive culture development through, 211;

About the Center for Creative Leadership

The Center for Creative Leadership (CCL) is a top-ranked, global provider of executive education that develops better leaders through its exclusive focus on leadership education and research. Founded in 1970 as a nonprofit, educational institution, CCL helps clients worldwide cultivate creative leadership—the capacity to achieve more than imagined by thinking and acting beyond boundaries—through an array of programs, products, and other services.

Ranked in the top ten in the *Financial Times* annual executive education survey, CCL is headquartered in Greensboro, North Carolina, with campuses in Colorado Springs, Colorado; San Diego, California; Brussels, Belgium; and Singapore. Supported by more than five hundred faculty members and staff, it works annually with more than twenty thousand leaders and three thousand organizations. In addition, sixteen Network Associates around the world offer selected CCL programs and assessments.

CCL draws strength from its nonprofit status and educational mission, which provide unusual flexibility in a world where quarterly profits often drive thinking and direction. It has the freedom to be objective, wary of short-term trends, and motivated foremost by its mission—hence, our substantial and sustained investment in leadership research. Although CCL's work is always grounded in a strong foundation of research, it focuses on achieving a beneficial impact in the real world. Its efforts are geared to be practical and action oriented, helping leaders and their organizations more effectively achieve their goals and vision. The desire to transform learning and ideas into action provides the impetus for CCL's programs, assessments, publications, and services.

Capabilities

CCL's activities encompass leadership education, knowledge generation and dissemination, and building a community centered on leadership. CCL is broadly recognized by sources such as *BusinessWeek*, *Financial Times*, the *New York Times*, and the *Wall Street Journal* for excellence in executive education, leadership development, and innovation.

Open-Enrollment Programs

Fourteen open-enrollment courses are designed for leaders at all levels, as well as people responsible for leadership development and training at their organizations. This portfolio offers distinct choices for participants seeking a particular learning environment or type of experience. Some programs are structured specifically around small group activities, discussion, and personal reflection, while others offer hands-on opportunities through business simulations, artistic exploration, team-building exercises, and new-skills practice. Many of these programs offer private one-on-one sessions with a feedback coach.

For a complete listing of programs, visit http://www.ccl.org/programs.

Customized Programs

CCL develops tailored educational solutions for more than one hundred client organizations around the world each year. Through this applied practice, CCL structures and delivers programs focused on specific leadership development needs within the context of defined organizational challenges, including innovation, the merging of cultures, and the development of a broader pool of leaders. The objective is to help organizations develop, within their own cultures, the leadership capacity they need to address challenges as they emerge.

Program details are available online at http://www.ccl.org/custom.

Coaching

CCL's suite of coaching services is designed to help leaders maintain a sustained focus and generate increased momentum toward achieving their goals. These coaching alternatives vary in depth and duration and serve a variety of needs, from helping an executive sort through career and life issues to working with an organization to integrate coaching into its internal development process. Our coaching offerings, which can supplement program attendance or be customized for specific individual or team needs, are based on our ACS model of assessment, challenge, and support.

Learn more about CCL's coaching services at http://www.ccl.org/coaching.

Assessment and Development Resources

CCL pioneered 360-degree feedback and believes that assessment provides a solid foundation for learning, growth, and transformation and that development truly happens when an individual recognizes the need to change. CCL offers a broad selection of assessment tools, online resources, and simulations that can help individuals, teams, and organizations increase their self-awareness, facilitate their own learning, enable their development, and enhance their effectiveness.

CCL's assessments are profiled at http://www.ccl.org/assessments.

Publications

The theoretical foundation for many of our programs, as well as the results of CCL's extensive and often groundbreaking research, can be found in the scores of publications issued by CCL Press and through the Center's alliance with Jossey-Bass, a Wiley imprint. Among these are landmark works, such as *Breaking the Glass Ceiling* and *The Lessons of Experience*, as well as quick-read guidebooks focused on core aspects of leadership.

CCL publications provide insights and practical advice to help individuals become more effective leaders, develop leadership training within organizations, address issues of change and diversity, and build the systems and strategies that advance leadership collectively at the institutional level.

A complete listing of CCL publications is available at http://www.ccl.org/publications.

Leadership Community

To ensure that the Center's work remains focused, relevant, and important to the individuals and organizations it serves, CCL maintains a host of networks, councils, and learning and virtual communities that bring together alumni, donors, faculty, practicing leaders, and thought leaders from around the globe. CCL also forges relationships and alliances with individuals, organizations, and associations that share its values and mission. The energy, insights, and support from these relationships help shape and sustain CCL's educational and research practices and provide its clients with an added measure of motivation and inspiration as they continue their lifelong commitment to leadership and learning.

To learn more, visit http://www.ccl.org/community.

Research

CCL's portfolio of programs, products, and services is built on a solid foundation of behavioral science research. The role of research at CCL is to advance the understanding of leadership and to transform learning into practical tools for participants and clients. CCL's research is the hub of a cycle that transforms knowledge into applications and applications into knowledge, thereby illuminating the way organizations think about and enact leadership and leader development.

Find out more about current research initiatives at http://www.ccl.org/research.

For additional information about CCL, please visit http://www.ccl.org or call Client Services at 336-545-2810.